The publisher gratefully acknowledges the generous support of the Classical Literature Endowment Fund of the University of California Press Foundation, which was established by a major gift from Joan Palevsky.

Meta-Religion

Meta-Religion

Religion and Power in World History

James W. Laine

UNIVERSITY OF CALIFORNIA PRESS

University of California Press, one of the most
distinguished university presses in the United States,
enriches lives around the world by advancing scholarship
in the humanities, social sciences, and natural sciences. Its
activities are supported by the UC Press Foundation and
by philanthropic contributions from individuals and
institutions. For more information, visit www.ucpress.edu.

University of California Press
Oakland, California

Library of Congress Cataloging-in-Publication Data

Laine, James W.
    Meta-religion : religion and power in world
history / James W. Laine.
        p.   cm.
    Includes bibliographical references and index.
    ISBN 978-0-520-28136-3 (cloth, alk. paper) —
    ISBN 978-0-520-28137-0 (pbk., alk. paper) —
    ISBN 978-0-520-95999-6 (electronic)
    1. Religions—History.   2. Religion and politics—
History.   I. Title.
BL80.3.L34   2015
201'.72—dc23   2014020289

Manufactured in the United States of America

24   23   22   21   20   19   18   17   16   15
10   9   8   7   6   5   4   3   2   1

In keeping with a commitment to support
environmentally responsible and sustainable printing
practices, UC Press has printed this book on Natures
Natural, a fiber that contains 30% post-consumer waste
and meets the minimum requirements of ANSI/NISO
Z39.48-1992 (R 1997) (Permanence of Paper).

To my wife, Joy,
and our children,
Maria, Patrick, Claire, and Rosie

Contents

Illustrations

Preface

I have written this book because I am unhappy with the usual surveys of world religions.[1] Ambitious surveys of the world's religions—whether they are college textbooks or popular accounts—convey large amounts of data. You can usually find there a serviceable summary of the *Bhagavadgita* or the *Dao De Jing* (*Tao Te Ching*) alongside the Gospel of Luke, but perhaps far more arcane material as well.[2] There will be potted histories of the "major world religions," though besides the Big Five—Hinduism, Buddhism, Islam, Christianity, Judaism[3]—its not clear how to slot in the other traditions like Daoism, Sikhism, Jainism, Shinto, not to mention the tribal religions of Native Americans or sub-Saharan Africans. Usually, as an afterthought, there are attempts to relate all these traditions to questions we modern folk are raising (e.g., about environmentalism, feminism, violence), whether or not those were *their* questions. And finally, there will be a word or two about just what religion itself is, what defines this category in which we have included all these traditions. How much *do* we include here? What if Confucians or Buddhists claim they are not "religious"—can we count them anyway? And what about various clearly secular ideologies, especially Marxist ones; do they, in effect, replace religions in some societies? Do we study them *as religions?*

I do not mean to disparage these books, nor the noble efforts of their authors to portray fairly and accurately the religious lives of ancient and modern people all over the globe, and I cannot replace here what they accomplish in those books. Students interested in facts—facts about the authorship of the Christian gospels and the doctrines of early Buddhism, facts about the Hindu gods and their worship in temples, facts about Zen meditation and Islamic personal law—should turn to these textbooks. What the usual hefty survey lacks is not facts but clear arguments about how those facts were chosen. What argument about the very nature of religion lies behind the chapter-by-chapter account of particular religions? For example, it is often assumed that "real religion" is all about the interior experience of sincere individuals, and thus the religion of lukewarm or hypocritical conformists is ignored. In other words, we are concerning ourselves with a tiny minority, but nowhere is that explicitly stated. Many *Religions of the World* textbooks should be retitled *The Religious Life of Noble Persons.*

Why do we read surveys of the religions of the world? Partly because, in an effort to be less parochial and more cosmopolitan, we want to see how other people answer the big questions. And partly because, assuming that a survey will be a menu of personal options, we believe we can use it to consider the options and pick a religious path that appeals to us. The most popular among such books are those that appeal to the seeker, providing the reader with a taste of a variety of "spiritualities." Pursuing either or both of these aims depends on the idea that religion is a genus, comprising roughly equivalent species. And that each of these examples of religion—Hinduism, Buddhism, Islam—serves the same function in society, or at least *should* serve the same function in society that privatized Protestant Christianity serves in open, tolerant, secularized western societies. Religion in this view, or at least authentic religion, is a personal philosophy and set of private practices with virtually no political role.

I am also somewhat unhappy about the way religion is treated in the study of world history. Surely the study of the history of the world is strikingly less Eurocentric than it was a few decades ago, yet a certain ingrained narrative is there. We still tend to have lodged in our heads a seemingly obvious progression that leads from Mesopotamia to Egypt to Greece to Rome to England to Massachusetts to California. India and China are added in, but often as classical and timeless civilizations unrelated to our story, "the rise of the West."[4] The most striking things about that narrative is that *it ends up with us,* and that it rather sidelines the vast Islamic civilization that dominated world trade and cultural exchange for a thousand years (ca. 700–1700 A.D.).

Unquestioned assumptions—about models of world history or the ways religions evolve—produce other blind spots. Why are religions and civilizations treated like organisms that take birth, grow, flourish, decline, and die? Why is there often a survey of the most ancient Indian mythology, reflected in Vedic Sanskrit texts composed before 1000 B.C., as part of a historical narrative of Hinduism, while there is no similar account of Greek and Roman mythology as the first chapter of European religion? The simple answer is because organizing a book with chapters on major world religions will mean having chapters on Hinduism and Christianity. "Hinduism" includes a treatment of early Vedic ritual and mythology, even while Vedic priests did not think of themselves as belonging to a religion named Hinduism and the vast majority of modern Hindus know very little about ancient Vedic traditions, while "Christianity" *replaces* the pagan traditions of Greece and Rome. Its prehistory has been covered by the chapter on Judaism, which again is treated as an ancient tradition going back to Abraham, even while the Rabbinic religion of the Judaism we know today was largely the product of the first century and Abraham would hardly have thought of himself as a member of the religion of Judaism. (Some Muslims would interject here that Abraham knew that he was a Muslim.) So the prevailing view has it that some ancient religious histories are relevant and others are not. But consider the medieval Italian peasant, celebrating holy days on an annual cycle, in harmony with the rhythms of agriculture, and venerating saints at sacred sites with ancient pre-Christian roots. Certainly such a person would affirm that she was a Christian. But is her religion really the same as that of the first-century Christian participating in what the Romans would have seen as a nonconformist cult, anticipating the imminent end of the world? Or does she, in fact, have more in common with the Roman pagan, both following ancient traditions and both suspicious of novelty? Similarly, is Mexican Catholicism both a chapter in the history of Euro-American Christianity and a chapter in Native American religion?

The more important problem with popular and textbook surveys of world religions is that they are bloodless. They present each religion as though it were a museum piece. Here's what Hindus believe (or do). Here's what Muslims believe (or do). Here's what Christians believe (or do). Isn't that nice? They all have these uplifting ideas about being a good person! Behind the well-meaning blandness is an unspoken relativist theology based on humanist notions of fairness: all these religions are products of different cultures; all have good things to teach us; if we open our minds and learn about them we will accept each other with respect and good will. This unspoken argument shifts the discourse to a level where both reader and author are *above* the religions they study, "respecting" them but not taking them seriously in the religious way religious people take them. It avoids even the most basic arguments about how scholars deal with the problems of defining and studying religion and ascertain the boundaries to this field of inquiry. Are Christianity and Hinduism really two comparable species of the same genus (religion)? Should we present only portraits of only the noblest Buddhists and Muslims? Or the most representative? Most Buddhists do not meditate, and most Muslims do not pray five times a day; are these people accounted for in the usual summary treatments of Buddhism and Islam? And if most people in world history have been unwilling to relativize their own religious beliefs, if many of them were in fact willing to kill or die for them, how should we account for that without simply assuming a sort of smug pact between reader and author that we are somehow more advanced than those benighted, intolerant, and bellicose souls of the past, especially in light of the fact that the twentieth century was the bloodiest on record. If we moderns are not fighting about religion, and we often are, we are still fighting about something. And most often, we still prosecute our wars with a rather religious conviction.

. . .

My interest in the world historical framework for the study of religion was first provoked by my study of history with Otto Nelson at Texas Tech University in 1970, when he suggested that I read W.H. McNeill's *Rise of the West*. That interest was extended when I read M.G.S. Hodgson's *The Venture of Islam* at the suggestion of my fellow graduate student Kevin Reinhart, now a professor of Islamics at Dartmouth College. I thank these dear friends for their inspiration and for all their wonderful, intellectually stimulating and enriching companionship over the last decades. While at Macalester, several colleagues in the History Department also gave me much to think about. I want to thank especially Paul Solon, Jim Stewart, Peter Rachleff, Karin Velez, and David Itzkowitz.

Outside my own field of specialization, I have also been inspired by the work of biblical scholars, especially Gene Gallagher and the late George W. MacRae, and my friends at Macalester College, Calvin Roetzel, Allen Callahan, Susanna Drake, and Andy Overman. Andy and I have taught a course and an NEH seminar together, and those many conversations resulted in the way I have conceived the first third of this book. I am extremely grateful to these friends.

In the 1980s I ventured into the field of Islamics, especially in order to understand the ways Hindus and Muslims in South Asia relate. This resulted in my book *Shivaji: Hindu King in Islamic India* (Oxford: Oxford University Press, 2003), and made me realize the limitations of studying Hinduism in an isolated way. In this field, I have been much influenced and aided by Carl Ernst, Stewart Gordon, Bruce Lawrence, Brendan Larocque, SherAli Tareen, and Mashal Saif.

Many other colleagues at Macalester assisted me as I ventured far outside my specialty. I want to thank especially Brett Wilson, Barry Cytron, Erik Davis, Joëlle Vitiello, Kiarina Kordela, Terry Boychuk, David Martyn, Satoko Suzuki, Arjun Guneratne, Paula Cooey, and the late Juanita Garciagodoy. I also received useful advice and counsel from Van Dusenbery, Daniel Williams, Andy Fort, Roland Jansen, Shana Sippy, Jeanne Kilde, Richard Davis, and Bruce Forbes.

Prior to undertaking this work, my studies have mostly dealt with India. In that field, I have continued to benefit from the generous help of a number of prominent South Asianists. I thank especially Alf Hiltebeitel, Vasudha Narayanan, James Hegarty, Richard Gombrich, Charlie Hallisey, Eleanor Zelliot, Irina Glushkova, Jim Masselos, Philip Lutgendorf, Paula Richman, Lynn Zastoupil, Fred Smith, Christian Novetzke, Lee Schlesinger, and Wendy Doniger.

My department at Macalester has been a congenial place to work, especially because of the constant help and unwavering support of my brilliant administrative assistant, Toni Schrantz. I would also like to thank our student worker Joanne Johnson, who provided much help with securing images for the book. I am sure I tried the patience of several people at the University of California Press. I thank my editor Eric Schmidt for his early encouragement, and for the patient work of Andrew Frisardi, Cindy Fulton, and Maeve Cornell-Taylor. Thanks also to Alex Trotter for his work on the index.

Macalester students in my course World Religions and World Religions Discourse have provided me with much to think about, as have my students in Introduction to the Religions of the World at the University of Minnesota. It is primarily for students such as these that I have written this book.

Of course, all my work would be impossible without the love and support of family and friends. I am grateful for the hospitality of my English relatives, Olivia, Dave, Barbara, Betty, Ahmad, Jamal, Kareem, and Yussef. My Texas family has been behind me from the beginning. Thanks to Rick and Nancy, and especially my mother, Marie. I've appreciated the encouragement of my oldest friend Bill Walter. Thanks also to Richard and Jill Michell for their constant friendship. Jill graciously provided two fine drawings for chapter 3. Finally, I have had the enduring affection of my children, Maria, Patrick, Claire, and Rosie, and had the best of companions in my wife, Joy. From England to India to Connecticut and Minnesota, as a scholarly advisor, partner, and friend, she has been there every day. To her and our children, I dedicate this work.

For eight beautiful years, my loyal dog Patches led me on daily walks. He didn't give a damn about religion or power but probably helped me more than anyone to stop and think. I hope the results honor his memory.

James W. Laine
Saint Paul, Minnesota
July 10, 2014

Introduction

In order to avoid the sort of bland detachment and presumed political neutrality of the usual world religions survey, I will pursue a particular argument that I believe takes religion more seriously than is usually the case in the academic world, where religions are "appreciated" more than fought over. My argument is a simple one: If you have discovered the truth, will you not want to live in a world governed by that truth? In other words, if God has spoken to you in a revelation; or the subtle nature of Reality has appeared to you in meditative experience; or you have perhaps only felt that all was right with the world as you participated in a stately ritual of renewal—will you not extend all your efforts to bring your world into congruence with the truth you have reached? And will not such efforts necessarily involve attempts to exercise power, and thus involve participation in politics? Is not the story of religion inseparable from political and military history? Is religious tolerance really such an obvious value and really the primary goal of studying religion? Or is something more complicated going on?

I am following an old argument in the sociology of religion, one Peter Berger expressed in his classic book *The Sacred Canopy:* "Every human society is an exercise in world-building. Religion occupies a distinctive place in this enterprise."[1] Berger goes on to develop a perhaps overly static model, in which human beings create a world to inhabit, begin to experience that world as fully natural, and thrive to the degree they are successfully socialized to live harmoniously in that world. Those not fully socialized seem to be on the road to serious mental imbalance. More recently, scholars influenced by Michel Foucault see culture, in more dynamic terms, as a place where dominant cultural patterns are continually resisted. There might be a dominant culture and a reigning orthodoxy, supported by the elite classes, but there are always people who are less influential and powerful, who "push back," employing the "weapons of the weak" to claim their vision of society.[2] While they may never win, they are also never vanquished.

Whatever model of society one adopts, the fact remains that religion is almost always a fundamental part of "world building." It plays a role in the *constructive* phase, when prophets argue articulately about how to conceive the truth, but also in the less noticeable phase of *maintaining* the taken-for-granted views of the world that have become habitual, natural, and thus almost beyond argument.

Now, if many of us in modern western culture find it possible to inhabit a world where religion does *not* play a primary role in creating that world, where religion is not congruent with what is seen as natural—a condition which holds for many people who nonetheless still affirm conventionally religious beliefs[3]—we have two fundamental questions to ponder before we proceed. First, if religion nowadays is not taking, as Berger would have it, a "distinctive place" in the enterprise of world building, what has replaced it? And second, if the religions we do see around us are not playing that role, what, exactly, are they doing? We might also ask whether this condition, usually referred to as secularism, is a condition unique to the modern western world. When one hears the assertion about a religion, "It's not so much a religion; it's a way of life," one has to wonder what kind of religion is *not* a way of life.

Before we explore possible answers to these questions, it is probably necessary to consider briefly the way scholars imagine religion operating in societies where it has a primary function in creating and maintaining the objective world. At the risk of creating too sharp a divide between the traditional and the modern, we can, for the sake of argument, consider a "traditional" society one where religion reigns supreme, maintaining an authority in matters of morals and metaphysics, and deeply embedded in everyday life. In Hindu India, one avoids eating with the left hand, *not* because it is *evil* to do so, but because one has internalized the sense that it is impure and has the special function of washing after defecation. A fully socialized Hindu might feel nauseated by the idea of eating with the left hand; in other words, not eating with the left hand is more an instinct than a consciously followed external rule. In a traditional Catholic society, people accepted the authority of the Catholic Church in matters of theology. Children were baptized and confirmed, were taught to declare allegiance to the creed, and were sternly warned against heresy. They grew up with a calendar formed by Christian culture, where holy days were the holidays; the private world of desire for food or sex was governed by religious notions; and everyday greetings were religious declarations, the religious "God be with you" (*adios, adieu*) slowly giving way to the neutral-sounding "goodbye." If the church's authority in theological matters was threatened, it might exercise explicit temporal powers in prosecuting heresy. But it was in another sense that it exercised its power in more self-assured, unselfconscious ways. On Easter Sunday, the individual in this society experienced that calendar date as an objective fact: it *felt* like Easter, and virtually everyone participated in expected behaviors that reinforced that reality. The more profound power of religion is not coercive; it is not an external pressure, but a seemingly natural inner impulse. Even in the modern world, we can see that whenever adults smile benignly on a little group of girls in their Easter dresses, they reinforce a custom that will make it likely for those girls to grow up wanting their own daughters to observe Easter similarly, and thus continue traditions that are less about theology than they are about belonging.[4]

Now, my portrayal here of traditional Catholic culture is probably tainted by nostalgia. Close historical studies have revealed more tension in the actual religious worlds of medieval Catholics than one might suppose.[5] Similarly, lower-caste Hindus—wildly underrepresented in the literature—might also inhabit a world much less fussy in matters of ritual purity. Nonetheless, even contemporary anthropological accounts of village culture in our own times, both Hindu and Catholic, often capture a way of life in which religion is not a set of abstract ideas *about* the world but something embedded *in* the world that people inhabit.[6] One has to note here that nostalgia for a village community where religion reigns supreme may drive the very modern phenomenon of the American exodus from city life, the escape to exurbs beyond the reach of government, where megachurches supply many social services and the notion of the separation of church and state seems less and less apt.[7] On the other hand, for those unmoved by this nostalgia—those for whom religion is a matter of private belief—the comprehensive way of life of the exurban megachurch is not just odd but incomprehensibly cultic and perverse.

Just as the origin of the systematic study of society in Europe— the discipline of sociology—coincides with the rise of individualism, the origin of the comparative study of religion coincides with the European Enlightenment demotion of religion from its preeminent role. Only after the fracture of the Holy Mother Church could "the Faith" be replaced by multiple "religions," and only once Christendom was replaced by nation-states (after the Enlightenment exalted Reason to replace God), could the power and authority of religion in European society be assumed by secular institutions. And only in such secular institutions could one take up a position *above* the variety of religions and presume to study them fairly and comparatively. Thus the academic study of religion, a discipline that is less than two centuries old, takes place in a context in which the nation-state has already assumed the right to adjudicate a multiplicity of religions (including alien religions, it should be noted, encountered in the colonies). We all know this, but it is a fact that often slips from consciousness when we are going about the business of studying religions, some of which are part of cultures where they take a royal position, and some of which are part of a world more familiar to us, where religion has been dethroned. And forgetting that fundamental difference, we proceed to talk about both kinds of religion as though we are talking about the same thing.

To anticipate the extended argument that will inform this book, religion is in many cultures a constituent of the world-building process, often the most important constituent, and thus, not surprisingly, engaged in struggles for power. It is thus inseparable from politics. But in the modern West, especially in Europe, this typical situation seems not to be the case, as secular institutions, governed by values of the Enlightenment (democracy, individual freedom, reason—all revered, by the way, as sacred) have replaced religion in its political and world-building role.[8] Even in America, where resurgent evangelical Christianity is taking a more confident political role, the secular values of democracy and freedom are also taken for granted, though unrecognized as the products of Enlightenment.[9] The modern condition, where religion as the bedrock of taken-for-granted assumptions has been replaced by less explicitly religious ideas and institutions, makes it hard for us to understand traditional religion and its relationship to power, and it also blinds us to the fact that our secular institutions are not a neutral ground for the fair adjudication of multiple religions, but the coercive instruments of something that effectively stands in for the One True Faith; the one reasonable, just authority. We might find it incomprehensible that people go to war for their religion, while we find it perfectly reasonable that we carry out military strikes to "defend freedom" or even "protect our way of life."

Since the treatment of religion as something neatly separate from politics is misleading, I want to attend to the place of religion in world-historical contexts often defined by the history of politics and war—religion as a critical part of the construction of the real world of legitimate power. I begin with the age of Alexander the Great and end with the contemporary world, the age of "the war on terror." It is a story that often crisscrosses Mesopotamia, the region of modern Iraq. So, as a corrective to the sort of world history that centers on Europe, we will see how Mesopotamia, the most ancient center of civilization, is the crossroads of religion and power in the ancient world, connecting Egypt, Greece, Persia, India, and China, while today it is, among other things, the battleground of the crusaders for democracy and the oil-rich Muslim critics of American imperialism. Both Alexander the Great and George W. Bush talked to God before invading Iraq. Both spoke of bringing democracy to the region. Both men were personally religious but sought to encourage vague and universal values, religious and political, rather than promote the particular doctrines of a specific sect or religion. (And both had sinking poll numbers late in their careers!)

Of course, a comparison of the lives and policies of Alexander the Great and George Bush would be abstract and fruitless. But the relation between religion and politics has not changed as much as we might initially think. If one is to exercise military and political power over a large area, one must encourage and promote values that are consistent with one's political agenda. And since often such populations are committed to multiple religions, and therefore are committed to what might be incommensurate worldviews, one must offer a vision of something that transcends and supersedes these religions. In the modern world we often talk rather blandly and bloodlessly about promoting tolerance. Certainly if we are to live together we must "tolerate" each other's religion. But while much ink has been spilled defending this virtue, we also find that even the most tolerant person has a commonsense measure by which the religions of others are evaluated and then affirmed, tolerated, or rejected as barbarous. The Sunnis and Shi'is of Iraq should tolerate each other, we aver, but the sacredness of democracy is above debate, and its opponents subject to censure and attack. The precondition for the multicultural acceptance of multiple religions (tolerance) is the shared acceptance of something above religion, something with the power to set the political conditions of shared community. But since religion often speaks the language of ultimacy, how do we imagine that something that would transcend it, and thus demote it?

In my analysis of religion and power, I will use two pairs of terms in the following specific ways:

Inclusivism here means the intellectual or political approach to religion, which assumes that differing religions can be included within an overarching system. When the Hindu accepts Jesus as an avatar, he is an inclusivist, accepting Jesus into an alien system in which he is one avatar among many.[10]

Particularism here means an assumption that different people in different times and circumstances should have different religious beliefs and ethical standards. The particularist would argue that a monk should be a vegetarian, but a soldier should not. Particularism is consistent with the ideology of the caste system, and the ideas of karma and rebirth.

Exclusivism here means the assertion that a particular truth or religion is exclusively true and thus involves the rejection rather than the inclusion of others. This position is often characteristic of monotheism and religions like Christianity that emphasize orthodoxy (strictly defined belief, as opposed to practice).

Universalism here means the assumption that a particular truth or religious doctrine is true for all people in all times and circumstances. So the Buddhist Four Noble Truths are assumed to be always true, regardless of context.

The thesis of this book is that the usual textbook account of the world religions, acquainting the reader with all that is good and noble in Buddhism, Christianity, Islam, and other religions, does little to acquaint us with the central issues of the study of religion. It fails to deal with the fact that if religious cultures "create worlds," the inhabitants of those worlds share not only doctrinal beliefs (Jesus is the Son of God; everything is impermanent; there is no god but God)—doctrines the contemporary ecumenist would have us treat as personal opinions to be politely discussed—but more importantly, convictions that have become so taken for granted that they seem embedded in the very nature of reality (human beings have equal dignity; karma produces a particular rebirth; history is the theater of God's Will in the world). What serves as tolerance is often the willingness to set aside the doctrinal as long as the practical concerns of governance operate under assumed notions of the Good, notions that appeal to the vast majority and exclude only the weak minority who can be classified as barbarous. These appeals to taken-for-granted values can form what I will call a "meta-religion,"[11] whether they are the reasonable ideas of Pax Romana or the United Nations' Universal Declaration of Human Rights.[12] They become the basis for dealing with multiple religions in the context of a common political community, in other words in a world where religion is more than private individual opinions about abstract metaphysical problems ("hobbies" as Stephen Carter would put it).[13] When Barack Obama expresses his respect for "all people of faith" and reaches out to Muslims, he embraces those Muslims who are ready to share his politics, those whose religion is thus congruent with "democratic values."[14] On the other hand, those who would counter American or European exercise of military power with their own weapons in the name of Islam are not "people of faith" but perpetrators of a perverted ideology. They are terrorists. And their religion, in the minds of most westerners, is not the real thing.

If we are now beginning to see the ways the taken-for-granted Enlightenment values of secularism serve as a meta-religion, we may also benefit from seeing the ways in which premodern people found to articulate encompassing ideologies that stood above the multiple religions of cosmopolitan societies. All premodern empires encompassed peoples with a variety of religions. Few were completely tolerant and supportive of all manner of religious life, but none achieved absolute religious conformity either, and most found ways of accommodating and in many cases, even supporting a diversity of religious practices. This means that the Enlightenment project of demoting religion had several predecessors, from the ancient Greco-Roman world to the Mughals in early modern India.

What we have noticed about the traditional approach to the study of the "world religions" is the assumption that encyclopedic coverage will mean neatly demarcated chapters on well-known religions like Christianity, Buddhism, and Islam. Each is treated in a summary way, a process that leads to what scholars bemoan as "essentialism," a kind of boiling down of the diversity of the tradition into some ideal form. In such an approach, however, the religion in question is presented as having an essential identity, changing over time, like a growing organism, but persisting through history, having a single career. Traditional surveys of world religions fail to take account of the internal debates within these religions, debates that reflect such significant internal diversity that we fail to grapple with the fact that any given Christian might have more in common with any given Buddhist or Muslim than he or she has with another Christian.

Buddhism (whose earliest doctrines stressed that all phenomena were in flux, lacking identity and permanence) seems to pose the biggest challenge to the usual paradigm, since Buddhists developed a bewildering array of doctrines and practices as they spread to Southeast Asia, Tibet, China, Korea, and Japan. Especially in East Asia, aspects of Buddhism seemed not only to differ from the Buddhism of South Asia, but seemed fully at odds with it. Is it meaningful to think of Nichiren Buddhism of Japan (which encourages prayers for prosperity while rejecting meditation as futile), and the Theravada Buddhism of Sri Lanka (which honors the lives of poverty and meditation of monks) as in any way the same religion? Would it not be better to study the Buddhism of East Asia in relationship to the other traditions of that region and civilization (especially Daoism and Confucianism), rather than a religious kernel buffeted by historical and geographical change, but somehow enduring across time and space?

Once we begin to raise such questions, we realize that all religious traditions are *fundamentally* and not just superficially affected by the historical and geographic location, the culture within which their adherents live out their faith. Believers may assume that their religion is grounded in a universal, unchanging, and eternal truth, but any critical student of religion will have to assume that religion is best studied as a dimension of the culture in which it is fully immersed. And once again, we must remind ourselves that we cannot favor some proponents of any given religion on the grounds that they have virtues consistent with what we prefer, and reject others for their violence or intolerance or sexism, without admitting that we are developing a *critique* of the world's religions more than we are engaged in dispassionate description of the lives of the majority of the world's religious people.

The approach I will follow here will be to take up critical world-historical contexts to examine the way people of a variety of religious allegiances live their lives as participants in the agreements and arguments that sustain cultural discourse. The approach cannot be fully comprehensive or encyclopedic, but will follow the theme of religion and power and the role of meta-religion in imperial projects across a broad swath of world history. Examining the relationship of religion to the exercise of political power in a wide variety of historical contexts will involve examination of multireligious cultures where traditions are upheld and shaped by people actively contesting and debating and fighting. We must relate discussion of those traditions intimately to the issues of political power so often ignored in the study of religion, for otherwise we present misleading portraits of depoliticized Hindus and Buddhists and Muslims functioning like Presbyterians in an American suburb. Points of religious conflict are too often treated as embarrassments, unfortunate incidents where religious people failed to live up to their ideals, or simply ignored as "political" and "not really about religion."

The first section of the book will treat the relation of religious communities to the empires of the ancient world, beginning with the empires of the Macedonian Alexander the Great (d. 323 B.C.) and the Indian Ashoka (fl. 250 B.C.), and concluding with the rise of Islam (632–711 A.D.). In this millennium, we see the rise of large empires that comprehend peoples of numerous languages, ethnicities, and religious allegiances. In many ways, it is the foundation of the world we now live in, and we see that the region around Iraq is the crossroads of military, political, and religious currents that shaped the destiny of the Eurasian landmass for centuries. My concern will be to examine the ways in which religion and imperial power relate, first in the age of Alexander and Ashoka, then in the age of the Persian and Roman contests, to the age of the first Christian emperor, Constantine (d. 337 A.D.), and finally in the age of Muhammad (d. 632 A.D.) and the early caliphs, whose military successes led to the formation of an Arab empire that stretched from the western Mediterranean to India and most closely approximated Alexander's dream: one ruler, one culture, one people, centered at Baghdad, a stone's throw from ancient Babylon. How do dreams of universal empire, of forging people into a single kingdom, relate to dreams of a single religious community? What strategies did political leaders employ to deal with diversity, especially religious diversity, while at the same time creating unified empires and commonwealths where money, goods, and ideas could travel widely with little hindrance? And what were the political implications of the rise of monotheism, and its rejection of the ideas of polytheistic pagan inclusivism?

The second historical context will be what I call the Islamic Millennium (ca. 700–1700), from the rise of the Arab empire and the building of Baghdad, to the great Islamic empires of the early modern period (ca. 1500–1700): the Persian Safavids, the Turkish Ottomans, and the Mughals of India. In the eighth century the first Arab rulers (called caliphs) oversaw the dramatic rise of Arab power in the Eurasian heartland centuries before a majority of their subjects embraced Islam. Almost a millennium later, in an age when Europe was torn apart by religious conflict (the seventeenth century), the last great Muslim emperors, whose culture was Persian and whose bloodlines were Turkish, ruled as divine kings (like their Christian counterparts) and assumed the centrality of the *Qur'an,* but coped far more successfully with the fact of religious diversity in their realms. The old dream of an undivided Islamic world might have seemed shattered, as these emperors in Turkey, Iran, and India recognized no single overlord, and yet the degree of Islamic wealth, power, and cultural influence throughout much of the world seemed still regnant. How can we characterize Islamic cosmopolitanism in this period, especially in India, where Muslim rulers ruled only with the cooperation of important Hindu military support? Of special interest here is the emperor Akbar (d. 1605), admired in the modern world for his seeming tolerance and support of the different religions of his realm, as he broke with orthodoxy to cancel discriminatory taxes on non-Muslims and brought Hindus, Christians, and others to his court to debate openly with Muslim intellectuals. Was his religious ideology a precursor to the styles of modern secularism that encourage tolerance, diversity, and multiculturalism? And how did his religious policy relate to his political and military goals?

The third section will concern the modern world, beginning with a reflection on the eclipse of Christendom and the roots and rise of European secularism. This discussion begins with the last great Christian monarchs, who struggled to maintain power and legitimacy in a Christendom fractured by Protestant-Catholic rivalries. With that background, we can consider the peculiar nature of religion as it emerged in the modern world, and begin to comprehend the nature of our current popular and scholarly understanding of the very category *religion,* a term that takes on special meaning after the Reformation. Finally, after an analysis of the Enlightenment and its effects on France and early America, I will consider the relation of religion and power in the contemporary world. Of particular interest is the secular experiment of the European Union, lauded and feared as a check on the warring European nation-states, a new empire encompassing the old central lands of Christendom, but now under the banner of the secular values of the French Enlightenment and human rights. One might see the European Union as the culmination of the process whereby religion is removed from the halls of power, privatized and restricted, while at the same time, new, more secular doctrines of the good, the true, and beautiful are invoked though not fully articulated as the basis for the humane society of Europe, no longer at war, but unified. At this moment of culmination, Europeans face, however, a new challenge. The assumed values of post-Christian secular liberalism (strategically left inarticulate) will have to be defended in a generation that contemplates the entry of Turkey (with a 99 percent Muslim population) into the European Union, and sees already the growth of a substantial Muslim minority population (for example, 10 percent in France). Does the European Union have a way of dealing with multiple religions in ways that recall or go beyond the inclusivist policies of Ashoka and Akbar?

Modern India, China, and especially the United States are, like Europe, sites of economic, political, and military power, and places of internal diversity. Each has its own version of secularism—India with its Gandhian heritage, China its Maoist, and the United States its Jeffersonian. India reveres Mahatma Gandhi (d. 1948) as the father of the nation, for leading the cause of independence against the British and formulating a very religious-sounding ideology that nonetheless opposed a Hindu state that would oppress the considerable Muslim minority in South Asia. Similarly, China sees Mao Zedong (d. 1976) as the revolutionary who forged a communist ideology to oppose western imperialism, an ideology that, while rejecting traditional religion as oppressive and bourgeois, itself took on many aspects of religion. Like the ancient imperial kingdom that preceded it, the contemporary Chinese state continues to be deeply suspicious of any sectarian movement (Islam, Christianity, Falun Gong) that offers personal salvation and might challenge the state in its role as the sole voice of authority and meaning. And finally the great superpower, the United States, using the heritage of Jeffersonian democracy to prosecute what many see as a worldwide imperial project. After two generations of opposing global communism in the name of freedom, now since 9/11, America is seen as a crusader for democracy and freedom against an Islamist threat. While western Europe and China have embraced a very thoroughgoing secularism, India and the United States have retained policies that evoke more explicitly religious resonance, and yet they too proclaim social and political goals that are consonant with what they believe to be the assumed values of the secular world.

These three chapters in world history will be the basis of my study of religion within the real world of authority, contest, and power. I assume, then, that any time we see religion as something *outside* the political arena, we are probably witnessing a political struggle that is authorized by other forces not explicitly religious, but forces defended with all the fervor that most people in most times and places have recognized as religious. When that happens, the truth that is defended with the exercise of every effective instrument of power is a truth that I will call a meta-religion: a truth so taken for granted that its proponents see it as consistent with what is only natural and reasonable. Neither Alexander the Great nor Ashoka, Akbar nor Napoleon claimed a doctrinal religious authority for their deeds, but operated in the name of truth and reason for principles that were above particular religions. They presaged the policies of modern European and American world leaders. Their voices are now echoed in the United Nations. And their principles, rooted in their meta-religions, may be articulated as enlightened policy, but they are also the result of values that have become so naturalized as to make their opponents' views seem barbaric, unworthy of consideration, and thus unworthy of the tolerance we assume the great religions deserve. All these leaders tolerated a diversity of religions, but could only tolerate those religions that would surrender their claim to ultimacy, to being the highest authority in the exercise of power. One who presumes to lead can never be a true relativist. Indeed, perhaps no one can be.

So let us find that meeting place of power and religion, or power and that which stands above, and in the place of, religion. Let us attend to the relationship of religion to political community.

PART ONE

Religion and Empire in Antiquity

330 B.C.–710 A.D.

323 B.C.	Death of Alexander the Great
322–185	Maurya Dynasty
232	Death of Ashoka Maurya
221–207	Qin Dynasty
202 B.C.–220 A.D.	Han Dynasty
130	Death of Indo-Greek ruler Menander (aka Milinda)
100	Approximate date of the *Bhagavadgita*
14 A.D.	Death of Emperor Augustus
33	Traditional date for the death of Jesus
70	Roman destruction of the Second Temple in Jerusalem
100	Approximate date of the *Lotus Sutra* and the *Laws of Manu*
220	Fall of the Han Dynasty
274	Death of Mani, founder of Manichaeism
325	Council of Nicaea
224–651	Sasanian Dynasty
337	Death of Emperor Constantine

415	Death of Hypatia
565	Death of Justinian I
579	Death of Khusraw I
320–550	Gupta Empire
632	Death of the Prophet Muhammad
711	Arab armies reach Spain and India
618–907	Tang Dynasty

CHAPTER I

Alexander and Ashoka

Cosmopolitan Empires and Religious Policy
from Egypt to India, 330–230 B.C.

One obvious place to begin a broad reflection on the history of religion
is with the founders of great religions—Gautama Buddha, Jesus Christ,
Confucius, Muhammad—and then their immediate followers. But if we
are to take seriously the issue of the way that religion is enabled and
constrained by political power, perhaps the less obvious path of investi-
gating the place of religion in the imperial polity will be more fruitful.
How did the imperial state patronize Buddhism or Christianity? In late
antiquity, how did the state adjudicate between the conflicting claims of
multiple religions? How did minority religions carve out space for their
subcultures to flourish? We begin here the thousand-year story that will
span Eurasia (what the Greeks called "the *oikoumene*") and will produce the world in which Buddhism, Hinduism, Judaism, Christianity,
and Islam could be imagined and find their geopolitical places ranged
round the crossroads of the ancient world.[1]

In addressing these questions, we can begin with the empires of two
great kings whose stories, in a sense, overlap: Alexander the Great
(r. 336–323 B.C.) and Ashoka Maurya (r. 269–232 B.C.). Both were long
remembered as religious and political unifiers. Both grappled with religious and cultural diversity. And from their era onward, the Mediterranean would be part of the same world as distant India: Greek and
Indian universalists reached out toward one another.

The Macedonian Alexander, who succeeded his father in 336 B.C. as
a military and political leader of the League of Corinth, and in his short

career, defeated the Persians and created an empire that stretched from Egypt and Greece to the Indian Punjab. He had been the student of Aristotle as a teenager, and was a champion of Greek culture. If his empire broke apart shortly after his death in 323 at the age of 33, the effects of this wide dispersion of Greek culture were long-lived. At the other end of the *oikoumene*, the Indian Ashoka ruled an empire that stretched from south India to Bengal and Afghanistan. His grandfather had hosted at court the Greek writer Megasthenes and he himself trained as a viceroy in Taxila (in modern Pakistan), one of the cities through which Alexander passed on his campaign in the Punjab. Since Greek women were part of his father's harem, some even believe Ashoka had Greek blood in his veins. More importantly, though this monarch is most well known for his patronage of Buddhism, his carved edicts included, not only declarations of Buddhist doctrine, but often rather Stoic-sounding statements of policy and philosophy in Greek and Aramaic in the northwest corner of his empire where Alexander had left his mark, and he is known to have sent embassies to Alexander's successors as far away as Egypt and Macedonia. India was a long way from Rome, but East and West were wings of the same "inhabited world," and although the military, political, religious, and material culture was diverse and varied, it was nonetheless comprehensible to cosmopolitan, "ecumenical" folk from the age of Alexander to that of the Muslim caliphs at Baghdad. By the second century B.C., Rome would be connected to India and China by land and sea routes, and with trade came the spread of religious ideas and the urgent need for universal principles by which these diverse ideas and institutions might be comprehended, managed, and governed. Alexander and Ashoka were early pioneers in the creation of this universalistic cosmopolitanism.

In world-historical terms, Alexander's dream of world conquest led him from Macedonia and Greece, to Egypt and the Middle East, to India's northwest. Throughout this realm he left behind Greek institutions and opened up the channels through which Asian cultural products would flow westward. In religious terms, he maintained his pious Greek observances throughout his expanding realm, while beginning to incorporate traditions that he encountered at the most ancient Egyptian and Mesopotamian centers of human culture. Alexander did not spread his own religion as he spread his *imperium;* rather he incorporated the religions he met, giving them a place within a broadly cosmopolitan Hellenism. In most ways, however, he was impressed by the high culture of Persia (whose notions of divine kingship endured from at least 600

B.C. to 1721 A.D. and beyond), and adopted it rather than imposing his own, perhaps too rough Macedonian ways upon those he conquered. It is noteworthy that Alexander visited Athens only one time in his life, and after his return from India, settled in Mesopotamia to consolidate his Greco-Persian empire. He died prematurely from a sudden illness, but it is clear that he had certainly been in no hurry to return to Greece or Macedonia. His sense of world empire drew him to the most ancient centers of human civilization, while his sense of the divine depended on a Hellenistic reading of ancient polytheism.

Alexander's flexible approach to religion remained the basic imperial pattern for empire builders until Constantine (d. 337 A.D.) began the process of transforming the Roman Empire into a Christian one and western monotheists began to follow patterns quite at odds with their Indian contemporaries. In the meantime, two generations after Alexander, Ashoka also developed a broadly inclusive religious policy, one that involved both a patronage of Buddhism, the universalist religion to which he converted, and a broader support of other religious communities that brought peace and stability to his realm. His approach, while more consciously deliberate than Alexander's, would have made perfect sense to the Macedonian king, and we know that Ashoka sent emissaries from India to communicate something of his views to Alexander's successors in the Mediterranean world.

Given our extant sources, it is difficult to get inside the head of either Alexander or Ashoka. We know something of Alexander's specific acts of piety and we know of his experiments in forging collaboration with the Persians of his new empire. We can further speculate on the lasting effects of his philosophical education, and what seems to be the lasting imprint of Greek philosophy on the expanded Hellenistic world and its role in the imperial policies of Alexander's successors, especially the Romans. In the case of Ashoka, we do have his edicts, carved as public monuments along the roadways of his far-flung empire, but the exact meaning of his religious policy remains a matter of scholarly debate.

As a Macedonian, Alexander was not a child of Athenian culture but a product of the Greek cultural frontier. And though he was a supporter of Greek culture and much enamored of Greek classical literature himself, he was to spend most of his astonishing military career in what he thought of as "Asia." Upon his accession to power at the age of twenty, he quickly confirmed his control over the Greek lands his father had won, and then moved decisively to undertake the quest that was to be his life's work, namely the conquest of Persia. The Greeks had seen the great Persian Empire as their primary adversaries since the golden age of Athens, when they survived Xerxes' massive Persian invasion in 480 B.C. Knowing this history, Alexander probably began his military venture as an act of revenge, replying to the Persian invasion and liberating the Greek colonies in Asia Minor from Persian rule.

When we refer to Persia in this period, we mean the great empire that centered itself not in Iran but in Mesopotamia (what is today Iraq), near the most ancient sites of culture and civilization in the Tigris-Euphrates Valley, the region of Babylon and Nineveh. Crossing the Hellespont in 334, Alexander landed in Asia Minor (modern Turkey), a twenty-two-year-old general, thrust his spear in the ground, and declared Asia to be his, the gift of the gods to whom he immediately gave worship. We may see this as a move from the center (what could be more central than Athens?) to the East, but it may have been more a case of moving from the periphery to the center, to the crossroads of world culture and the oldest sites of civilization. He not only aspired to defeat the Persians in battle, but to incorporate them and to replace their king in their ancient Mesopotamian capital.

Alexander visited ancient Troy (or the town claiming to be such), but quickly began his military conquests and his pursuit of his opponent, the emperor of Persia, Darius III. When he "freed" Greek cities, he pronounced them democratic city-states, while still assuming imperial overlordship. Alexander won a decisive victory over Darius in 333 in southern Turkey, capturing Darius's family but not the emperor himself, who fled the field. Turning to Syria and Phoenicia, he won difficult victories on the eastern Mediterranean coast, at Tyre and Gaza, before marching triumphantly into Egypt, which welcomed him as a liberator from the Persians and crowned him Pharoah. In the winter of 332, he visited a famous oracle in the Libyan desert, the shrine of Amon at Siwah. Such a shrine, though administered by Egyptian priests, would be a place equivalent to Delphi, where supplicants could put questions to the god represented there and receive answers, however inscrutable those answers might be. The god in this case, Amon, already known to classical Greek writers like Herodotus and Pindar, was a high god, associated with the sun and equated with Zeus.

We might pause here with Alexander, to consider what his religious acts in Siwah meant to him, what his understanding of religion was. Alexander, like most people from Macedonia to the Middle East, to Egypt, and even, for that matter, to India, was a pious man who worshiped the gods of specific locations while at the same time believing those

FIGURE 1. Siwah today, an oasis in the Libyan Desert. Arian Zwegers, photograph courtesy of Creative Commons.

gods equivalent to universal forces named differently in different cultures. He thought of himself as a descendant of Herakles, who had, according to legend, supplicated Amon at Siwah. Alexander had taken considerable trouble to follow in the footsteps of his heroic ancestor, and, upon receiving the word that he was destined to be king of Asia, set forth to conquer with a divine approval that reached beyond the borders of Greece and Macedonia. Perhaps the priests also revealed to him that he was the Son of God (Amon, Zeus), supporting a claim his mother had made. He certainly claimed thereafter a divinely sanctioned royal legitimacy for Macedonian rulers that was to last in Egypt until the days of Cleopatra, three centuries later.

Returning to Mesopotamia, Alexander spurned Darius's offers for peace, occupied Babylon, and defeated him again near the Tigris. Graciously installing Darius's family in comfortable circumstances at Susa, the capital, Alexander pursued his prey, but finding the fleeing Darius murdered by a disloyal vassal, he arranged for an honorable royal funeral in Persepolis. Confirming what he learned in Egypt, Alexander began to think of himself, not as a Macedonian invader, but as the legitimate emperor of Asia, the successor of Cyrus the Great (r. 559–529 B.C.), the Persian emperor who swept down from Iran to topple the ancient Babylonian kingdom and liberate the Jews from exile.[2] In this light, he began to envision Macedonians and Persians administering a common empire and manning a common army, a vision not often shared by his Macedonian comrades. Moreover, he began to adopt Persian royal dress and experiment with Persian royal etiquette.

Consolidating his power across the Persian Empire and deep into Central Asia, Alexander turned to India in 327 B.C. He had some success there, reaching the Punjab, where King Porus sued for peace and allied with him before Alexander's weary soldiers mutinied and demanded to return home. As it turned out, the journey home proved almost more difficult than the life of conquest, and those returning both by sea and land suffered terribly from hunger, illness, and thirst.

Finally arriving back in Mesopotamia in 324, many of his Macedonian soldiers chose to retire home, but Alexander, maybe now fully inhabiting the role of Persian emperor ("Lord of Asia"), remained at Susa, just east of the Tigris River, where he married Darius's daughter and arranged a mass wedding of ten thousand Macedonian men and Persian women, a social experiment known as his policy of "racial fusion." He arranged a funeral in Babylon for his beloved companion, and while there, planned future campaigns into Arabia. However, at this point when he might have consolidated his empire, while residing in the ancient palace of Nebuchadnezzar II, Alexander suddenly died of illness at the age of thirty-three, and his empire soon broke apart, his successors including, among others, the Ptolemies of Egypt and the Seleucids of Syria and western Asia, both bearers of Greek-speaking culture, and both known to Ashoka. For the next thousand years, Indians would write about "Greek" invaders (Yavanas, Yonas) from the northwest, ultimately applying that title to Muslim soldiers of largely Turkish stock. After Alexander, India was never to be cut off from contact with the Mediterranean world.

Like Alexander, Ashoka was something of an outsider to the high culture of his own realm. He did not come from a properly royal (or *kshatriya*) family, and he patronized the heterodox religion of Buddhism and developed a critique of some aspects of the orthodox teaching of the high-caste brahmin priests. He inherited a Mauryan Empire that, under his rule, expanded to include almost all of the Indian subcontinent, extending into the northwest as far as the upper Indus Valley, even into regions of what is Afghanistan today. The legends of King Ashoka are numerous, but reliable historical information is more difficult to obtain. We know little of his military success but do know that his

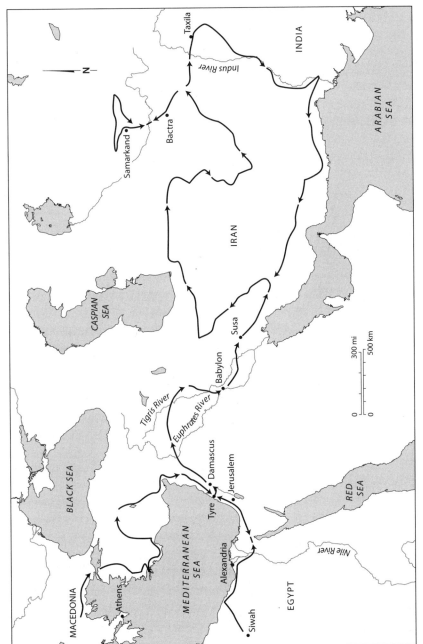

MAP 1. The empire of Alexander the Great.

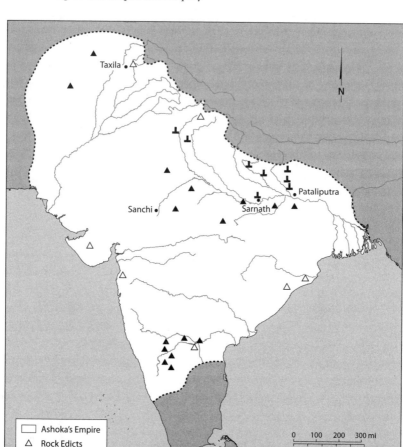

Taxila

Sanchi

Sarnath

Pataliputra

N

	Ashoka's Empire
△	Rock Edicts
▲	Inscriptions
⊥	Asokan Pillars

0   100   200   300 mi
0   100 200 300 400 500 km

MAP 2. The empire of Ashoka.

empire was extensive, uniting India in a way not seen again until the Mughal Empire or perhaps even British times. Most importantly, however, we have epigraphical sources, the inscriptions he commissioned as statements of his policies. In his own words, he pursued a policy of *dharma,* a word variously translated as "religion," "truth," "piety," or "righteousness," and these proclamations were etched in stone, left for us to decipher today. As a political unifier of ancient India, he is taken as an icon in modern India, his symbols covering contemporary Indian currency, with his watchword, *dharma viyaya* ("the victory of *dharma*") subtly replaced by the Gandhian phrase *satyam eva jayate* ("truth alone conquers").

While Alexander was a man of action, much admired for his military genius, we have but a few tantalizing clues to about the nature of his religious beliefs and his dreams for a world empire. Perhaps his experiments in uniting Persians and Greeks grew out of his commitment to Greek cosmopolitanism, and a belief in a kind of destiny and natural law that gives legitimacy to the victor. Ashoka, however, provides us with a more clearly articulated religious policy. He proclaims that his primary role as emperor is to foster *dharma*, not in the narrow sense of Buddhist teaching (about which he mentions very few specifics), but in the broadest sense of good conduct, piety, and truth. After the time of Ashoka, the precise meaning of *dharma* becomes a primary point of debate between orthodox brahmins and Buddhists. But already in Ashoka's inscriptions, *dharma* is translated into Greek and serving as a broadly cosmopolitan policy toward religious diversity. Ashoka's "*dharma* policy" was an imperial meta-religion designed to manage the religious diversity characteristic not only of India but of the entire Eurasian *oikoumene* in the third century B.C.

Ashoka was a Buddhist, and while we can discount legends that have him end his life as a monk, it is clear that he took his religion very seriously. By his own account, he converted to Buddhism as an act of remorse, following the great battle against Kalinga:

> The Kalinga country was conquered by King Priyadarsi, Beloved of the Gods [Asoka], in the eighth year of his reign. One hundred and fifty thousand persons were carried away captive, one hundred thousand were slain, and many times that number died.
>
> Immediately after the Kalingas and had been conquered, King Priyadarsi became intensely devoted to the study of Dharma, to the love of Dharma, and to the inculcation of Dharma.
>
> The Beloved of the Gods, conqueror of the Kalingas, is moved to remorse now. For he has felt profound sorrow and regret because the conquest of a people unconquered involves slaughter, death, and deportation.
>
> But there is a more important reason for the King's remorse. The Brahmanas and Sramanas . . . as well as the followers of other religions and the householders—who all practiced obedience to superiors, parents, and teachers, and proper courtesy and firm devotion to friends, acquaintances, companions, relatives, slaves and servants—all suffer from the injury, slaughter, and deportation inflicted on their loved ones. Even those who escaped calamity themselves are deeply affected by the misfortune suffered by those friends, acquaintances, companions and relatives for whom they feel undiminished

affection. Thus all men share in the misfortune and this weighs on King Priyadarsi's mind.

[Moreover, there is no country except that of the Yonas (that is, the Greeks) where Brahmin and Buddhist ascetics do not exist] and there is no place where men are not attached to one faith or another.

Therefore, even if the number of people who were killed or who died or were carried away had been only one-hundredth or one-thousandth of what it actually was, this would still have weighed on the king's mind.

King Priyadarsi now thinks that even a person who wrongs him must be forgiven for wrongs that can be forgiven.

King Priyadarsi seeks to induce even the forest peoples who have come under his dominion to adopt this way of life and this ideal. He reminds them, however, that he still exercises the power to punish, despite his repentance, in order to induce them to desist from their crimes and escape execution.

For King Priyadarsi desires security, self-control, impartiality, and cheerfulness for all creatures.

King Priyadarsi considers moral conquest (that is conquest by Dharma, *Dharma-vijaya*) the most important conquest. He has achieved this moral conquest repeatedly both here and among the peoples living beyond the borders of his kingdom, even as far away as six hundred yojanas [about three thousand miles], where the Yona [Greek] king Antiyoka rules, and even beyond Antiyoka in the realms of the four kings named Turamaya, Antikini, Maka, and Alikasudara, and to the south among the Cholas and Pandyas [in the southern tip of the Indian peninsula] as far as Ceylon.

Here in the King's dominion also, among the Yonas [inhabitants of the northwest frontier province, probably Greeks] and the Kambojas [neighbors of the Yonas], among the Nabhakas and Nabhapanktis [who probably lived along the Himalayan frontier], among the Bhojas and Paitryanikas, among the Andhras and Paulindas [all peoples of the Indian peninsula], everywhere people heed his instructions in Dharma. . . .

This edict on Dharma has been inscribed so that my sons and great grandsons who may come after me should not think new conquests worth achieving. If they do conquer, let them take pleasure in moderation and mild punishments. Let them consider moral conquest the only true conquest.

This is good, here and hereafter. Let their pleasure be pleasure in morality [dharma-rati]. For this is good, here and hereafter.[3]

In this, one of Ashoka's lengthiest inscriptions, found in the Himalayas less than two hundred miles north of Delhi, we find specific historical data as well as clues to his religious mentality. On the one hand, he mentions the Hellenistic kings Antiochus II Theos of Syria (Antiyoka), Ptolemy II Philadelphus of Egypt (Turamaya), Antigonus Gonatas of Macedonia (Antikini), Magas of Cyrene (Maka), and probably Alexander of Epirus (Alikasudara), all ruling in the eastern Mediterranean

FIGURE 2. Ashokan Pillar, from Sarnath, northern India. Similar pillars with four lions are found in several sites in northern India, and the standard image is used today on Indian currency. Getty Images, photograph courtesy of iStockphoto.

about 250 B.C. Since we know that Greek women were present in the harem of Chandragupta, Ashoka's grandfather, Ashoka may have heard of Alexander the Great from his grandmother and we know that his father invited a Greek philosopher to court.[4] Thus it is quite plausible that Ashoka would send embassies to Alexander's successors and sought to share with them his religious views. This is all the more interesting in light of the Greek and Aramaic versions of Ashokan inscriptions found near Taxila, discussed below. In this text, he uses the word Yona, a Persian word for Greeks (Ionians) and is aware that orthodox Brahmins and Buddhist monks do not exist among the Greeks.

In terms of religious ideology, it is clear that Ashoka associates his new reverence for *dharma* with the virtue of nonviolence. This is consistent with his declarations in numerous other inscriptions where he praises not only restraint from waging war but the adoption of vegetarianism. He uses the rhymed pair *brahmana*s and *sramana*s, a phrase even attested in Megasthenes (the Greek ambassador to Chandragupta's court), to refer to Vedic priests (brahmins) and "ascetics" (sramanas) of heterodox orders, primarily Buddhists, but members of other groups as well. In a socially conservative, almost Confucian way he values obedience to superiors and sees dharma as a kind of unspecific but humane morality, and assumes that it can spread even in those realms beyond the reach of Indian monks and teachers.

What we do not see here is any mention of specifically Buddhist monastic teaching about meditation or the attainment of enlightenment (nirvana), nor even elucidation of the moral requirements for Buddhist laypersons. Some scholars conclude then that Ashoka used the word dharma in the broadest and most inclusive sense,[5] and, though he patronized the Buddhist monastic order, followed a religious policy that encouraged obedience and morality rather than the adoption of any particular religion. Others,[6] however, emphasize that his role as the lay Buddhist patron par excellence required him to rule in such a way that produced a prosperous, peaceful realm within which Buddhist monks could pursue their lives as religious virtuosi. And late in his career, Ashoka does mention that he "set out for enlightenment" and went on a "dharma tour." This suggests that while playing his role as lay royal patron, he to some extent hankered after the religious life.[7]

Besides encouraging moral and respectful behavior alongside vegetarianism and nonviolence, we see from other edicts that Ashoka saw his royal role as that of a patron of religious institutions, a benefactor concerned with public welfare. He created special officials, dharma mahamatras, as agents of the empire assigned to oversight of religious institutions like monasteries and pilgrimage sites. He commissioned wells and rest homes and concerned himself with the availability of medical care for his subjects. In all these ways, he was concerned with doing good, with morality, and he saw the ritualistic side of religion as a waste of time. In that sense, though he supported a variety of religious communities, his support was not indiscriminate. He discouraged both animal sacrifice and the sort of ritualism that was the vocation of many brahmin priests (cf. Rock Edict 10).

Ashoka encouraged religious tolerance, stating explicitly "I have honored all religious sects with my offerings" (Pillar Edict 6):[8]

> King Priyadarsi honors men of all faiths, members of religious orders and laymen alike, with gifts and various marks of esteem. Yet he does not value either gifts or honors as much as growth in the qualities essential to religion in men of all faiths.

This growth may take many forms, but the root is guarding one's speech to avoid extolling one's own faith and disparaging the faith of others improperly, or, when the occasion is appropriate, immoderately.

The faiths of others all deserve to be honored for one reason or another. By honoring them, one exalts one's own faith and at the same time performs a service to the faith of others. By acting otherwise, one injures one's own faith and also does a disservice to the faith of others. . . .

The objective of these measures is the promotion of each man's particular faith and the glorification of Dharma.[9]

This makes it clear that for Ashoka, *dharma* is above particular religions, a meta-religion that serves as the guide for adjudicating the value of the numerous traditions that might contribute to the peace of the realm. The word he uses here for "sects" is *pasanda,* which seems to carry no negative connotations for Ashoka but is used by later writers to connote heresy.

Disparagement of another's religion is characterized here as an example of the sin of not controlling one's tongue. Though control of speech is certainly a Buddhist virtue, it would resonate well in Stoic Greek circles as well. Much of this declaration was copied in the Aramaic and Greek inscriptions of the northwest, where *dharma* is translated as *qyst* (Aramaic for "truth") and *eusebeia* (Greek for "piety"). The word "sect" (*pasanda*) is rendered in Greek as *diatribos,* conveying the sense of a school involved in debate with other schools. A Kandahar inscription values the man who is master of himself and controls his tongue (*gloses egkrates*)—displaying, in other words, virtues recognizable to wise men in Buddhist and Greek philosophical circles, but derived from a universal *dharma.*

Both Alexander and Ashoka were religious men in their personal lives who ruled vast cosmopolitan empires in which their subjects would have followed a bewildering variety of religious practices. And despite our tendency to separate East from West, their empires overlapped and shared much in common. What then can we ascertain about the relation of religion and power in the policies of these two emperors?

Although both men were cultural missionaries, neither sought to impose his personal religion upon the subject population. In Ashoka's case, despite the considerable expenditure and effort to have religion policed by his bureaucrats (the *dharma-mahamatras*), we have seen that he discouraged his people from religious disputation. His goal was to promulgate what he thought of as a reasonable public morality as a meta-religion, serving as the umbrella under which a variety of sects and movements could be nurtured and encouraged. He called his meta-religion *dharma,* which seems to have been the impetus for a veritable explosion of religious texts over the next five hundred years in which the nature of *dharma* is debated. In his own time, he was confident enough of the inclusive power of these ideas to send emissaries to Alexander's successors—ruling foreign realms where *brahmana*s and *sramana*s were not to be found—and still predict victory for *dharma/eusebeia.*

In Alexander's case, he was himself a personally pious devotee of Greek gods, thought of himself as the descendent of Achilles and Herakles, and felt a divine calling to pursue his destiny. As his extraordinary achievements began to confirm what he hoped or thought to be his invincible (*aniketos*) greatness, he began to claim divinity. But though he remained pious in his reverence for the gods of the Greek pantheon, even setting up images of them in India, his brush with divinity went beyond the classical Greek religion. Not only did he undertake the extraordinary and difficult pilgrimage to Siwah, where his party lost its way in the Libyan desert, only to survive by following flocks of birds (divinely sent, of course) to the oasis, but he was confirmed there as son of Amon and further received divine sanction for his Persian conquest. In other words, Alexander began to enter a cosmopolitan religious world in which he did not think of himself so much as the avenger of the Greeks, the liberator of fellow Greeks in Asia, and the proselytizer of a superior Greek culture, but rather as the recipient of a more universal divine approbation. Never really an insider to Greek culture, and certainly never accepted by the elite citizens of Athens, he began to have royal ambitions stoked by the conquest of far more ancient sites of civilization than Greece. He became pharoah, a divine king acclaimed by the Egyptian priesthood, and would later occupy Babylon as king of Asia, a successor of Cyrus. Divine kingship, resisted by Greeks and Jews and only cautiously embraced by some Roman emperors, was one of Alexander's legacies in the West, a tempting claim of final authority and claim for allegiance always dangerously at odds with the jealous claims of other gods.

Classic treatments of Alexander, especially Tarn,[10] celebrate the great conqueror as a man who brought democracy to Asia and promoted a universal brotherhood by encouraging and patronizing the intermarriage of Macedonians and Persians. When one reads of the ruthlessness of Alexander's campaigns, it is hard to see the great hero as a bearer of enlightenment, and more recently, scholars have emphasized his military genius more than any putative cultural program he might have promoted.[11] Nonetheless, after Alexander, we have a cultural arena at the crossroads of Eurasia, in which the Greek language spread, and cultural products flowed back and forth from Egypt to India. It was a cosmopolitan, multicultural world, and Alexander's successors, like Alexander himself, would have to develop policies that both enhanced their power by claiming final authority over the multiple centers of divine power spread across their realms.

We see the stress points of Alexander's own multicultural experiment in the resistance of his Macedonian soldiers to accept either his claims of divinity or his demand to be bowed down to as the Persian monarch. The rough soldiers in the Macedonian frontier kingdom expected their leaders to have the common touch. Their reluctance to bow down to a Persianized divine king make them precursors of those pious Muslims a thousand years later, who resist the pretensions of the caliphs who adopted Persian royal styles and adopted the title "shadow of God on earth."

Jonathan Z. Smith has called our attention to the distinction of "difference" and "otherness"; the first is the situation of two cultural groups recognizing their differences in order to work out a method of communication, the second a situation of such incommensurability that no communication is possible.[12] Clearly the imperial premises of both Alexander and Ashoka in regard to religion were based on the recognition of difference, not otherness. Alexander preferred his own gods, and rendered them worship even when he was in a region as distant as India. But he did not assume that his gods were universal and must be worshiped by the Asians he conquered. On the contrary, he quickly adapted himself to whatever religious culture he found himself in, and sacrificed reverently to local deities. In many cases, his practice, assumed to be the most natural one, was based on a rather facile identification of Greek gods with Asian or Egyptian equivalents. So instead of imagining a host of deities with limited regional jurisdictions and powers, the assumption is of a single set of universal deities worshiped under numerous names. Like negotiating foreign languages, foreign religions simply required proper translation.

Such an inclusivist theology would have seemed quite reasonable to Indians, and has remained, in fact, the standard Hindu approach to pluralism to the present day. Ashoka, however, seems to have thought through a rather more rigorous approach to religious pluralism. He subjected all religions to a critique based upon common criteria. Thus while he accepted the legitimacy of numerous religious groups in his realm and discouraged intolerant denunciation of any sect, and even while he himself patronized numerous religious groups outside his own preferred Buddhism, he saw all groups as valuable for the lives of his subjects insofar as they promoted *dharma,* taken here as meaning a kind of universal human morality. This provided him with a more clearly articulated meta-religion, a basis for a rational and moral adjudication of religions, on the basis of which, for all his tolerance, he felt justified in criticizing blood sacrifice and what he saw as the superstitious good-luck rituals of popular piety.

A meta-religion of moral and rational assumptions, rooted in an understanding of nature itself, provides the sort of universalist umbrella under which to shelter a multitude of ethnic sects and cults found in any large empire. In the Mediterranean world, Greek philosophy provided such a meta-religion, though it is vaguely defined in the policies of Alexander the Great. By the time of the Roman Empire, we see a fully developed meta-religion that made it possible to include and patronize a wide variety of religious groups, and yet maintain a claim on authority, not to be superseded by the theocratic claims of any group.

Thus from India to Rome, great kings claimed legitimacy using the language of religion, while still assuming a diversity of gods and sects across their realms. To govern this diversity, and comprehend it required the cultivation of universal standards of reason and morality. In the age after Alexander and Ashoka, universalists found a language that transcended traditional religion without displacing the local gods with the One. For Indians, it was the language of *dharma;* for those in the Hellenistic world, something similar was crafted. Shortly after Alexander created the conditions for cosmopolitanism (to use a Greek word), they began to write of the "animating Reason of the universe," a principle they called *logos.*

CHAPTER 2

Imperial Religion

China to Rome, 250 B.C.–250 A.D.

Short-lived as it was, Qin [Shih Huangdi] bequeathed a
heritage that has informed every type of government in China
thereafter, be it imperial, republican, Maoist, or post-Maoist.
This is seen in the acknowledged principle that authority
throughout the realm stems eventually from a single source of
power and that in this way the peoples and lands governed
by that power form a unity.

—Michael Loewe[1]

In fact, who is so demented, so mentally incapacitated as to
deny that there is one highest God. . . . With many names we
call upon his powers spread through the created world, since
we are all ignorant of his proper name.

—Maximus of Madaura[2]

How was religion related to the exercise of power in the centuries after
Alexander? In distant China, as well as in India and the Greco-Roman
world of the Mediterranean, religious diversity flourished, but under the
careful management of those who wielded power and influence: in
China, the emperor and the bureaucracy of scholar-officials; in Rome,
something similar; and in India, far more loosely, the priestly caste, the
brahmins. India will be the subject of the next chapter as we now concentrate on the two imperial wings of Eurasia, Rome and China, who
opened trade channels and exalted emperors to divine status in the centuries before and after Christ.

In 210 B.C., the First Emperor of China was buried with a massive
army of exquisitely carved terracotta warriors and their forty thousand

FIGURE 3. Terracotta warriors. Chensiyuan, photograph courtesy of Creative Commons.

bronze weapons.[3] After his stunning career as the first man to unify China into a centrally governed empire, Qin Shih Huangdi prepared to rule for eternity in heaven. On this earth, however, his brief dynasty, the Qin,[4] was to last only a few more years, to be followed by the glorious Han (202 B.C.–220 A.D.), whose writers disparaged the great First Emperor as a tyrant even while building on his many achievements.

Those achievements included the standardization of the writing of the Chinese language, standardized coinage, measurements, legal procedures, and the undertaking of massive public works projects (e.g., the building of the first stages of the Great Wall and a national road system). While Confucius had looked back to a mythic golden age of sage-kings, China was never politically or even culturally unified before the Qin Dynasty, but thereafter, the unified state became the ideal throughout Chinese history. As Michael Loewe, historian of the Qin and Han Dynasties notes above, the legacy of the Qin Dynasty was the continued belief in the unitary nature of the Chinese state and its people. Traditionally, historians argued that that initial unification came at the cost of a harsh authoritarianism backed by anti-Confucian, "Legalist" (*Fa Jia*) scholars, including a program of thought control by burning classical books and executing numerous recalcitrant scholars.[5] Some such activity was authorized by the regime, though it was probably far less ruthless than Han writers and politicians portrayed it, as they were eager to discredit the dynasty they had replaced. It is nonetheless true

FIGURE 4. Chinese Emperor Qin Shih Huangdi. Dennis Jarvis, photograph courtesy of Creative Commons.

that Qin Shih Huangdi vigorously pursued the goal of politically and culturally unifying the Chinese Empire and breaking with tradition (and the majority of Confucian scholars) in order to weaken the wealthy feudal lords in the former principalities of the realm. When the Han Dynasty assumed power, it restored the prestige of the Confucian ideology, but did so in a way that retained the central power of the emperor.

Two centuries after the First Emperor of China took the title Huangdi ("August Thearch"), Octavian (d. 14 A.D.), Rome's first emperor, gained a similar title, Augustus Caesar, Son of the Divine. He too ruled over an expansive empire, conquering lands all around the Mediterranean, including Judea and Galilee, where an obscure preacher named Jesus of Nazareth would be executed by his successor. Improbably, Jesus too would gain the title of Son of the Divine, and one day be revered even by Roman emperors as Christ the King. In the Augustan age of the Pax Romana, however, Jesus's sort of exclusivist monotheism was hardly the norm, and seen by powerful Romans as the belief of weird cultists. Augustus preferred a revival of traditional religion and would oversee the restoration of eighty temples to old Roman gods in his capital. Even while the cult of the emperor was cultivated as a mark of imperial unity, Rome was also becoming the home of many temples to foreign gods. Until the imperial adoption of Christianity, this would be the pattern: an inclusive adoption of foreign gods, an emphasis on piety and tradition, all under the aegis of a divine or semidivine emperor. Only those groups resisting inclusion and thus disloyal to the emperor, would suffer persecution.

CHINA DURING THE HAN DYNASTY: IMPERIAL CIVIL RELIGION AND THE SECTARIAN CHALLENGE

Though remote from South Asia and the West, China made its first sustained contact with both civilizations in this period, just as the Qin and Han Dynasties established cultural norms that were to endure through most of Chinese history. In China today, the dominant ethnic group refer to themselves as "Han Chinese," and it was during the Han that a certain Confucian orthodoxy became the basis for imperial policy and civil religion.[6]

Traditional descriptions of Chinese religion often give accounts of Confucianism, Daoism (Taoism), and Buddhism, as though most Chinese had a clear sense of three distinct traditions. As a corrective to this misleading view, scholars emphasize that there are broadly shared Chinese values like harmony, and that only certain intellectuals might be strongly invested in one tradition—Confucianism, say—and opposed to another—Buddhism, for example. At a folk religion level, most villages would have a local deity unaffiliated with any literate tradition. Moreover, any adequate account of Chinese civilization needs to emphasize that for most of Chinese history, the imperial center had great importance, and that managing religion was a task the imperial regime took very seriously. Thus the careers of the various Chinese religious traditions must in large part be viewed in terms of their relation to the Chinese imperial project.

After a period of anti-Confucianism during the Qin regime, the Han Dynasty made Confucianism the officially sanctioned ideology of the state. Among other things, this involved the state examinations, which ambitious young men took as a pathway to lucrative careers as civil servants. This role for Confucian orthodoxy was to remain a feature of high culture in China until the early twentieth century. So, what was the nature of this Confucianism, and how did it relate to popular culture and to the high culture of the imperial state?

What we know of Confucius (d. 480 B.C.) comes to us from the work attributed to him, known as the *Analects,* but after the Qin Dynasty, the extant text clearly contains much material added long after Confucius died. Thus we have a kind of received version of Confucius's values, and much of standard Confucianism is the result of several centuries of reflection by Confucian scholars. Most prominent of these values would be the virtues of ritual propriety (*li*), involving filial piety (*xiao*), and leading to a posture of humane interaction (*ren*). The goal of the Confucian program is to produce cultivated gentlemen who will revere tradition and govern selflessly. It is a conservative program that presumes that ego is conquered through submission to the rules of etiquette, and that a hierarchical society governed by such rules will be one of harmony, where human interaction is gracefully choreographed. Confucius's putatively autobiographical statement in the *Analects* traces his life of cultivation through reverential study: "The Master said, At fifteen I set my heart on learning. At thirty, I had planted my feet firm upon the ground. At forty, I no longer suffered from perplexities. At fifty, I knew what were the biddings of Heaven. At sixty, I heard them with a docile ear. At seventy, I could follow the dictates of my own heart; for what I desired no longer overstepped the boundaries of right" (*Analects* 2.4).[7] In large part, for two thousand years, this remained a human ideal, the ideal of the sage. The Confucian goal of humble submission to ritual etiquette and the cultivation of learning in the pursuit of gentlemanly virtues produced armies of civil servants who governed the Chinese Empire. It was clearly a powerful ideology, but Confucianism spoke little of divine beings or prayer, so was it a religion? Perhaps not in the sense of those traditions that offered salvation to individuals, but certainly its emphasis on ritual, selflessness, and duty produced a tradition that jealously guarded its role as the highest standard for human behavior, and the proper philosophy for the governance of the Chinese Empire. And more broadly, if the Chinese have long revered harmony as a primary human goal, the Confucian belief that harmony is achieved by common submission to ritual meant that most Chinese felt that the map of the heavenly Way (*Dao*) was ritual propriety. One elliptical saying in the *Analects* captures this spirit: "The Master said, 'As for governing through non-assertion (*wu-wei*), was not

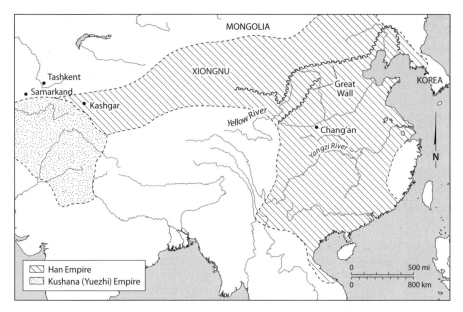

MAP 3. The Han Empire, ca. 100 A.D.

Shun an example of this? What did he do? All he did was make himself reverent and face south in a correct posture, that is all'" (15.4).[8] In other words, by submitting to the ritual, the ancient sage king Shun achieved harmony and exercised moral force (*de*), without assertive action. Here we see how the Confucian might use the language generally associated with Daoism (*wu wei,* nonaction) to describe the effective and peaceable actions of nonegotistical ruler.

In Han times, especially under the long reign of Emperor Wu (r. 141–87 B.C.) and his official the scholar Dong Zhongshu (d. 104 B.C.), not only was Confucianism made the orthodox creed of the ruling class, it was supplemented by numerous references to *yin-yang* cosmology. The emperor put a great deal of time and thought into his role as Son of Heaven, carrying out elaborate rituals intended to establish proper, harmonious relations with Heaven and Earth. In this, his actions often mimicked those of Qin Shih Huangdi. He also resembled the First Emperor in his reliance upon harsh punishments to maintain order. Dong argued that the king should carry out executions in the winter, when nature's chastising force (*yin*) was ascendant, and not as *yang* waxed with the coming of spring, summer, and new life. The actions of the ruler might be thus ritualized while nonetheless brutal.

Of course, not all Chinese agreed with Confucian ideas. Besides the Qin Legalists, some great thinkers of the third century B.C., especially Zhuangzi (Chuang Tzu), argued that the individual attained harmony with Dao by living spontaneously, attaining "naturalness" (*ziran*) and casting off convention. Calling themselves Daoists, the authors of these ancient texts developed ideas that appealed to many individuals, especially those for whom civic life was not satisfying. We can certainly see the appeal of Zhuangzi's writing and the text of the *Dao De Jing* (*Tao Te Ching*), for a civil servant who lost his job because of war or political intrigue.

Often ridiculing Confucius, Zhuangzi writes in language that sounds very Buddhist, but he penned these lines centuries before the first Buddhist set foot in China: "Do not be an embodier of fame; do not be a storehouse of schemes; do not be an undertaker of projects; do not be a proprietor of wisdom. Embody to the fullest what has no end and wander where there is no trail. Hold on to all that you have received from Heaven but do not think you have anything. Be empty, that is all. The Perfect Man uses his mind like a mirror—going after nothing, welcoming nothing, responding but not storing."[9] Written before the rise of the Qin, a text like this would gain popularity in the third century A.D., when the great Han Dynasty fell to northern barbarian invaders and cultivated Confucian gentlemen lost their roles as "undertakers of projects" and "proprietors of wisdom." But in the prosperity and optimism of the early Han, it was Confucius who was mostly venerated, as the patron saint of filial piety, respectful obedience, and service to the emperor. Because of its enlarged social role, Confucianism in this period changed from being simply a set of philosophical reflections on ethics, character, and government, to being a civil religion. If the emperor was the Son of Heaven and state-supported rituals kept the earth in harmony with heaven, the emperor's regime should suffice in supplying the Chinese populace with a sense of meaning. Popular religion of ancestor worship and supplication of village deities could merge with this ethos, but sectarian religion, promising an alternative source of meaning and personal salvation, was a threat to the state's jealous claims to ultimacy. Such "cults" or "secret societies," from the perspective of the emperor and his loyal ministers, would always be viewed with suspicion.

In the second century A.D., as the Han Dynasty began to crumble, two Daoist sectarian movements arose that formed the template of future "alternative" religions that rose up to challenge the state's claim to have a monopoly on meaning and truth. They were called the Yellow

Turbans and the Celestial Masters. These "religious Daoists" (*Dao Jiao*) are generally distinguished from the world-weary gentlemen or "philosophical Daoists" (*Dao Jia*) who read the *Dao De Jing* and Zhuangzi as a means to cultivate the spirit of detachment.

The Yellow Turbans were active in eastern China during the 180s, spreading among landless peasants and landowners in a period of floods and famine. Led by faith healers promulgating a scripture called *Tai Ping Jing* (Scripture of Great Peace), the sect welcomed women and men, and preached an apocalyptic, utopian message. Given the weakness and corruption of the Han emperor in this period, the Yellow Turbans initially gained a significant following, and were a real threat to the regime. Expecting a New World in 184 A.D., they rose up with a force of 360,000 rebels, and suddenly all of China was at war. Crushing them involved a major military operation that left the dynasty mortally wounded.

In western China, a similar movement, the Celestial Masters, gained numerous followers among both the Han Chinese and other ethnic groups. Also known as the "five-bushels sect," they too began as a utopian and millenarian movement, taking donations of rice from all, and seeking to take over China, again in the name of a promised "Great Peace" (*tai ping*). Under the grandson of the founder, they were able to establish a regional theocratic state. Although never officially breaking with the Han Dynasty, in effect sectarian priests replaced government officials, and the sect's leader (the "Celestial Master") assumed ultimate authority in the region. Conquered by a warlord in 215, the Celestial Master made peace with his conqueror and intermarried with his family, and his followers were dispersed throughout China. Although they never again assumed real political power, this sect became part of a Daoist church organization that has survived to the present day, especially in Taiwan.

Thus we see in the Han Dynasty a wealthy and powerful empire surviving for four centuries, a sort of mirror of Rome,[10] where the state found support in the kind of sober civil religion of duty and tradition that Roman elites would surely understand. Before the coming of Buddhism, Daoist cults—popular, egalitarian, apocalyptic, and utopian—challenged the status quo and won significant battles against a weakening and corrupt imperial regime in the 180–220 A.D. period. After the fall of the Han, in a period of political division that would last from 220 to 589 A.D., Buddhism would enter China and win many followers among those for whom the staid and worldly traditionalism of Confucius was unsatisfying. It would also provide "barbarian" rulers in the north an alternative state religion to Confucianism and a cadre of monks to replace the Confucian scholar-officials who saw them as usurpers of the Han. But for now, we can note that a basic religious pattern had been established in China that would endure: a state religion of traditional reverence, living comfortably with popular village religion, but threatened by sectarian movements that might provide an alternative system of meaning to those oppressed by the state, or those in need of a personal salvation not supplied by the civil religion.

HELLENISTIC AND ROMAN CIVIL RELIGION AND THE MONOTHEISTIC RELIGIONS

The Han emperors authorized the exploration and colonization of the Central Asian trading oases that would eventually produce what we call the Silk Road. But before the Chinese fully developed a lucrative trade with distant Rome, the West was following political and religious patterns that paralleled Chinese ones. Here we consider those patterns in the period before Christianity became politically important in the West and Buddhism became politically important in China. Kings in the period 250 B.C. to 250 A.D. from China to Central Asia, Iran, and the West all claimed some version of religious legitimacy, and all repressed any religious community that seemed to discourage reverential loyalty to the regime.

In the Macedonian successor kingdoms to Alexander's empire, especially the Seleucids, who held much of the old Persian realm, and the Ptolemies of Egypt, we see a continuation of both the promotion of Greek culture, and the sort of religious inclusivism that made a place for local deities and cults. In such a world, the Greek language was the lingua franca, and Greek philosophy provided a cosmopolitan way of understanding religious diversity. What had faded was the Greek ideal of the independent, democratic city-state or *polis*, for which fifth-century Athens served as the ideal. In that sort of community, citizens had debated the affairs of the day and felt they had a real voice in politics. Their Olympian religion, what was called paganism after the rise of Christianity, was one of duty and tradition ("good form"). It compares well to Han Confucianism. Scholars have noted that even when classical thinkers began to have philosophical doubts about their belief in the gods, they still attended to the proper pieties expected of them by tradition. Such a religion, resting on a sense of assured gesture and communal tradition rather than articulate belief and intense interior experience, was wholly congruent with the shared social and political life of tight-knit communities. In contrast, the Hellenistic world of cosmopolitan cities, where the average person felt cut off from politics and social life, was fractured and diverse, and produced many sectarian movements we today might call "cults," small communities of adherents given to a devotional religion of mystery or ecstasy, focused not on the gentle satisfactions of tradition but on the palpable experience of transcendence and salvation. Whereas in China, sectarians were impoverished peasants crushed by excessive land rents, in the Hellenistic world, it was the lower-class population of cities that turned to religions of salvation. Thus while the so-called Hellenistic world saw the spread of the Greek language and aspects of Greek culture, there was also the spread of non-Greek religion from Egypt and Babylon, foreign gods and goddesses that offered solace and salvation to the alienated populations of great cities from Alexandria to Antioch, Corinth to Rome. Most of these could be tolerated and absorbed as "popular religion," as in China, but some did appear to represent a political threat.

One community might seem the most likely one to disrupt the dominant imperial paradigm of inclusivist polytheism: the Jews. Of course, despite their uncompromising monotheism and the fact that their sacred biblical texts recalled a time of political independence under the great kings David and Solomon, the Jews had by this period both dispersed in large numbers to places like Alexandria and Babylon, as well as worked out a modus vivendi with their Hellenistic overlords to maintain an unencumbered religious life in Jerusalem. While many Jews could never really accept the status of their god and cult as simply one among many—the claims of Yahweh were too jealous for that—most nonetheless acculturated to the Hellenistic world. They learned Greek and read the Bible in that language. Left alone to practice their religion, many of the Jewish elite were quite happy to live in a world where their political masters spoke Greek and established a Hellenistic public life of gymnasiums, theaters, and schools. Just as many American Jews today, especially of the Reformed tradition, want to live in the mainstream of a public life governed by a public ideology that does not recognize their religion but happily tolerates it, many of the Jews of late antiquity embraced Hellenism with enthusiasm.

In the centuries after Alexander, we can learn much from the fate of Jews in the Mediterranean world about the possibilities and limits of imperial inclusivism. There were many such submerged religious subcultures, but none that we know as much about as we do the Jews. We will consider here two different stories: first the Maccabean revolt, and second, the appeal of the famous Jewish intellectual, Philo of Alexandria, to the Roman emperor.

For the person familiar with the Bible, it is important to recognize that from the perspective of the great Hellenistic empires of the Mediterranean world, the little principality of Judea, and even the broader community of Jews dispersed throughout these empires, were of relatively little importance. Pious legends have Alexander making pilgrimage to Jerusalem during his campaigns in the Near East, but these are fictional. His concern was with greater centers of power—Memphis, Tyre, Persepolis, and especially Babylon—than with Jerusalem, and while he reverenced the pagan gods of these cities, seen as parallels to the Olympian gods he worshiped, he had no time for the God of Abraham.

Alexander's successors, up to and including the Romans, would have had a similar outlook, seeing the importance of local temples as sources of power and revenue, and largely respecting the right of local peoples to maintain their traditional religious practices. If the multiplicity of subordinate peoples of a great empire could be organized into a strong alliance, surely the many deities they worshiped could be similarly allied. If the Jews wanted to claim that their god alone was The God, the only deity deserving reverence, that was simply their view, an unimportant one as long as they did not seek to back up that claim militarily. Without an army, their resistant theology could be easily contained— and even, given the right gestures of collaboration, supported.

In the centuries after Alexander and prior to Roman rule, Jerusalem lay along the border between the Ptolemaic and Seleucid empires. Being Macedonian successor states, both promoted Hellenistic culture in the alien cultures of Egypt and the Near East. Until the famous Cleopatra, none of the Ptolemies bothered to learn the Egyptian language, even while counting on the indigenous Egyptian priesthood to legitimate their rule. The Jews of Judea also had the choice to favor the rule of one or the other and their own internal divisions often broke down along those lines, Ptolemy-supporters versus the pro-Seleucid faction.

During the reign of Antiochus III (223–187 B.C.), Jerusalem was under Seleucid control. Antiochus III was an ambitious and energetic ruler, eager to regain lost lands and push back his frontiers. Like Alexander, he brushed aside financial concerns as he pursued his military objectives and campaigned once again in the far eastern territories bordering India. Antiochus dealt with the Jews of Judea through the high

FIGURE 5. Second Temple in Jerusalem. Getty Images, photograph courtesy of iStockphoto.

priest of Solomon's ancient Temple in Jerusalem. At this time, the high priest was the equivalent of a petty prince, ruling in consultation with a governing council. The Jews of Judea lived then as a more or less self-governing state, while recognizing the ultimate authority of the Seleucid emperor. The emperor even supplied the Temple with a very generous supply of sacrificial animals, wine, oil, wheat, and incense. This sort of arrangement represents the Hellenistic norm, where great kings reign over all, but rule through intermediaries in a great diversity of states representing a multiplicity of cultures.

The Jews of Jerusalem, as well as those of the diaspora, largely ignored the attractions of foreign deities, but many were attracted to cosmopolitan Hellenistic culture. One could develop a less strict form of observance in order to participate more widely in the Greek-speaking world: reading their literature, attending their theaters, even exercising in their gymnasiums. So many Jews preferred Greek to Aramaic or Hebrew that the Bible was translated in Alexandria (as the Septuagint) during the reign of Ptolemy II Philadelphus (r. 283–246), one of the four Macedonian kings known to Ashoka.

So it is all the more surprising that in this broadly tolerant, pluralistic world, we discover the events of religious repression that led to a major

Jewish revolt, remembered by Jews today in the stories associated with the holidays of Hanukkah. When we read that Antiochus IV Epiphanes (r. 175–164) wantonly desecrated the Temple in Jerusalem by having Baal (equated with Zeus) worshiped there with a pig sacrifice, one wonders what possessed him to adopt religious policy so unlike that of his predecessors and successors. Is it a simple tale of an intolerant bigot trying to exterminate the Jewish religion in order to bring them into line with all his vassals by having all his realm worship his royal person as a god, as Zeus incarnate (Epiphanes)?

The morality tale found in the first book of Maccabees would certainly present it that way.[11] The text notes that after Alexander, a "sinful root" sprouted in the person of Antiochus IV. Some Jews sought accommodation with Greek or gentile culture:

> In those days lawless men came forth from Israel, and misled many, saying "Let us go and make a covenant with the Gentiles round us, for since we separated from them many evils have come upon us." This proposal pleased them, and some of the people went to the king. He authorized them to observe the ordinances of the Gentiles. So they built a gymnasium in Jerusalem, according to Gentile custom, and removed the marks of circumcision, and abandoned the holy covenant. They joined with the Gentiles and sold themselves to do evil. (1 Macc. 1:11–15)

In other words, before Antiochus IV's explicit acts of desecration, some of Jerusalem's Jews were quite ready to integrate with the high culture of Hellenism. But when Antiochus, strapped for cash after his expensive campaigns against Ptolemaic Egypt (and those of his grandfather Antiochus III), desecrated the Temple to plunder its wealth, Jerusalem's Jews were faced with a consequential choice: either they would rebel, to honor the sanctity of their most holy and ancient traditions, in which case they would be branded as insurrectionist and Ptolemy sympathizers, or they could peaceably collaborate with a regime that had no respect for their religious tradition. Antiochus IV rather rashly seemed to think he could command the wholesale abandonment of the Jewish law. Many Jews, faced with execution, clearly did capitulate, as the first book of Maccabees readily admits (1 Macc. 1:41–52), but others were radicalized and began the guerilla movement known as the Maccabean Revolt, led by Judas Maccabeus ("the Hammer") and his brothers.

Clearly, the king had overreached. Inheriting a Seleucid realm where many Jews were quite content to live in a vassal state and participate in the cosmopolitan culture of the Hellenistic world, Antiochus IV antagonized the majority of Judean Jews, not only the tradition-minded farmers of the countryside but the sophisticated, urban elites of Jerusalem as well. His demands were extreme indeed. When a thoroughly Hellenized high priest was willing to go so far as to make contributions for the sacrificial rituals to Melkart (a Phoenician deity associated with Herakles) at the athletic games in Tyre (171 B.C.), a gesture of recognition of the pagan civic religion, Antiochus managed to horrify and alienate even him. The conflict began over money, but while this was an uncomfortable fact of what we might call Seleucid colonialism—where the high priest was understood to be a collaborationist conduit of funds to the imperial center—we see that Antiochus's demand to enter the Temple directly and to personally extract funds from the treasury crossed a critical threshold. Grudging acceptance of the status quo suddenly gave way to open rebellion.

Supporting in response a really extreme faction of pro-Seleucid collaborationists, Antiochus IV began policies intended to completely eradicate all vestiges of Jewish observance. He banned circumcision and observance of the Sabbath. He forced Jews to eat pork and ordered sacrifices performed to Baal Shamin, the Phoenician deity in his mind equated with Zeus, but for Jews, the epitome of the false idols of their ancient Canaanite enemies. Most commentators read the biblical book of Daniel as a not-so-veiled reference to the abominations of Antiochus Epiphanes: "Forces from him shall appear and profane the Temple and fortress, and shall take away the continual burnt offering. And they shall set up the abomination that makes desolate. He shall seduce with flattery those who violate the covenant; but the people who know their God shall stand firm and take action" (Dan. 11:31–32).

It is noteworthy that Antiochus did not make similar demands of Jews living in other parts of his empire. His bloody repression in Jerusalem seems to have been primarily motivated, not by a crazed desire to have Jews worship him, but out of a need for money and a misguided belief that he could succeed by backing the most Hellenized of the Jewish elite class. Yet he only succeeded in provoking a nationalist revolt of uncompromising religious zealots who not only wanted the restoration of the right to practice their traditional religion, but also developed a thirst for political independence, and a desire not only to cleanse the Temple, but to remove all members of the Hellenizer faction from the priesthood. Although Antiochus Epiphanes realized his mistake just before he died, sending word to the Judean Jews that they could revert to their traditional religion and all its practices, he still sought to work with the most Hellenized among them. Resistance continued under the

Maccabee brothers, resulting in the establishment of relative freedom for the Jewish nation for almost a century.

It is important to note here that the fourth book of Maccabees, while recounting the grisly details of seven brothers tortured to death by Antiochus for remaining true to Jewish law, argues in the language of Stoic philosophy that the brothers' martyrdom was evidence of the victory of Reason over the claims of emotion. Reason, in the service of piety (*eusebeia*),[12] allows the "philosophical" martyrs to face torture and death with heroic equanimity (4 Macc. 1:1–6; 4 Macc. 5:18–31). So even in the heroic struggle to defend a Jewish way of life from the repressive policy of Hellenizers, colonized Jewish intellectuals used the very language and philosophy of their colonizing oppressors.

The peculiarity of the religious struggle between observant Jews and Antiochus IV brings into sharp relief the nature of the more usual, moderate policies of Hellenistic kings. While Alexander's pretensions to divinity were tentative, and mocked by his fellow Macedonians, the later Hellenistic kings often successfully claimed divine status and were rendered due worship by their subjects. But in a polytheistic world, the multitude of deities made it possible for most people to do their patriotic duty while maintaining a traditional local piety or cultivating a devotion for one of the exotic deities like Isis or Mithras who offered personal salvation, and whose ecstatic cult spoke more directly to the heart than the staid and formal traditions of the civic cult. Under the Romans, even the Jewish priests worked out a compromise whereby they avoided the idolatry of sacrificing *to* the divine emperor, but were willing to offer sacrifice *on behalf of* the emperor to the One God who ruled the cosmos.

Once again, however, the relative peace won by tolerant inclusivism was shattered when an emperor overreached. When Gaius Caesar, known as Caligula (r. 37–41 A.D.), demanded to have his image installed in all temples, including the Jewish Temple in Jerusalem and in synagogues throughout his realm, resistant Jews stood out as disloyal cranks. In this case, however, crisis was averted without armed rebellion, but more interestingly, we see in the work of Philo, a thoroughly Hellenized Jew of Alexandria, an argument that sought to win a place for the particular Jewish religious observances by means of universalistic Greek philosophical ideas. In other words, Philo was a proponent of a minority religion (a religion that has sometimes proved most resistant to inclusion), who made use of Greek philosophy to reestablish his claim of loyalty to the empire. So unlike the emperor, who might develop a sort of meta-religion in order to establish his inclusive hegemony over the many faiths of his realm, here the meta-religious ideology is employed by a man without hegemonic power, willing to give up any demands that others abide by his religion, but hoping only to find a niche for his group within the broad cultural and political framework of Hellenistic cosmopolitanism.

Philo was a contemporary of the apostle Paul, and like him, was conversant with the Hebrew scripture but wrote exclusively in Greek. He wrote numerous philosophical treatises in which he balanced a commitment to biblical texts with his commitments to a Greek philosophical discourse. He portrayed the law-giver Moses as a kind of ancient philosopher, read scriptures allegorically, and developed a concept of God consistent with notions of a cosmic law of reason. Jewish particulars were read as expressions of universal truths. Jews expressed these truths in the language of law, allegory, and myth, while the Greeks employed the language of philosophy. The truths were the same. Thus, for Philo, circumcision is simply commanded of Jews, but *is reasonable* as a practice that symbolizes excision of improper pleasure, even as it leads to health and vitality.

Philosophically then, Philo was convinced that Jewish religious practice had a reasonable place in the world of Hellenistic thought, just as he believed the Jewish people could be loyal Roman citizens. In appealing to universalism, he employed the word *logos,* often somewhat misleadingly translated as "the Word" as in the prologue to the Gospel of John ("In the beginning was the Word ... "). *Logos,* like Ashoka's *dharma,* and perhaps the Chinese *Dao,* implies a universal Reason, upon which the comprehensible patterns of nature and human community are founded. Using this concept, so popular among the Stoic philosophers of his day, Philo was able to read biblical references to God's speech and action as expressions of His reasonable ordering of His creation. *Logos* linked the transcendent God to this world.[13]

It is not surprising, then, that given his finding of a congruence of Jewish law and Reason, Philo looked forward to a day when all people would affirm their common truths. He believed that even in his own day the wise Emperor Augustus had recognized the fundamental truths that Jews proclaimed. He welcomed converts to Judaism and awaited the day when "each nation would abandon its peculiar ways, and, throwing overboard its ancestral customs, turn to honoring our [Mosaic] laws alone."[14]

Given his intellectual preeminence, it is not surprising that Philo was chosen by his community to lead a delegation to Emperor Caligula to win for the Jews the right to maintain their religious practices by avoiding the inclusion of the emperor's image in their synagogues. (Meanwhile Petronius, a more cautious official in Jerusalem, was stalling, hoping to avoid a crisis.) Philo writes of this task in two texts, *Legatio ad Gaium*, (*Delegation to Gaius*, i.e., to Caligula) and *In Flaccum* (*Against Flaccus*, the Roman official in Alexandria executing Caligula's orders).

Philo and his colleagues had two primary objectives. First they had to refute the charges of some non-Jewish Alexandrians that their religious scruples were signs of political disloyalty. To this, Philo replies that Jews recognize the Roman Empire as the very center of world civilization, noteworthy for its noble system of laws. Indeed the Jews' only request was to be treated as other people under Roman law were treated; they should be allowed to maintain their traditional religious practices. The second objective followed the first, namely convincing the emperor that worshiping his image in their Temple and synagogues was for Jews tantamount to apostasy.

In reporting on the broader diplomatic effort to persuade the emperor to desist from a direct assault on the religion of the Jews, Philo gives an account of the arguments of King Agrippa, Gaius's friend and the successor of King Herod in Judea and Galilee. On hearing of Caligula's order to defile the Temple, Agrippa falls into a faint, from which, according to Philo, he recovers enough to write a long letter pleading the case of the Jews. His argument follows the one of Philo, asserting that the religious practices of Jews deserve respect but that does not make the Jews less patriotic than others:

> It fell to me to have for my grandparents and ancestors kings, most of whom had the title of high priest, who considered their kingship inferior to their priesthood, holding that the office of high priest is as superior in excellence to that of the king as God surpasses men. For the office of one is to worship God, of the other to have charge of men. As my lot is cast in such a nation, city and temple I beseech you for them all. For the nation, that it may not get a reputation the reverse of the truth, when from the very first it has been so piously and religiously disposed to all your house. For in all matters in which piety is enjoined and permitted under their laws it stood not a whit behind any either in Asia or in Europe, in its prayers, its erection of votive offerings, its number of sacrifices.[15]

It is striking that Agrippa can hope that Caligula might be persuaded by an argument that emphasized the difference in worshiping the one God and governing men. What is more striking, however, is Agrippa's emphasis on the *religious* activities Jews undertook to show their devotion to the Roman emperor. They would not worship the emperor but they certainly worshiped on his behalf. More than once in this passage we find the word *eusebeia,* "piety," the very word Ashoka employed to translate *dharma,* and here as well it carried the connotation of proper duty, divinely sanctioned but linked to political authority. Representing the sort of Roman client that mediated between the Jewish people and the Romans, Agrippa might appeal to the emperor as a reasonable sort, his own power dependent upon the Romans. Meanwhile, the restive, overtaxed peasants, who were suspicious of both their own collaborationist leaders as much as the Roman overlords, began to protest openly in the tens of thousands.

Face to face with Caligula, an emperor determined to be worshiped as a god, and moreover, a mentally unbalanced and unpredictable man, the members of Philo's delegation were subject to his mocking scorn but succeeded in disputing the charge of political disloyalty. On the second matter, they left without any clear word on the future of emperor worship in their synagogues. Within a year, however, Caligula was dead, and his successor, Claudius, rescinded the order. The Jews of Alexandria returned to a life of religious freedom within the context of their participation in a fully Hellenistic cultural life.

For modern-day Christians, the experiences of the Jews under Seleucid and especially Roman rule are read as preludes to the experience of the early Christian martyrs. They identify with the Jews as a people unfairly persecuted for their devotion to the one true God by an oppressive, tyrannical regime. One might note, however, that from the Roman perspective, the political exercise of authority, and the peace and prosperity that issued from the effective exercise of that authority, depended on certain broad cultural agreements. Religious diversity was largely accepted, but only insofar as one's group took its place alongside the others, under the umbrella of a philosophically grounded, meta-religious ideology, consistent with Roman law and reverence for the emperor. For much of this period, elite diaspora Jews were able to live amicably in this context, and Philo's intellectual project is consistent with the goal of preserving the particulars of Jewish practice while seeking common ground with the rulers on the basis of a shared philosophical universalism, all the while avoiding any challenge to the legitimacy of Roman imperial rule. However, in the aftermath of Antiochus's repression, the Jews of Judea both accentuated the marks of their religious identity and pursued a quest for real political independence. After a period of some success, their fortunes were to decline, suffering the

Roman destruction of the Temple in 70 A.D., and again in 132 A.D., the context in which early Christians, seen first as a sect of Jews, began to work out their relationship to imperial power. But before turning to this next episode, we should try and inhabit the imaginations of those Roman authorities suspicious of the religious communities resisting full integration into the broader society of the Roman Empire. In Philo's Alexandria, the Jews were fairly successful in making their claim to be Alexandrians and not foreigners and exiles, as their opponents accused. Like all the diverse peoples of the eastern Roman Empire, they spoke Greek and lived in a thoroughly Hellenistic culture, and even Caligula judged them "unfortunate rather than wicked."[16] Strictly observant separatists, whatever their early military success, were no match for the Roman Empire; even the Temple was abandoned for a new Judaism of study and prayer in synagogues.

What is clear from this history is that imperial power can tolerate religious diversity, as long as a certain cultural agreement is reached with regard to a shared social and political life. Those Romans in authority were like the modern French government, happy to accommodate a variety of religious communities until those communities reject cultural integration and challenge the authority of the state. At that point, any sign of religious identity—language, dress, circumcision—could be seen as an expression of disloyalty to the state and the broader community.

We need to keep in mind here that there was no one Judaism in this period, and that the social locations of Jews in Jerusalem or the countryside of Judea, Samaria, Galilee, and the diaspora had everything to do with how Jews viewed Roman imperialism. Just as the Seleucids and Ptolemies sought out compliant Jewish elites who would not only embrace Hellenistic culture but would legitimate their rule and taxation policies, so too did the Romans. King Herod, who ruled Judea from 37–4 B.C., was an especially favored client of Emperor Augustus; his brutal repression of the people and his ruthless extraction of taxes are revealed in the New Testament gospels, while Roman sources treat him as a loyal and successful leader. The New Testament not only in portrays Herod as the evil king, but paints a general picture of peasant poverty and disease, social ills that Jesus addressed in his itinerant ministry.

Scholars like John Dominic Crossan and Richard A. Horsley have emphasized that Jesus can not be accurately viewed as a humble preacher of wise sayings to isolated individuals, but must be seen as one of many protesting against the injustice and oppression produced by the Roman imperial project.[17] Judea, Samaria, and Galilee were *colonies,* and like the colonies of modern European imperial powers, produced leaders who identified with the ruling invaders and profited by their alliance. The client kings and the priests of Solomon's Temple were Jews, but exercised power and legitimacy as the agents of the Romans. Those without power or wealth, on the other hand, hoped against hope for a new world order. They called it the Kingdom of God. And such a kingdom appeared a troublesome rival to the first Roman emperor. In that period, a Roman civil war had pitted Marc Antony and the Macedonian queen of Egypt, Cleopatra, against Octavian, adopted son of Julius Caesar. It ended with Octavian's victory at Actium in 31 B.C. Thereafter, Octavian, now called Augustus Caesar (r. 27 B.C.–14 A.D.), was celebrated as "the Savior" (*Soter*) and Bringer of Peace. Horsley quotes from an Augustan inscription:

> The most divine Caesar . . . we should consider equal to the Beginning of all things . . . ; for when everything was falling [into disorder] and tending toward dissolution, he restored it once more and gave to the whole world a new aura.
>
> Whereas providence, which has regulated our whole existence . . . has brought our whole life to the climax of perfection in giving to us [the emperor] Augustus, whom it [Providence] filled with strength for the welfare of men, and who being sent to us and our descendants as Savior, has put an end to war and has set all things in order; and [whereas,] having become [god] manifest (*phaneis*), Caesar has fulfilled all the hopes of earlier times . . . in surpassing all the benefactors who preceded him . . . , and whereas, finally, the birthday of the god [Augustus] has been for the whole world the beginning of good news (*euvangelion* [= gospel]) concerning him [therefore let a new era begin from his birth].[18]

It was a peace that did little for oppressed peasants of the empire, and those hoping for God's Kingdom looked for a different kind of savior and a different gospel. At the conclusion of Herod's repressive rule, there were massive revolts, and the Romans turned to increasingly harsh methods to put them down. Anyone claiming to be anointed by God (*messiah*), the successor of King David and the proclaimer of liberation and God's reign, would be a dangerous figure to the Romans. Jesus was not the first of such figures and certainly not the last. The Romans crucified thousands of rebels and enslaved tens of thousands in suppressing the revolts.[19] Clearly the early followers of Jesus would have had a much less positive view of Roman rule than Philo had.

The Romans who crucified Jesus and countless other bandits and revolutionaries spoke the language of peace and reason and even divine legitimacy. Pompey's initial invasion of the east (66 B.C.) was under-

FIGURE 6. Augustus Caesar. Getty Images, photograph courtesy of iStockphoto.

taken to "pacify" bandits/terrorists/pirates (*latrones*),[20] who blocked the flow of grain from Egypt and Asia back to the metropole. He was content to reinstate the high priest as a sort of religious and political leader in Jerusalem, but only as a conduit of Roman power. Anyone claiming that Roman power should be resisted, that indeed the only legitimate ruler was the One God, appeared to the Romans the way Islamists appear to Americans today, as extremist fanatics. Those Jews, whether they carried daggers to assassinate collaborators (the Sicarii) or retired to the Dead Sea Qumran community to live a life of strict purity, awaiting the end of time, could not accommodate themselves to Roman authority and economic exploitation. Unlike Philo, they could see in Rome only a colonialist oppressor.

The early Christians began as a similarly alienated and distrusted group, though within a generation or two, began to make their appeals to Rome that they could live within the empire as good citizens even while not participating in emperor worship and the broadly patriotic civil religion of traditional Roman culture. The earliest material in the gospels reflects the first situation, while later layers of gospel text and Pauline writings, the second.

Consider *Mark* 6:14–29, which tells of Herod Antipas, son of Herod the Great, who executed John the Baptist but wondered if Jesus's ministry to the poor and oppressed of Galilee represented a kind of return of John. As a client of the Romans, whose job was to extract taxes from the Galilean peasants who had long supported prophetic resistance to all monarchical repression (even the kings of Israel), Herod had reason to worry: "King Herod [Antipas] heard of it [Jesus's healings and exorcisms] for Jesus' name had become known. Some said 'John the baptizer has been raised from the dead; that is why these powers are at work in him.' But others said, 'It is Elijah.' And others said, 'It is a prophet like one of the prophets of old.' But when Herod [Antipas] heard of it, he said, 'John, whom I beheaded, has been raised.'" (Mark 6:14–16).

Would a prophetic figure of the north anoint a rebel king? In ancient times, the northern tribes had rebelled even against Solomon who had built the Temple with forced labor. The northern peoples, especially Galileans, remembered these stories, how Elijah spoke truth to power and was vindicated by his God. So it was natural to wonder whether Jesus was not only another John the Baptist but another Elijah.

The scant historical material related to Jesus is testimony to the fact that Jesus's execution was but one of many that the Romans carried out to crush messianic revolts in the first century. After the great revolt in 66 A.D. and the destruction of the Temple, Jews largely abandoned their political quest and adopted a religious life that centered upon the observance of Jewish law and the study of the scriptures. The Rabbinic Judaism of these Pharisees was the only survivor of these turbulent times (producing what we think of as the nonpolitical *religion* of Judaism today), as the rebels finally gave up, the Dead Sea Community of Qumran either died out or was destroyed, and the optimistic Hellenizers like Philo failed to sustain a living Jewish identity.

Of course one other Jewish community continued: those who believed that Jesus was God's messiah. In Paul's mission to the gentiles of the Roman world, however, Christianity ceased to be simply a version of Judaism, and became more like the other religions of salvation that arose in the East and captured the hearts of the alienated urban folk who were unmoved by the traditions of patriotic Roman paganism. But if Christians were not mounting a political rebellion in Galilee or Judea, they were still a suspicious cult, made up of people unwilling to worship the emperor or participate in the rhythms of the civic cult and calendar. Roman aristocrats found them "superstitious," and several nervous emperors persecuted them with efficient brutality. It is often claimed that the courageous willingness to die as martyrs gave Christians a mystique that strengthened their movement, but they nonetheless sought in many ways to prove themselves respectable and unthreatening to Roman authority. In the three centuries before Constantine legalized Christianity, Christians very slowly accommodated themselves to the inescapable reality of Roman power.

In the meantime, while bringing a palpable salvation to many, Christians followed a variety of beliefs and diversity of gospels. Even the canonical gospels reflect the transition from belief in the imminent return of Jesus and a final judgment, to an acceptance that the world might not end so soon. With such a shift came a certain acceptance of Rome, and Jesus's death comes to be blamed, not on the Romans who crucified him, but on "the Jews,"[21] that is, the priests of the Temple (John 19:12). John's gospel, written last, about 90 A.D., after the destruction of the Temple, portrays Jesus less as a Jewish messiah figure, and more as a Hellenistic Divine Man, speaking with mysterious, divine foreknowledge:

> But the Counselor, the Holy Spirit, whom the Father will send in my name, he will teach you all things, and bring to your remembrance all that I have said to you. Peace I leave with you, my peace I give you; not as the world gives do I give to you. Let not your hearts be troubled, neither let them be afraid. You have heard me say to you, 'I go away, and I will come to you.' If you loved me, you would have rejoiced, because I go to the Father. . . .
> But when the Counselor comes, whom I shall send to you from the Father, even the Spirit of truth, who proceeds from the Father, he will bear witness to me. (John 14:26–28 and 15:26)

When John begins his gospel, not with a birth narrative or with references to Herod, but with "In the beginning was the *Logos* . . . ," he identifies Jesus with a cosmic and timeless Reason, not rooted to a specific time and place and group of people. Moreover, John stresses that the Kingdom of God is not so much in the future, to be awaited, but made present in Jesus (5:25). John was addressing the Hellenistic world. Had he been asked to translate the texts for Buddhists, who may have visited Philo's Alexandria in this period, one can imagine him writing, "In the beginning was the *dharma* . . . " The appeal to *logos* is the appeal to the eternal. Consider the gnostic *Gospel of Truth,* in which the impulse to abstraction is full-blown: "This is the perfection in the thought of the Father, and these are the words of his meditation. Each one of his words is the work of his one will in the revelation of his word. While they were still in the depth of his thought, the word, which was first to come forth revealed them along with a mind that speaks the one Word in silent grace."[22] This is a very different Christology than one finds in the earlier Gospel of Mark: "Again the high Priest asked him, 'Are you the Christ, the son of the blessed?" And Jesus said, "I am; and you will see the Son of man sitting at the right hand of the Power, and coming with the clouds of heaven'" (Mark 14:61–62). Mark uses the imagery of Old Testament prophecies of the messiah (e.g. Dan. 7:13), whereas John's Jesus is a lofty, mysterious figure with more in common with the saviors of gnostic groups, Christian and non-Christian.

The variety of Christian groups has become abundantly clear to scholars since the discovery of the cache of gnostic texts at Nag Hammadi, Egypt in 1945. What seems striking about these texts is the degree to which they claim a kind of mystical authority, bequeathing vision and insight but offering no political challenge of the sort embedded, though somewhat obscured, in the earliest canonical materials. The apocalyptic, early texts, the descendent of Persian-influenced Jewish apocalyptic literature, hint darkly at God's imminent overthrow of the powerful and corrupt. The abandonment of the apocalyptic and the embrace of mysticism suggests the abandonment of revolutionary hopes, the tacit acceptance of this world as the inescapable, irredeemable realm of the flesh, with the hope of the individual's salvation through entrance into the other world, that of the spirit.

In the second century, Christians not only contended with the Romans who would persecute them, but internally, as a wide variety of groups read and followed a host of gospels, those which made it into the canon, and those that lost out and were declared heretical. Presumably, to Roman authorities, these differences made little difference, and Christians, whether slaves or philosophers, appeared obstinate and peculiar. In his famous letter to the Roman emperor Trajan early in the second century, Pliny, a governor in Asia Minor, writes: "This is the course I have taken with those who were accused before me as Christians. I asked them whether they were Christians, and I asked them a second and a third time with threats of punishment. If they kept to it, I ordered them off for execution, for I had no doubt that whatever it was they admitted, in any case they deserve to be punished for obstinacy and unbending pertinacity.... As for those who said they neither were nor ever had been Christians, I thought it right to let them go, when they recited a prayer to the gods at my dictation, and made supplication with incense and wine to your statue."[23] Pliny's cavalier dismissal of eccentric Christians and his callous willingness to execute them should not blind us to the fact that he goes on to claim a kind of policy of moderation, which Trajan endorses. One should not seek them out or accept anonymous charges against them. One's political goal is not religious uniformity, but political stability and public order. Christians seemed to be a suspect group, unwilling to endorse wholeheartedly the imperial project, but that did not necessarily make them all revolutionaries.

In seeking a place for Christianity in the Roman world, the author of the Gospel of Luke and the Acts of the Apostles, subtly alters the received traditions. Biblical scholars note that Luke, like the earlier Gospel of Mark, makes note of a Roman soldier at the foot of the cross. Mark writes: "And Jesus uttered a loud cry, and breathed his last. And the curtain of the temple was torn in two, from top to bottom. And when the centurion, who stood facing him, saw that he thus breathed his last, he said, 'Truly this man was the Son of God [huios theou]!'" (Mark 15:37–39). Luke follows the text, but adds: "Now when the centurion saw what had taken place, he praised God, and said, 'Certainly, this man was innocent!'" (Luke 23:47). Both authors have a gentile recognize Jesus, but Luke's further point is that Jesus was not guilty of any crime.

When Luke continues his account of the early church in Acts, he avoids condemnation of Roman rule, and even though Paul was imprisoned and probably executed by officials in Rome, Luke concludes his account with the following surprising statement about the apostle's life there: "And he [Paul] lived there two whole years at his own expense, and welcomed all who came to him, preaching the kingdom of God and teaching about the Lord Jesus Christ quite openly and unhindered" (Acts 28:30–32). Such a turn had occurred already in the first century, after the Roman destruction of the Temple, and as Christianity spread among the non-Jewish urban population of the empire. During the second century, biblical texts like the pastoral epistles (1–2 Timothy, Titus, attributed to Paul, but surely written a century later), make even more explicit attempts to urge a respectable behavior for Christians seeking acceptance in Roman society, including, among other things, a concern that women be silent in church.

> Now a bishop must be above reproach, the husband of one wife, temperate, sensible, dignified, hospitable, an apt teacher, no drunkard, not violent, but gentle, not quarrelsome, and no lover of money. He must manage his own household well, keeping his children submissive and respectful in every way. (1 Tim. 2:2–4)

> Women should adorn themselves modestly and sensibly in seemly apparel, not with braided hair or gold or pearls or costly attire, but with good deeds, as befits women who profess religion. Let a woman learn silence with all submissiveness. I permit no woman to teach or have authority over men; she is to keep silence. (1 Tim. 2:8b–12)

> Bid the older men be temperate, serious, sensible, sound in faith, in love, and in steadfastness. Bid the older women likewise to be reverent in behavior, not to be slanderers or slaves to drink; they are to teach what is good, and so train the young women to love their husbands and children, to be sensible, chaste, domestic and kind, and submissive to their husbands, that the word of God may not be discredited. Likewise urge the younger men to control themselves. Show yourself in all respects a model of good deeds, and in your teaching show integrity, gravity and sound speech that cannot be censured, so that an opponent be put to shame, having nothing evil to say of us. (Titus 2:2–8)

Clearly a century after Jesus's death, Christians—at least those whose texts became canonical—were seeking to establish themselves as a movement to be distinguished from the ecstatic and Dionysiac cults that also offered salvation to spiritually adventurous seekers, those unsatisfied with patriotic civil religion. The doctrine of domestic respectability is, however, a far cry from the revolutionary words of Jesus found in earlier texts:

> And when they bring you to trial and deliver you up, do not be anxious beforehand what you are to say; but say whatever is given you in that hour, for it is not you who speak, but the Holy Spirit. And brother will deliver up brother to death, and the father his child, and children will rise against parents and have them put to death; and you will be hated by all for my name's sake. But he who endures to the end will be saved. (Mark 13:11–13)

> I came to cast fire upon the earth; and would that it were already kindled! . . .
> Do you think that I have come to give peace on earth? No, I tell you, but rather division; for henceforth in one house there will be five divided, three against two and two against three; they will be divided, father against son and son against father, mother against daughter and daughter against mother, mother-in-law against daughter-in-law, and daughter-in-law against mother-in-law. (Luke 12:49, 51–53)[24]

In moving from a revolutionary gospel to a doctrine of respectable domesticity, well before Roman emperors adopted Christianity as part of a policy of imperial unification, Christians were already laying a foundation for the case that their religion, with its universal claims, was better suited than paganism to support an empire made up of diverse peoples.

Before examining Christianity as a Roman cult or sect, we must distinguish the paganism of popular religion from the inclusivistic traditionalism of intellectuals intent on preserving both their old ways and their privileges as masters of a cultural elite. The latter involved the project of presuming a framework, what we have been calling a meta-religion, which was universalistic and encompassing, and built upon a foundation of Greek philosophy. Garth Fowden writes of the "seeds of polytheist universalism," while Jeremy Schott discusses the philosophers of late antiquity who were committed to the idea of a divine rationality or *logos* discernible in the diverse traditions present in the Roman Empire.[25] For Schott, the intellectual project of finding the universally true inherent, even buried, within a diversity of foreign myths is the intellectual counterpart of imperial conquest. It creates the possibility of claiming authority; you provincials represent the particular, while we cosmopolitans represent the universal. You have value, but value fully realized in being a part of the universal empire.

A philosopher like Plutarch (d. 120 A.D.), for example, believed in One God who transcended all the gods, and he read the myths of barbarians allegorically to find the rational basis for their beliefs. As Erich Voegelin notes, Plutarch finds parallels between Alexander the Great and Julius Caesar, and concludes that the king is superior to the philosopher because he realizes in deed what the philosopher can only imagine. Referring to the philosopher Zeno, the founder of Stoicism who lived just after Alexander, Plutarch says: "Men should not live separated under the laws of their respective poleis and peoples, but form one polity and people with a common life and order common to all. What Zeno only dreamt, Plutarch continues, Alexander put into effect; for to Zeno's reason (*logos*) he supplied his deed (*ergon*)."[26] Plutarch saw in Alexander the great unifier, sent by the gods to realize the unity philosophers discovered in the *logos* that governed the world and gave all people a common life.

By the middle of the second century, Plutarch had philosophical counterparts among the Christians. They too had a universalism that resisted pure abstraction by its focus on one man; in their case, Jesus

Christ rather than Alexander. They opposed any portrayal of Christianity as just one more barbarian tradition among many, and a novel one at that. For example, a thinker like Justin Martyr (d. 165 A.D.) agrees with his pagan interlocutors in seeing Divine Reason (*logos*) as manifest among many peoples, but their vague grasp of this principle is now superseded by the Christ-event; *logos* is now made manifest, is incarnate (John 1.1, 14: "In the beginning was the *logos* . . ." and "the *logos* became flesh"). In effect, Justin turns the tables on those who see Greek thought as the lens through which all traditions can be reconciled. Although born a pagan in Palestine and comporting himself in the style of a philosopher, Justin converted to Christianity and made Christ-as-*logos* the one transcendent principle by which all other traditions might be judged. The fact that Justin was executed for his beliefs shows us that the struggle to maintain a dominant framework or meta-religion that would *manage* the diverse traditions of the Roman Empire was mortal combat indeed. But well after the Roman emperors embraced Christianity as the religion of the realm, there were many intellectuals who, like Augustine's interlocutor Maximus, quoted above, preferred an inclusive monotheism that embraced all the gods in a manner not unlike the Hindus. As late as the fourth century, many North Africans and North Indians would have found much to agree upon, philosophically, politically, and religiously. And so, to India.

CHAPTER 3

The Debate over *Dharma*

Hindus and Buddhists Compete for Ideological Dominance in South Asia

But those whose minds are clouded by desires resort to other gods, following a variety of rituals, bound by their material natures. Whatever form a devotee worships in faith, I make that faith firm. That devotee, disciplined by faith, propitiating that deity, obtains results, ordained only by Me.

—*Bhagavadgita* 20–22[1]

While political and cultural unity of China or Rome was never assured or fully achieved, the very fact that it was an ideal contrasts markedly with India, where cultural diversity remained the norm, and perhaps surprisingly, even the goal of those governing the society. Whereas Ashoka had accepted a measure of religious diversity, his promulgation of a universal, meta-religious *dharma* might have resulted in a cultural ideal and policy for rule that promoted unity. But in the centuries after Ashoka, brahmin intellectuals met the challenge of Buddhist universalism with a project to reclaim the word *dharma*, and to develop a "particularist" or "context-sensitive" cultural ideal: different truths for different people in different times and circumstances. Particularism is the hallmark of gender and caste hierarchy. And brahmin men were at the top of that hierarchy.

In the five centuries after Ashoka, we see an explosion of South Asian religious literature devoted to the word *dharma*, most prominently the great Sanskrit epics and the *Laws of Manu*, as well as a transformation of religious art. Much of this material can best be interpreted as conservative brahmin responses to the challenge of Ashoka's pro-Buddhist policies. If Ashoka can be compared to Constantine as an emperor supporting a reformist religion at the expense of the old traditions,[2] the consequent difference in the histories of South Asia and the West might lie in the fact that in India, the old traditions were, although reformulated, reaffirmed.

Often Indian historians concentrate on the great empires of the Mauryas (321–185 B.C.) and the Guptas (319–500 A.D.), the first providing a model of Buddhist kingship in Ashoka's reign, the second an era of classical Hinduism. But it was between these two, in an era of invasion and complex cultural interchange, that we find conditions ripe for articulating ideologies and practices that relate religion to power in consequential ways. The Sanskrit literature of the period represents the intellectual project of reaffirming the role of brahmins as defenders of orthodoxy and orthopraxy at a time when they were challenged by Buddhists and other heterodox teachers and by the foreign invaders who often supported them. The record of religious art and architecture in this period represents royal patronage of a visual piety that both satisfied the longings of ordinary people and reflected the glory of their kings. Tellingly, Romila Thapar has covered this period in her *History of India,* in separate chapters entitled "The Disintegration of Empires" and "The Rise of the Mercantile Community," the first a dizzying account of the military fortunes of one ruler after another, and the second an account of the increasing wealth of traders who marketed their wares over longer and longer distances, leading to a world that linked India with Greece, Egypt, and Syria, as well as to Central Asia and China.[3] Put simply, it was a time of change, struggle, and ferment, and cultural products of that period suggest what a watershed it was for Indian civilization.

If we list some of the historical monuments of the period we can begin to see the outline of a narrative:

The Maurya Dynasty fell in 185 B.C. to a rebellious brahmin courtier, who founded the Shunga Dynasty and instituted policies that restored brahmin orthodoxy and preeminence.

The Bactrian King Milinda, known in the West as Menander, ruled an Indo-Greek kingdom in the northwest (155–130 B.C.) and converted to Buddhism. The famous text *The Questions of King Milinda* is a kind of Buddhist catechism in the form of a Platonic dialogue.

The Chinese of the Qin Dynasty built the Great Wall to defend against the nomadic peoples of the steppe lands. With the success of the Chinese in defending their borders during that brief dynasty

(Qin, 221–207 B.C.) and during the formative Han Dynasty (202 B.C.–220 A.D.), successive waves of barbarian hordes pushed into Central Asia and down into northwestern India. The first of these were Scythian tribes, called Shakas, who conquered Bactria and Gandhara and extended their power as far as Mathura. The Shakas gave way to another Central Asian tribal people, known as the Yuezhi to the Chinese, but as the Kushanas to the Indians. The reign of most famous Kushana king, Kanishka, is difficult to date exactly, but he probably flourished about 130 A.D., as a celebrated patron of Buddhism, thus known as a "second Ashoka."

Monumental religious architecture, perhaps begun by Ashoka, flourished, and gave rise to a rich iconography, especially iconography of the Buddha. The reliquary mounds known as stupas are first attested in this period, predating the construction of Hindu temples. Sculpted depictions of the Buddha also seem to predate the rise of a similar Hindu religious iconography. We find two types of Buddhas sculpted in this period, one strikingly Greco-Roman, with Buddha portrayed as a kind of Apollo in a flowing toga, the other a more indigenous form, emphasizing his yogic power. The first type is referred to as Gandharan, as the region it comes from is in the northwestern region of Gandhara, adjacent to Bactria, in what is today near the Pakistan-Afghanistan border region; while the other is from the city of Mathura, just south of modern Delhi.

The classical Indian epics the *Ramayana* and the *Mahabharata* were composed in their final literary form in this period. These enormous works (the *Mahabharata* is over a hundred thousand verses) represent a deep reflection on *dharma,* the proper role of kings, and the rise of the heroic avatars Rama and Krishna. The *Mahabharata* includes the famous *Bhagavadgita*—a small but crucial part of the great epic. The *Mahabharata* mentions Shakas, Kushanas, Greeks, and even the Chinese (*Cina*s, using a word, as in English, related to the brief Qin Dynasty, when cultural contact was first made).

Besides the extensive treatment of *dharma* in texts of epic poetry, we find the classic *Laws of Manu* bringing together in one text the traditions of scholastic legal reflection on *dharma.* Like the epics, Manu reflects an emphatic brahmin response to heterodoxy (especially Buddhism), and an apologetic defense of brahmin privilege and traditional caste roles.

The enormously influential *Lotus Sutra,* written in hybrid Sanskrit, portrays the Buddha as a cosmic divine figure, and becomes one of the fundamental texts of the Mahayana Buddhist movement. Mahayana seems to absorb Iranian eschatological themes, for example, the return of a future Buddha at the end of our age, as it spreads along the Silk Road and into China.

These seven points deserve fuller discussion in turn, but to anticipate the argument, we can see that, taken together, they tell a story of expansive empires, monumental religious art, and the ideological battle of those who upheld the status of brahmins and a society ordered by caste roles against those who challenged that structure by making religious truth a quest open to all men (if not all people).

As we have seen, Ashoka had his edicts inscribed at public sites throughout his vast empire. His understanding of *dharma* as a rather inclusive public morality, expansive but colored by Buddhism, effectively disenfranchised brahmins who felt that knowledge of the truth was something gained from the scriptural revelations of which they had custody. It is noteworthy that the Vedic scriptures had never been written down, but were painstakingly memorized by brahmin boys, a practice which kept them free from scribal error and away from the uninitiated. Ashoka's inscriptions, however, were meant to be public, written in stone and available to all who could read the vernacular. For Ashoka, *dharma* was a meta-religious frame that seemed tolerant and inclusive, but as with all such frames, could not include all.

Of course, for the majority of people, who were not literate, impressive monuments taught the essential religious and political stories. While Vedic religion was aniconic, after Ashoka, Hindus, Buddhists, and others developed shrines and temples that attracted lay people, giving rise to a visual piety that would remain characteristic of Indian religion to the present day. Legend has it that Ashoka distributed the ashes of the Buddha to eighty-four thousand reliquary mounds called stupas. Doubtless this claim is fictional, but it is a fact that in the centuries after Ashoka, architecturally impressive stupas were built that appealed both as abstract expressions of Buddhist teaching, even as they were embellished by a sculpture that incorporated many elements of folk religion. The surviving stupa of Sanchi, near modern-day Bhopal in central India, is a fine early example of these monuments. Viewed diagrammatically from the top, the stupa is a perfect circle, with four cardinal points marked by gates, with a square platform or altar in the center.[4]

Viewed from the side, we see the elaborately carved gates, adorned with elephants and fertility goddesses (*yakshi*s), as well as bas-relief depictions of the great stories of Buddhism (e.g., the Buddha's "going forth" into the ascetic life; his previous lives or *jataka*s; the *bodhi* tree,

FIGURE 7. Sanchi Great Stupa. Getty Images, photograph courtesy of iStockphoto.

FIGURE 8. *Yakshi* at Sanchi Stupa. Getty Images, photograph courtesy of iStockphoto.

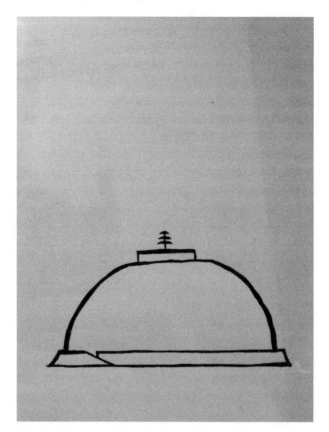

FIGURE 9. Stupa. Original drawing by Jill Michell.

etc.). The massive dome, suggesting the dome of heaven, is topped by an altar where the Buddha's relics represent the sacrificial offering of desire, burned up by his wisdom and restraint. The Buddha himself is not depicted, except perhaps in a schematic way, the whole structure suggesting a figure seated in meditation, again with the altar containing the relics of burned-up desire.

In a short time, especially during Kushana times, we begin to see the Buddha sculpted, both in a realistic Hellenistic manner that suggests that the artisans, if not the patrons, were Indo-Greeks, and in a more indigenous style that depicts the Buddha in a less realistic, more dynamic and yogic fashion.

Some have argued that the Hellenistic Buddhas are evidence of a spread of "superior" Greco-Roman techniques in this period, while

FIGURE 10. Seated Buddha. Original drawing by Jill Michell.

others have argued for the temporal primacy of more indigenous Mathuran images.[5] Without going into these chauvinistic debates, we can see that Kanishka's realm linked the region of Delhi to Central Asia and absorbed Hellenistic, Persian, and Indian cultural traditions at the same time. His patronage of a Buddhism that made a place for visual piety, policies perhaps underway during his predecessors, would be further impetus for brahmins and their supporters to respond intellectually, politically, religiously, and artistically.

It is in texts, however, that we find articulate evidence of the brahmin response to Buddhism. Two prominent scholars of the *Mahabharata*, Alf Hiltebeitel and James Fitzgerald, agree that the great epic was composed in its present form as a response to the reign of Ashoka and the general threat that heterodox religious movements posed for the social

FIGURE 11. Mathura Buddha. Photograph by Patrick Laine.

and religious order envisaged by conservative brahmins.[6] The *Mahab-harata* purports to be an epic recounting events of the ancient past, but the extant text clearly reveals the context in which it was written. Although the *Mahabharata's story* is set in the distant past, at the end of the previous age, thousands of years ago, its mention of kings and peoples of the period after 200 B.C. clearly establishes the time of the text's final composition.

The story involves a disputed royal succession leading to war, with long passages devoted to the problem of discerning *dharma*, what is right. The conflict is between two sets of cousins, the sons of Pandu, the Pandavas, and the sons of Dhrtarashtra, usually called the Kauravas. It recounts several generations of an extremely convoluted genealogy, making it impossible to determine the proper line of descent that would

FIGURE 12. Kushana Emperor Kanishka. Biswarup Ganguly, photograph courtesy of Creative Commons.

determine the legitimate king. Thus, although the Pandavas are portrayed as the "good guys," especially since they are allied with Krishna, God Incarnate, their rival cousins are not without good argument that they too have a claim on kingship. The problem that the *Mahabharata* poets pondered was the subtlety of *dharma*. The difficulty of discerning true *dharma* is a central concern both in the main story and in countless related tales and didactic passages.

The Pandavas are five brothers, most important of which is the eldest, Yudhisthira, called the Dharma King, and his younger brother

Arjuna. Yudhisthira, often beset by indecision and given to intellectual debate and restraint, is not the usual heroic king. Arjuna, however, is a true warrior and conforms more to the image of a great hero, but like Achilles, with whom he is often compared, he also has an intellectual side. It is to him that the great revelation known as the "Song of the Lord," or *Bhagavadgita*, is given on the eve of the war. This, too, is a reflection on the difficulty of discerning *dharma*.

Early in the story, the Pandavas have lost their kingdom to their cousins, the result of Yudhisthira's willingness to take part in a disastrous dice game. The game is an image of blind fate, and Yudhisthira's willingness to bet everything and lose is a sign of his fatalism. After losing the game, Yudhisthira and his brothers and kin have to accept a thirteen-year exile. As they wander the forest, they have ample opportunity to meet with wise ascetics and sages. During one such encounter, they hear the ancient sage Markandeya's prophecy of how the world will decline in the age to come, when *dharma* is at its weakest. This so-called prophecy of the future describes, however, the contemporary age of the epic's poets:

> In that time, there is a substitute for the sacrifice, a substitute for almsgiving, and indeed, a substitute for taking vows. Brahmins do the work of Sudras, and Sudras acquire wealth, and . . . even follow the dharma of Kshatriyas. In the Kali Yuga [Age of Decline], brahmins cease to study the Veda or the sacrifice, [cease to] make offerings to the ancestors, and begin to eat any food [regardless of its purity]. My son, brahmins then will not pray, while Sudras are intent on prayer. Then with the world upside down, [we have] the portent of destruction. O King, the many barbarian kings will then rule the earth, intent on lies, evil, and following deceitful policy. [They will be] the Andhras, Shakas, Pulindas, Greeks, Kambojas, Aurnikas, Shudras and Abhiras. . . . No brahmin at all will live according to his caste-dharma and Kshatriyas and Vaishyas will have the wrong jobs. (*Mahabharata* 3.186.25–31)[7]

According to this apocalyptic view, the signs of the end-times are the reigns of kings who are either foreign barbarians (Shakas, Greeks), tribals (Abhiras), or, like Ashoka, members of non-*kshatriyan* castes (Andhras, Shudras). The whole hierarchy of caste, with each group attending to its proper duty, will go awry. Markandeya goes on to describe a time of natural disaster and especially moral decay, when women become shameless, traders cheat, and ascetics grow long hair and don the monk's robe as a cover for a life of wining, dining, and illicit sex (3.186.34–44). The conclusion of this decline is the necessary destruction of the world before its cyclic restoration. This text is an extraordinary lament over the abandonment of caste society governed by the *dharma* of brahmins, made possible by the ascendance of heterodox Buddhist and foreign kings in the 200 B.C. to 200 A.D. period.

The most famous declaration of ideology in the eighteen-book *Mahabharata* is the eighteen-chapter *Bhagavadgita*. In terms of the epic story, the *Gita* is placed just before the great war, when the Pandavas' great hero, Arjuna, loses heart at the prospect of facing his kinsmen and gurus in battle. He is counseled by Krishna, God incarnate as well as his best friend and charioteer. The teaching of the *Gita* is usually summarized as a resolution to a deep ideological conflict between those who argue for obedience to caste duty and social role (*svadharma*), and those who claim that salvation comes to those who renounce the world, giving up their particular social roles in favor of the universal quest for liberation. Those renouncers, followers of Buddhism or Jainism, or a wide range of practitioners of yoga, do not worry about the values of a well-ordered society, but pursue rather the individualistic goals of detachment, serenity, peace of mind, *nirvana*.

In despair at the prospect of killing his cousins, revered teachers, and old comrades, Arjuna cries out, "Would it not be better to eat alms than kill my gurus, for having killed them, I would be consuming food smeared with blood" (*Bhagavadgita* 2.5). In other words, Arjuna says that the worldly action of fighting and winning a battle for the sake of kingship—surely an ancient path of heroes—is tainted by sin. It would be better to be a renouncer, a monk, begging for alms, than to enjoy the postwar banquet won by shedding the blood of cousins and teachers.

The *Gita* is usually read, then, as a reflection on the debate between those who favor worldly action and those who favor renunciation, and its resolution is something like the Christian idea of being "*in* the world but not *of* the world." Krishna enjoins Arjuna to be a yogi, detached from the fruits of his actions but committed to action nonetheless. His duty as a *kshatriya* is to fight and rule. He is to fight, not because of a desire for wealth and glory, but to be obedient to the task given him, performing it as a sacrificial, devotional act to God the Creator. However we might evaluate the nobility of the *Gita*'s philosophical and theological message, read as a timeless classic, it is important to see that if the *Mahabharata* as a whole was composed in its extant form as a response to Ashoka's rule, surely the condensed ideological message of the *Gita* should be read, in large part, as a critique of Buddhism and a defense of the role of brahmanic orthodoxy. Since Buddhist monks are called *bhikshu*s (mendicants, almsmen, or more literally "beggars"), Arjuna's question about taking up a life of begging alms (*bhaikshyam*) suggests that he is considering the validity of the claims of Buddhist monks. Worldly life, tainted by desire and violence, should be abandoned for the monastic or solitary life. In many ways the *Gita* is a sustained argument against this Buddhist position. It makes adherence to particular caste duties a central value and thus disparages the renouncer for avoiding those responsibilities.

In contrast to such particularism, *The Questions of King Milinda*, which is to some degree set in the same sociopolitical world (e.g., it too mentions Shakas, Greeks, and Chinese), not only assumes that the religious life is open to all men, but in a very interesting passage, explains how the Buddha himself is both a brahmin and a *kshatriya*, essentially by making neither a matter of birth:

> A Brahman . . . means one who has passed beyond hesitation, perplexity and doubt. And because the Tathagata [Buddha] has done all this, that therefore also is he called a Brahman. A Brahman . . . means one who has escaped from every sort and class of becoming, who is entirely set free from evil and from stain, who is dependent on himself, and it is because the Tathagata [Buddha] is all these things, that therefore also is he called a Brahman. . . . The appellation "Brahman" was not given to the Blessed One by his mother, nor by his father, not by his brother, nor his sister, not by his friends, nor his relations, not by spiritual teachers of any sort, no, not by the gods. It is by reason of their Emancipation that this is the name of the Buddhas, the Blessed Ones. (*The Questions of King Milinda* 4.5.26)

> And the Blessed One . . . making the army of the Evil One, those given over to false doctrine, mourn; filling the hearts of those, among gods or men, devoted to sound doctrine, with joy; raises aloft over the ten thousand world systems the Sunshade of his Sovranty, pure and stainless in the whiteness of emancipation . . . the symbol of his mighty fame and glory. That too is why the Tathagata [Buddha] is called a king. (4.5.27)[8]

This sort of thinking is for Arjuna precisely the road not taken, but present to him as a tempting, universalistic ethic "beyond hesitation, perplexity and doubt," "free from evil and stain."

Krishna *does* encourage Arjuna to be a yogi, and even prescribes some typical yoga practices to him (*Bhagavadgita* 6), but not as a way of renouncing all action (*karma*). Indeed, Krishna argues, the renunciation of action is impossible, as even monks and ascetics have to do *something* just to maintain their physical existence (3.5). Acting in his role as Creator God involves action (*karma*), Krishna emphasizes (3.22–4), and He is the one who created the caste system (4.13). And, whenever there is a decline of *dharma* and the rise of its opposite, he comes into the world as an avatar (4.7–8). But actions alone do not stain him, nor do they stain anyone. The classical sacrifices were always conceived of as *karma* (ritual action, or action in general) producing worthy results, and Krishna supports the maintenance of sacrifice (3.11–14), but all actions can be done as sacrificial acts if one performs them devotionally and not from personal desire.

The clearest evidence of the *Gita's* conservative commitment to the ideals of brahmins comes in Krishna's declaration that it is better to perform one's prescribed duty (*sva-dharma*), even poorly, than to perform another person's task well. In other words, God has prescribed the roles of the caste system, and one should stay in one's place (3.35). This is true in part because all creatures have a particular biochemical make-up (we would say DNA), and they can only really act effectively in conformity with it (3.27–8, 31). Men are men, women are women, brahmins are brahmins, and servants are servants. Those who teach otherwise (like the Buddhists) are deluded and lost (3.32).

Now, if under the rule of Buddhist and foreign kings, from Ashoka to Kanishka, we see non-*kshatriyas* ruling and members of all castes taking on the role of religious teacher, we see the *Mahabharata* as a whole, and the *Gita* in particular, to be both a lamentation over the decline of *dharma* (as they understand the word), and a rallying call for all people to be obedient to their caste *dharma*. The strategy of the epic poets was not, however, to turn back to the Vedic orthodoxy of sacrifice and reject all aspects of the novel religious world present in India by the year 100 B.C. Rather, they included some of those new elements, but placed them carefully within a hierarchy that preserved brahmin authority and privilege.

Their first task, as we have seen, is to make a place for yoga, but not as an alternative way of life that removes the individual from society. The practice of yoga may allow one a certain detachment and peace of mind, a realization of the true self's freedom, but one still performs one's essential duties prescribed by caste. Yoga may even bring one to ultimate salvation, described in the *Gita* as *brahmanirvana* (6.15), a compound word that embeds the rather Buddhist word *nirvana* within the cosmic Hindu principle of ultimate reality. But in addition to this inclusion of the traditions of yoga and even Buddhism, the poets go on to conceive of a higher form of yoga, a devotional yoga (*bhaktiyoga*) whereby detachment is achieved, not through meditation and asceticism, but in making all one's acts devotional gifts to God.

If the rise of Buddhism witnessed not only the challenge to the brahmin's authority but the rise of a popular visual piety, the *Gita* responds by offering its own version of a simple piety for laymen. Krishna declares: "Whoever offers Me a leaf, a flower, a fruit, or even water, with devotion, such an offering I accept from one who is truly devout" (9.26). Such acts of offering, already in evidence at Buddhist stupas in 100 B.C., and still the primary devotional acts in modern popular Hinduism, are here for the first time given legitimacy by brahmins in a Sanskrit text.

But perhaps the most striking inclusion in the text is the choice of Krishna to be the all-powerful Creator God. The *Gita* is not just a revelation of a particular doctrine, but God's self-revelation. In a series of dramatic statements, Krishna identifies Himself with the sacrifice, the Vedas, a host of gods, the sacred syllable *Om,* the Self, the very ground of Being (*Bhagavadgita* 9–10),[9] and then shows to Arjuna his Cosmic Form, a terrifying embodiment of his all-consuming nature as Time itself (*Bhagavadgita* 11). All of this makes sense as a powerful inclusivist theology, but why would brahmin poets writing in Sanskrit choose to identify Krishna, a black-skinned, heroic deity associated with cow-herding tribal groups, with God Almighty?

Stories about baby Krishna and Krishna the youthful prankster and lover make their way into orthodox Sanskrit literature at a later date, but may reflect the kind of popular tales revered by common folk from a very early period, before Brahmin scholars adopted him as the spokesman for their very brahmanic, conservative theology of the *Bhagavadgita.* The contrast between the two Krishnas could not be greater. The first is a naughty but loveable child, who grows into a flute-playing cowherd, summoning the women of the village away from their wifely duties to cavort with him in the woods. This Krishna—as we learn in the medieval Sanskrit *Puranas*—has been raised by foster parents, cowherds of the country, to protect him from the murderous intent of an evil uncle. According to the brahmin storytellers reworking these folktales, he is, in fact, a boy of royal blood and, in the *Mahabharata,* he returns to his proper life as a prince and warrior. The rustic tales of the country exalt the love of God that transcends social convention—valorizing even the adulterous love of married women for Krishna—whereas the teaching of the *Gita,* as we have seen, commends obedience to social role.

Perhaps, once again, it is the challenge of heterodoxy, especially Buddhism, to the social order that explains the adoption of a popular, cow-herd god into the Sanskrit literature of conservative brahmins. If Buddhists were winning lay support by incorporating popular devotional religion into what might be seen as its antithesis, it would make sense for conservative brahmins to choose a popular god as spokesman for their conservative orthodoxy. In adopting Krishna, they take the stories of his cow-herding youth and make them a temporary phase, his real identity being the royal figure of the *Mahabharata*. Both roles are, of course, even further subordinated by his true identity as God Almighty.

Krishna's self-revelation also includes a dramatic epiphany in which he shows his cosmic form to Arjuna. This passage (*Bhagavadgita* 11) also relates to the emergence of the visual piety that preceded the literary adoption of devotional religion by Buddhists and Hindus of this period, and it is paralleled in the early Mahayana text the *Lotus Sutra:*

> A vision of many wonders, with many mouths and eyes, many divine ornaments, many divine and uplifted weapons, many divine garlands and garments, divinely perfumed and anointed, this universal miracle, the omniscient, infinite God!
>
> The light of the noble one would be like that in the sky of a thousand suns shining forth simultaneously.
>
> Then the Pandava [Arjuna] saw in one place, within the body of the God of gods, the whole world, divided and manifold.
>
> Then, filled with amazement, his hairs on end, Dhanamjaya [Arjuna] bowed and saluted the God and said:
>
> "O god, I see in your body all the gods, and the other types of beings as well. . . .
>
> "I see you, infinite in form, in every direction, with many arms, bellies, mouths and eyes, O Lord of All! O Universal Form! I see no end to you, no middle, no beginning!
>
> "I see you ablaze, luminous all around, crowned and armed with discus and club, [but] hard to look upon, with the immeasurable splendor of flaming fire and sun everywhere!
>
> "You are the Imperishable, the highest object of knowledge; you are the reservoir of the universe. You are the everlasting, perpetual governor of *dharma*. I consider you the eternal Cosmic Man [Purusha]." (*Bhagavadgita* 11.10–18)[10]

The *Lotus Sutra* offers a similar vision of the deified, cosmic Buddha at the very beginning of the text:

> And at that moment there issued a ray from within the circle of hair between the eyebrows of the Lord. It extended over eighteen hundred thousand Buddha-fields in the eastern quarter, so that all those Buddha-fields appeared wholly illuminated by its radiance, down to the great hell Avici and up to the limit of existence. And the beings in any of the six states of existence became visible, all without exception. Likewise the Lords Buddha staying, living, and existing in those Buddha-fields became all visible, and the law [dharma] preached by them could be entirely heard by all beings. And the monks, nuns, lay devotees male and female, Yogins and students of Yoga, those who had obtained the fruition (of the Paths of sanctification) and those who had not, they, too, became visible. And the Bodhisattvas Mahasattvas in those

Buddha-fields who plied the Bodhisattva-course with ability [*upaya kaus-alyair*] due to their earnest belief in numerous and various lessons and the fundamental ideas, they, too, became visible. Likewise all the Lord Buddhas in those Buddha-fields who had reached final Nirvana became visible, all of them. And the Stupas, made of jewels and containing the relics of the extinct Buddhas became visible in those Buddha-fields.[11]

This revelation—that the historical Buddha is a sort of incarnation of a cosmic being, indeed God of gods (*devadeva*)—assumes the sort of devotional Buddhism in which, again echoing the Gita, "those who offered flowers or perfumes to the relics of the Tathagatas, to Stupas . . . images of clay or drawn on a wall (they have all reached enlightenment)."[12] Even more striking are some of the Buddha's self-revelations: "Hearken to me, ye hosts of gods and men; approach to behold me: I am the Tathagata, the Lord [Bhagavan], who has no superior, who appears in this world to save. I am Dharmaraja, born in the world as the destroyer of existence. I declare the law [*dharma*] to all beings after discriminating their dispositions."[13] The *Lotus Sutra* can be read as a direct response to a text like the *Gita*; the Buddha, not Krishna, is the Lord and king of *dharma,* and in the cosmopolitan world of northwest India and into the Central Asia of Kanishka, the *Lotus Sutra* was to have an enormously influential career. Once translated, it became a beloved text not only in Central Asia but among Chinese and Japanese Buddhists as well.

In India, however, we see other determined efforts to capture the word *dharma* and rescue it from Buddhist control. We are fortunate to have both Wendy Doniger's and Patrick Olivelle's recent studies of *The Laws of Manu;* both conclude that the text must be read alongside the *Mahabharata* and, like the epic, as a response to Buddhist rule.[14] Olivelle dates the composition of Manu to the end of this period, during the reign of King Kanishka, when not only was there the threat of heterodoxy but of foreign rule as well. *Manu,* like the *Mahabharata, The Questions of King Milinda,* and the *Lotus Sutra,* mentions the same groups of foreigners in the northwest (Shakas, Greeks), and knows of the Chinese, but takes an even more strident attitude in defending the place of brahmins in society. Olivelle concludes:

Reading the MDh [Laws of Manu] one cannot fail to see and to feel the intensity and urgency with which the author defends Brahmanical privilege. A major aim of Manu was to reestablish the old alliance between *brahma* and *ksatra,* an alliance that in his view would benefit both the king and the Brahmin, thereby reestablishing the Brahmin in his unique and privileged position within society. We hear the repeated emphasis on the inviolability of the Brahmin in his person and his property. He has immunity from the death penalty, from taxes, and from the confiscation of property. The king is advised repeatedly that a Brahmin's property is poison. Stealing a Brahmin's gold is one of the five grievous sins, and the death penalty is imposed on the perpetrator. Devotion to Brahmins is a cardinal virtue of kings: "Refusal to turn back in battle, protecting the subjects, and obedient service to Brahmins—for kings these are the best means of securing happiness" (7.88). The reason why foreign ruling classes, such as Greeks, Sakas, Persians and Chinese, have fallen to the level of Sudras ... is their lack of devotion to Brahmins: "By neglecting rites and failing to visit Brahmins, however, those men of Ksatriya birth have gradually reached in the world the level of Sudras" (10.43).[15]

Olivelle notes that Manu uses the word *Shudra* not as a dispassionate title for the fourth class of people, but pejoratively, to connote lower-class folk who, in days of moral decline, claim the status of rulers. He quotes *Manu* 4.61: "He [a brahmin] should not live in a kingdom ruled by a Sudra, teeming with unrighteous [adharmika] people, overrun by people belonging to heretical ascetic sects [pasanda], or swamped by lowest-born people." It is noteworthy here that Manu uses a word for "heretics" [pasanda] that, as we noted above, Ashoka employed, without any negative connotation, to mean "sect."

If, in the interest of stressing the role of *kshatriyas* as warriors, the *Gita* makes the surprising inclusion of popular *bhakti,* Manu makes a similar strategic inclusion in the service of his defense of the brahmin householder's role. In other words, the *Gita* argues that Arjuna should not renounce the world, but should carry out his duty as a prince and soldier. It makes yoga and the quest for detachment a matter of personal, inner spirituality while preserving the primacy of caste obligations. Manu makes a place for the ascetic life, but unlike the Buddhists, who see the life of the celibate monk as the highest calling for any man, Manu prescribes ascetic renunciation for brahmin grandfathers, men who had already fulfilled their social obligations:

> When a householder [grhastha] sees his skin wrinkled and his hair turned gray, and his children's children, he should take to the wilderness. Giving up village food and all his belongings, he should go to the forest, entrusting his wife to his sons or accompanied by her.
>
> Taking with him his sacrificial fires and the implements required for his domestic fire rituals, he should depart from the village to the wilderness and live there with his organs controlled [niyatendriya].
>
> Using various kinds of ritually clean sage's food, or vegetables, roots and fruits, he should continue to offer the same great sacrifices according to rule.

He should wear a garment of skin or tree bark; bathe in the morning and evening; always wear matted hair; and keep his beard, body hair, and nails uncut. (6.2–6)

Thus although Manu makes a *place* for the renouncer, and goes on to discuss various techniques of asceticism and yogic meditation (6.33–86), even a rather Buddhist reflection on the body [" . . . foul-smelling, filled with urine and excrement, infested with old-age [jara] and sorrow [soka], the abode of sickness, full of pain, . . . and impermanent"; 6.76–77], he preserves the preeminent place, not for the monk, but for the householder: "Student, householder, forest hermit, and ascetic: these four distinct orders [asramah] have their origin in the householder. All of these when they are undertaken in their proper sequence as spelled out in the sacred texts [sastra], lead a Brahmin who acts in the prescribed manner to the highest state. Among all of them, however, according to the dictates of the vedic scripture, the householder is said to be the best, for he supports the other three" (6.87–89).

If the *Gita* and *Manu* were thus willing to make concessions to important cultural innovations—the worship of popular deities and the lure of forest asceticism—they both stressed the primacy of social role as defined by caste, a hierarchy of values governed by brahmins, and we can judge their success by the evidence of the continued importance of caste in the society of India from that time to the present. The universalism of ascetic religion, especially Buddhism, which diagnosed one illness (desire) and one cure (self-control) for all persons in all times and places was to have a powerful appeal across much of Asia, but it never succeeded in displacing the particularism of brahmins in the land of its origin.

What we call Hinduism today—a loose federation (a meta-religion?) of caste-based religious practices, worship of both pan-Indian and local gods and goddesses rooted to place—finds its origins in this period, in its response to the universalistic challenge of Buddhism. Unlike the complex paganism of the Roman world, which gave way to Christianity, a religion of universalism and creed, Hinduism prevailed, as millions turned to their local gods and their kings found a way to sanction their pieties.[16]

CONCLUSION: INDIA, CHINA, AND THE WEST, 250 B.C.–250 A.D.

From the Mediterranean world to India, and to a lesser extent China, we see the growth of cosmopolitan empires in this period enabling—

and enabled by—religious ideologies that made sense of diversity by *including* a multitude of gods and rites into a framework that both valorized provincial religion and reasserted the authority of those who controlled a meta-religious discourse that evaluated, ranked, and spoke for the many traditions of conquered peoples. The primary strategy for managing religious diversity was inclusivism, a straining for unity and universalism that did not require the eradication of religious diversity in the name of a singular God and exclusive Truth. *Dao, dharma,* and *logos* were inclusive categories as well as sites of contest. In contrast to the situation in China and Rome, India's inclusivism was less related to a singular imperial authority.

In Han China, imperial officials could tolerate the popular religion of village peasants and even the philosophical Daoism of intellectuals, neither of which threatened their privilege and power as Confucian bureaucrats. What threatened the regime was the organized sectarian religion of millenarian cults. Not only did these rebellious groups manage military revolts of real significance in the late second century, they challenged the regime spiritually by offering an alternative system of meaning that disregarded the emperor's claim to be the singular Son of Heaven. They did not ultimately succeed, but became a model for apocalyptic cults of salvation that repeatedly arose to disrupt the religious and political status quo of every Chinese dynasty from the medieval period until the present day.

In India, Buddhism mounted a universalistic challenge to the religion of hierarchy that today we call Hinduism. Where Buddhism claimed a singular truth, the Buddha's *dharma,* for all persons in all times and places, and appealed to foreign invaders, the particularism of Hinduism, claiming different *dharma*s for different people depending on their sex, caste, and age, made a spirited comeback under brahmin leadership in this period. Embracing a multitude of gods and cults, brahmin thinkers formulated a tradition that asserted their spiritual and intellectual authority, and they produced an inclusivism that had room for many endogamous castes and their many styles of religious life. Such tolerance could only operate as long as these different religious styles, like the different castes that maintained them, could be ranked and relativized by brahmins, whose authority was forcefully backed by kings. What could not easily be tolerated was any tradition that rejected brahminical authority. Buddhists were the primary group to make such a challenge, and it was a serious one, but ultimately, Buddhism had far more success outside of India than within it.

Greco-Roman religion, like that in India, assumed that the diversity of cults we now call paganism could be included within an empire as long as these religions embraced the imperial cult and were willing to be included within a framework that recognized the intellectual authority of Greek-speaking universalists. As in China, only those groups that seemed to challenge the inclusivistic system and the imperial authority that authorized it, were subject to harsher methods of control. First Jews, then Christians, resisted in the name of a universalistic truth that did not happily admit of inclusion within the imperial system of discursive hegemony. However, unlike India and China, where the universalistic Buddhists were ultimately defeated, Roman emperors ultimately embraced, in the name of unity, the Christian universalism they once opposed. But that is a subject for the next chapter.

CHAPTER 4

Confessional Religion and Empire before the Rise of Islam

My Church is superior . . . to previous churches, for these
previous Churches were chosen in particular countries and in
particular cities. My Church shall spread in all cities, and its
Gospel shall reach every country.

—Mani (d. 276 A.D.)[1]

The Fertile Crescent was a high road that linked the priests of
Egypt at one end to the Chaldeans and the Magi at the other,
not to mention the sages of India beyond. . . .

    When Constantine became a Christian he created a golden
opportunity to unite a wholeheartedly universalist religion
and its abundance of scriptural authority and missionary
impetus with an empire's forces of political, military, and
economic expansion in order to create a genuine world
empire.

—Garth Fowden[2]

In the centuries leading up to the rise of Islam (300–700 A.D.), the great
empires of Eurasia transformed and were transformed by universalistic
and confessional religious movements. Rome became a Christian empire.
The Guptas in India saw a renewed Hinduism attain its classical form.
Buddhism found a home in China in a period of north-south political
division. The Sasanian Empire of Persia saw the revival and reorganiza-
tion of a national Zoroastrian church. And betwixt and between them
all, in the Central Asian bazaars and courts of the Silk Road, a rich variety of religious ideas found expression in cosmopolitan settings where
universalism was dictated by multiculturalism. In Central Asia, where

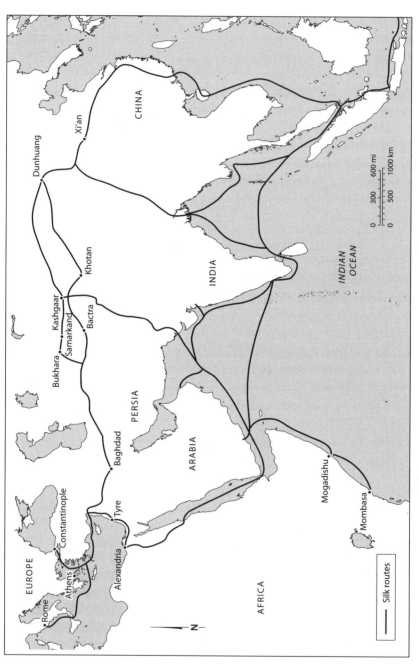

MAP 4. The Silk Road Eurasian trade routes.

no singular culture could reign supreme, we find Buddhists meeting Zoroastrians meeting Nestorian Christians meeting Jews meeting Manichaeans. As international trade brought exotic products to every corner of Eurasia, diverse religions came as fellow travelers.

The extraordinary transformation of Indian Buddhism, as it made its way into Central Asia, and from there to East Asia, is a main part of this story, but the lesser-known tale of the spread of Manichaeism from Mesopotamia to North Africa and China is no less interesting and perhaps even more instructive for our understanding of religious cosmopolitanism and inclusivism across Eurasia in the centuries before the rise of Islam. Once it broke with its Jewish parent, Christianity too developed a full-blown universalism, seeing itself as the true religion for all persons in all times and places, and not simply as a private faith. As Christianity was undergoing its profound transformation in the West from persecuted, "superstitious" sect to the favored religion of the Byzantine Empire, Zoroastrianism was reformed and established as the state religion of the Sasanians (the Persian Empire, 224–651 A.D.). While western Christians came to see the careers of Rome as universal empire and Christianity as universal religion as fatefully and providentially intertwined, eastern Christians from Persia to India still had to survive as minority groups. Various Christian churches, along with Jews and Manicheans, strove to find comfortable niches in Sasanian urban society, sometimes with success but never with the certain backing of the royal and military elites.

The question of what sort of religion suits the imperial project admits of no easy answer. Zoroastrianism and Hinduism were successful ethnonationalist religions allied with imperial states (Guptas and Sasanians), preferred over more universalist traditions available to Iranians and Indians. And while universalist traditions like Manichaeism and Buddhism were attractive to merchants and urbanites along the Silk Road, they struggled to win strong and lasting alliances with great imperial powers, though Buddhism was to play a profoundly important role in China, Japan, and Southeast Asia. Thus, until the rise of Islam, Christian Rome, in its successful founding of a singular imperial state under a single religion, was the exception.

Before turning to the headline events of this age, especially the coming of Christianity to Rome and the coming of Buddhism to China, we first turn to the Silk Road that connected the wings of the *oikoumene,* and served as the meeting place for religious people of many persuasions.

RELIGION ON THE SILK ROAD

If, in India, Buddhism evolved as a rival religion to that of orthodox brahmins, once Buddhist missionaries ventured to the northwest and on to the Silk Road linking China and the Mediterranean world, they were to encounter Zoroastrians, Jews, Christians, and Manicheans. The religions of all these diverse peoples would evolve through their mutual relationships and their relation to political power. Until the rise of Islam in Central Asia, the Silk Road region would connect several civilizations, and serve as a conduit not only for trade, but for cultural, and especially religious exchange as well.

Some scholars have thus argued that the Mahayana schools of Buddhism have their genesis in Central Asia.[3] From the first to the third centuries, the Kushanas built an empire that politically linked the area around modern Delhi with the regions north of what is Pakistan today. Under rulers who spoke an Indo-European language, the people in this realm met traders from Rome and China, and here Buddhism took on a new coloring and absorbed elements alien to India. While the theme of this book is the relationship of religion to power, especially imperial political power, the religion of the Silk Road was the religion of merchants, men who moved among Romans, Persians, Chinese, and Indians. The later Kushanas, especially King Kanishka (d. ca. 140 A.D.) enthusiastically supported Buddhism. Their patronage was not exclusive, however, and in their realms, Buddhism became thoroughly cosmopolitan. Whatever role the Kushanas might have had in patronizing Buddhism, the Silk Road arena remained fundamentally multicultural, and the character of Buddhism in this area was malleable and not rigidly doctrinal. Thus, in northwest India and Central Asia, Buddhist thinkers developed many of the ideas that were to be characteristic of the Mahayana schools that were most influential in East Asia.

Many students and scholars see in Mahayana a sort of protestant Buddhism that rejects the pretensions of monks and opens up a rich new freedom of interpretation of Buddhist truths. But although many Mahayana texts do disparage monastic pretension, the emphasis in Mahayana on literary texts and abstruse philosophical argument suggest that its first creators were themselves monks, and not humble lay people. In fact, Mahayana is not a school of Buddhism but a broad movement, difficult to characterize by any single, simple portrait. Here we will not consider the more sophisticated intellectual moves of Mahayana thinkers, but concentrate instead upon the religious culture produced by the followers of various Mahayana schools in Central Asia. To get a taste for Mahayana piety, we will return to some of the teachings of the *Lotus Sutra*, and then turn to the widespread devotion to the future Buddha to come, Maitreya.

As we have seen, the *Lotus Sutra* introduces us to a Buddha who is fully divine, not a human being who struggled heroically to attain enlightenment. It reinforces this novel view by having the Buddha claim that he teaches all manner of beings according to their capacity, employing "skillful means" (*upaya*). All the possible doctrinal differences in Buddhism might thus be accounted for by this device, this concept of *upaya*. Different persons at different levels of wisdom can learn Buddhism in different ways, according to their abilities. We are children in a burning house. Our parents call out to us, tempting us with a variety of toy carts, urging us to flee and thus save us.[4]

Such a comprehensive and inclusive view would prove an attractive way, not only of making sense of the doctrinal diversity within Buddhism, but of serving as a political model for managing a plethora of sects. Once freed from the idea of a single human Buddha who died in 480 B.C., never to be born again, one could now imagine a vast pantheon of celestial Buddhas and *bodhisattvas*, skillfully employing a whole range of ministries to countless suffering beings of vastly different temperaments. These divine beings, like patron saints, specialized in meeting the particular needs of different groups of devotees.

Unlike Christianity, where debates about the precise nature of Christ were to have important political consequences, the notion of *upaya* or "skill in means" allowed Buddhists to assume that the Buddha was multiple or could adapt himself. This, in turn, allowed Buddhism to avoid a sharp break with the all-inclusive pluralism of polytheism, whether in India, Tibet, China, or Japan. The inclusive nature of Mahayana Buddhism made it infinitely malleable, and thus so susceptible to compromise that Buddhism could be almost anything, in one form or another, and thus be rendered incapable of radical reformist critique of the status quo.

If anything characterizes Mahayana Buddhism, it is the idea of the *bodhisattva*, a sort of divine figure, poised to attain enlightenment, but turning back from final immersion in *nirvana* to reach out in compassion to a multitude of suffering beings. Instead of a focus on the historical Buddha Gautama, Mahayana Buddhists revered a host of celestial *bodhisattvas* and Buddhas not tied to time or space. For example, in the *Lotus Sutra* we read of the Buddha Avalokitesvara, a gracious savior who hears the prayers of those in trouble:

If one be thrown in a pit of fire, by a wicked enemy with the object of killing him, he has but to think of Avalokitesvara, and the fire shall be quenched as if sprinkled with water.

If one happens to fall into a dreadful ocean . . . he has but to think of Avalokitesvara, and he shall never sink down in the king of waters. . . .

If a man be surrounded by a host of enemies armed with swords, who have the intention of killing him, he has but to think of Avalokitesvara, and they shall not be able to hurt one hair of the body.

If a man, delivered to the power of the executioners, is already standing at the place of execution, he has but to think of Avalokitesvara, and their swords go to pieces. (*Lotus Sutra* 24.5, 6, 9, 10)[5]

This passage goes on to list a wide variety of calamities that an individual might escape through the grace of Avalokitesvara. It is noteworthy that the appeal here is not escape from the snares of temptation, lust, or other sins of weakness or heedlessness—the typical barriers a monk faces on the path to enlightenment—but external threats to the bodily health of the person. And several of the verses, including the last two quoted above, suggest a context in which the individual is endangered by the employment of military and judicial power exercised by the state. Avalokitesvara, later transformed into a female goddess of mercy in China (Guanyin) and Japan (Kannon), and thought by many Tibetans to be incarnate today in the Dalai Lama, was to have a great career as a savior of lay people beseeching help in the mundane matters of the world.

Another religion of faith and grace is found in the Buddhist devotional sects of Maitreya. Maitreya was an enormously complex figure, recognized by all manner of Buddhist sects, both Mahayana and non-Mahayana. Recognized as the Buddha of the future, and bearing a name linguistically related to the Persian Mithras (indeed to several Indo-European words meaning "friend" and "friendliness"), it is tempting to see Maitreya as a product of the Buddhist imagination as it encountered Zoroastrian ideas of a future savior, bringing judgment and salvation to the world at the end of time. The Zoroastrian figure of Saosyant, the product of Zoroaster's seed and a blessed maiden, awaited as divine savior and judge, and believed to initiate and win the last great battle against evil in the world, shares many characteristics with Maitreya.[6] In China, following in the footsteps of the Daoist Yellow Turbans, Buddhist followers of Maitreya sometimes tried to bring about a new utopian world through revolution. Some of these faithful soldiers followed charismatic leaders believed to be the very incarnation of Maitreya. But Maitreya is not simply a western apocalyptic savior in Buddhist clothes, although many of these traits seem to fit. He is also an Indian figure, believed to be of the brahmin caste, and he was revered not only in northwest India and Central Asia, but in Southeast Asia as well. Nonetheless, it is important to remember the importance of Maitreya during the age of the expansionist Kushanas when judging the claims that Buddhism is an otherworldly religion committed to a view of the world that is timeless and ahistorical.

Certainly the image of Ashoka, adumbrated in the Kushana king Kanishka, suggests that Buddhism could serve as the ruling ideology for a royal state, and, as we see in Stanley Tambiah's important study *World Conqueror and World Renouncer,* it did so in the Buddhist kingdoms of Southeast Asia.[7] But as a worldwide movement, Buddhism was never at the aegis of a political formation comparable to Christendom, however much particular polities might patronize one set of Buddhist institutions or another.

As Buddhism made its way along the Silk Road, another wholly new and universalist tradition arose in Mesopotamia to meet it: Manichaeism. Manichaeism is perhaps the most self-consciously constructed religion the world has ever known, the brainchild of its founder, the prophet Mani. Mani was born in Mesopotamia in 216 A.D. when this region was the fault line between the Roman Empire and the Persians. It was an area of religious diversity, with groups of Jews who had lived there since the time of the exile, Christians, ancient Babylonian mystery cults, and soon-to-be reformed Zoroastrian traditions. Mani's father followed the Mandaean religion, a baptist sect (revering John the Baptist, but not Jesus) that still survives in the marshes of Iraq, but the boy had a revelation experience at the age of twelve that convinced him that he was an apostle, a successor of Jesus Christ, though his understanding of Christianity was of a distinctly gnostic type, and his teaching always stressed a sharp dualism of flesh and spirit. He later traveled to India (probably the northwest where Persian and Greek influences were strongest), and he became convinced that he was to fulfill not only the mission of Christ but of the Buddha as well.

Mani accepted the ancient Zoroastrian dualism and had a similarly rich mythology of the struggle between the two primary elements of the world, but in his ascetic and gnostic reading, the struggle was not a simple matter of good and evil but of matter and spirit. Particles of spirit, trapped in the world of flesh and matter, had to be rescued and redeemed. The Son of God, called Jesus but hardly portrayed as an historical person, took the role of redeemer of Adam, revealing to him his soul of light but also the evil origin of his corrupt body. Mani was to take up this redemptive task.

During the reign of Shapur I, the first great Sasanian emperor, Mani seemed to find the perfect imperial patron. Shapur had spread his rule into the border regions not only of Mesopotamia, but Georgia and Armenia as well. He had even once captured the Roman emperor Valerian in battle. The time seemed right for a realignment of power between Rome and Persia, and perhaps a new religious dispensation as well. Whatever Shapur's ambitions, the western provinces of his empire were not very deeply Iranized, as Greek and Aramaic languages were still dominant, and only the rural nobility were interested in the traditional Zoroastrian fire cult. In the cities, his less Persianized subjects were followers of Judaism and a range of Christian and gnostic sects. Mani first succeeded in converting the emperor's brothers, and traveled with the emperor on campaign. Surely he began to hope that he could establish a religion that could speak to the expanding cosmopolitan world of both the Persian and Roman Empires.

The emperor had, however, another companion on campaign, the Zoroastrian priest Kartir, who restored and reformed Zoroastrian fire temples wherever they went. His goal was to Persianize the empire by establishing an organized and purified Zoroastrianism as a national church,[8] no doubt with himself as the pope, and he largely succeeded, at least in the Iranian heartlands and at the level of official policy. In fact, despite its exceedingly ancient roots, it is only in Sasanian times that the Zoroastrian tradition was fully organized, with a clearly established priesthood, and scripture (the *Avesta*), and, most importantly, imperial backing. While Shapur continued to support both Mani and Kartir, Kartir won the exclusive support of Shapur's son and successor, Bahram I (r. 273–76), and as Kartir's influence rose, Mani's fell. The successor of Buddha and Christ, the self-proclaimed "seal of the prophets," was thrown into prison, where he died a martyr, leaving his followers subject to official persecution.

Mani's dualism of flesh and spirit, light and dark, had resonances not only with spiritual traditions of Christian gnosticism and ancient Zoroastrianism, but with the thought of Indian yogis and ascetics as well. His was a universalistic doctrine indeed, meant for the whole world. In fact, although Manichaeism spread to northern Africa, where it won the brief allegiance of Augustine, and to China, where it survived until early modern times, it was never to achieve real prominence in the lands of Alexander the Great. Where it promised to eclipse its spiritual forebears as a universal religion par excellence, it failed to strike deep roots among the laity or gain firm political backing. Perhaps its sober pessimism about the corruption of the body limited its appeal for practical worldly folk, although the facile assumption that ascetic religion and politics don't work together overlooks the fact that for much of Christian history, ascetic traditions made monks and nuns the ideal models of human existence. In Manichaeism's case, the fluidity of its doctrines, encompassing so much, made it perhaps too malleable to be politically potent. And because of its ascetic ideals, the strict division between married laymen and "the elect" may have meant that only a tiny minority of the population ever fully embraced Manichaean thought and practice. Indeed, the Chinese had a hard time distinguishing Manichaeans from Buddhists.

Thus while Rome was becoming an officially Christian empire, Persia officially became a Zoroastrian one, the two great powers then facing off against each other at the crossroads of the *oikoumene* for the next three centuries.[9] But while emperors and generals might have repeated such a narrative as a way of inspiring their subjects and soldiers, the differences in the religious culture of the new Rome and that of the Persian Empire should not be overlooked. Most importantly, unlike Christianity, Zoroastrianism never became the heartfelt faith of the urban masses, and many were drawn to the more cosmopolitan and soteriological traditions like Nestorian Christianity, especially in the ancient urban centers of Mesopotamia. Here, as all across Eurasia, Judaism worked out a way to live as minority sect without political power (producing the Babylonian Talmud in Persia-ruled Mesopotamia). Manichaeism also survived, but only as an underground religion of salvation, a sect without deep cultural roots or political influence. Some Persian emperors chose to persecute minority religions, others not, but most took for granted the fact that many of their subjects, especially their non-Iranian ones, would follow faiths other than Zoroastrianism. Thus their fight with Christian emperors was not really a Zoroastrian crusade.

RELIGION IN INDIA, 320–820 A.D.

Across the eastern border of the Persian world, the Guptas (320–550 A.D.) established a dynasty often characterized as the golden age of classical Hinduism in North India. Although the Guptas consciously modeled themselves on the great Mauryan Dynasty, their polity was softer, depending more on feudal relationships than direct bureaucratic oversight of the petty kingdoms that made up their empire. What is most often noted about the era of the Guptas and their successors was the high degree of cultural sophistication attained by Indian writers and artists in this period. Writing in the classical Sanskrit language (a language similar in structure and function to classical Greek), playwrights, grammarians, philosophers, mythographers, legal scholars, mathematicians, and astronomers produced a vast corpus of art and learning that would characterize the classical, pre-Islamic Indian style. This was the age of the dramas of Kalidasa (read by Goethe), and the works of Aryabhatta, a mathematician and astronomer who accurately reckoned *pi* and knew the earth was a sphere rotating on its axis. The brilliant poet and scholar A.K. Ramanujan once asked, "Is there an Indian way of thinking?"[10] If there is, indeed, a distinctively Indian way of thinking (and being in the world), its style was formulated in this era.

Brahmin philosophers debated Buddhists in this period, both producing works of great rigor and complexity, a golden age of Indian philosophy that would last until the demise of Indian Buddhism in the twelfth century. Brahmins made an attempt to refute Buddhist universalism, the Buddhist system that would make truth something constructed, worldly, and available to all persons. To do so, they needed to make credible their belief in revealed scripture, and to uphold an ideology of caste to maintain their claims of spiritual and intellectual authority. We have seen that in the previous era the epic poets and *dharma* scholars responded to Buddhism by asserting the idea that *dharma* is an ethical system that sees different roles and standards for different people, depending on those persons' caste, gender, and age. In such a worldview, brahmins are, as it were, biochemically constituted to be priests and scholars, whereas kings are naturally inclined to wage war and rule. Brahmins should be vegetarians; kings should not. From the brahmins' perspective, the Buddhist rejection of such particularism in the name of universal truths endangers the proper foundations of society by confusing the roles of the different species of human beings. Such were the issues that continued to be debated throughout this period in India.

We can see how the Buddhist position might appeal to kings who were foreign or came from non-*kshatriya* castes. It might also appeal to any king who was unwilling to grant brahmins sole authority in matters of religion and philosophy. Just as in the West, there was always a tension between those who asserted religious authority and those who asserted political authority. But in India, the tug of particularism always seemed to win out, and the religion that supported the diversity of castes and roles, seeing it as altogether appropriate that different persons had different gods, different ways of life, even different ethical standards and principles—the religion we now call Hinduism—was to prevail.

In some ways, Hinduism was to prevail in part because it *did* recognize a universalism, but did so in a way that left pluralism intact. Toward the end of the period under review here, India's most influential philosopher, Shankara (d. 820), developed a universalism that recognized one Truth above all others, but left other, "lower" truths undisturbed. Shankara's fundamental principle was that there exists only one ultimate Reality, *brahman,* Being Itself, which is beyond all defining qualities (*nirguna*). In perceiving *brahman,* we most often misperceive its true nature and superimpose qualities that finally have no reality. Such misperception is like a fearful man seeing a snake, when in fact only a rope lies before him. This ignorance and misperception causes us to invest in a world that is finally not true. We are attached to fleeting and temporary "names and forms" (*nama-rupa*) that have no final reality. For Shankara, the mystical insight that all is *brahman* removes the false misperception and allows the seeker to be detached and removed from the vicissitudes of the phenomenal world.

But what is striking about Shankara's monistic (*advaita,* "nondual") philosophy is that while he sees the phenomenal world as only partially real and true, since only the One (*brahman* or "Being," *sat*) truly exists, he vigorously maintains the necessity of recognizing the validity of that very social world transcended by the higher truth. Thus while all the gods and the castes of human beings are not *finally* true, they still have a temporary role for those persons not ready to see the Final Truth. And those qualified persons are brahmin men ready to renounce married life and live as monks. So while critics accused Shankara of being a crypto-Buddhist, his influential philosophy took some of Buddhism's universalism, while retaining the particularism of caste Hinduism.[11]

What was at stake in India's cultural choices was the persistence of a society in which all manner of pluralism was embraced, if ranked hierarchically and managed. It was a system that pagan Greeks would have found comprehensible. But whereas they were superseded by a Christian universalism that declared one truth for all people in all times and circumstances, such exclusivism and egalitarianism never took hold in India. India would remain a country of innumerable castes and gods. Jews and Christians came to India early in the common era and could be absorbed as endogamous castes, followed later by Zoroastrians

(Parsees). But until the coming of Muslim rulers in the twelfth century, the system that governed these diverse religious communities would be a Hindu system. The vigor with which Hindu philosophers denounced Buddhist philosophers attests to their seriousness in defending a system with such enormous political and social consequences.

RELIGION IN CHINA, 220–845 A.D.

At the time of Mani's death in 276, the great Han Dynasty had fallen to northern barbarian invaders. From 220 to 589 A.D. China was politically divided; "barbarians" ruled the north, and the south was fractured by a host of warring princes. This political and military collapse also crushed any simple faith in the ancient Confucian traditions that were part of Han imperial culture; and since aliens ruled all of northern China, faith in ancient Chinese traditions over all was shaky at best. The new rulers in the north turned to Buddhism for literate advisors and for the religious legitimacy a cosmopolitan tradition could confer. Embracing a triumphalist caesaro-papism, they developed an ideology that saw the ruler as nothing less than the incarnation of the Buddha. In the south, among the aristocratic northern refugees, Buddhism took a more sensitive turn, where intellectuals interpreted its more philosophical ideas in the Daoist language of detachment, impermanence, and nature mysticism.

When China was finally reunited under the Sui Dynasty (589–618 A.D.) and the great Tang Dynasty (618–907), Buddhism was part of a mix of imperially patronized religious traditions, sometimes referred to as the "Three Teachings" (*san jiao*) of Confucianism, Daoism, and Buddhism. This formulation suggests the simplistic, oft-repeated idea that China had achieved an enlightened pluralism unimagined by intolerant dogmatists to the West. There were indeed periods during which Chinese emperors dispensed patronage to a variety of schools, but what complicates this irenic picture is the history of harsh government repressions of a variety of religious sects in China periodically from the late second century to the present day, a history ably covered in Daniel Overmyer's (inappropriately entitled) book *Folk Buddhist Religion*.[12] What this history shows is that however pluralist China might have been, it was a pluralism that presumed the primacy of the imperial state. Whenever any religious group seemed to threaten the cultural cohesion of the state, it was branded dangerous and was crushed. That some of these sectarian movements were indeed revolutionary, but others were not, did not matter. Like elite Romans, who first saw Christianity as a superstitious cult, the Chinese continued to harbor suspicions about any foreign sect, especially those that offered individual salvation and threatened to tear the fabric of a deeply traditional society.

During the fifth century, emperors of the Northern Wei Dynasty, originally northern barbarian warlords, began to adopt Chinese ways and became lavish patrons of Buddhism. They erected monumental statues of the Buddha, following a style already prominent on the Silk Road in places like Bamiyan.[13] Buddhist monasteries in China, as in Central Asia, were enriched by trade on the Silk Road, and in a time of political and military unrest, became places where traders both conducted business and atoned for sins. Many of the most successful traders on the Silk Road were Sogdians, an ethnic group coming from an area around modern Uzbekistan. Speakers of an Iranian language, they adopted Buddhism, and later Manichaeaism, and served as major culture brokers from China to the Middle East, but unlike the Kushanas, never established an empire.

During the period of political disunity, trade on the Silk Road continued, and numerous ethnic groups on China's northern and western borders found a place in China's cultural life. From Central Asia, nomadic warriors became allies and kings, and Buddhist monks translated scriptures. For all its political turmoil, this period set the stage for the rich cosmopolitanism of Tang China (618–907), when China became the most populous, wealthy, and sophisticated place on earth.

Tang emperors came to power in the seventh century, claiming to be reincarnations of the great Daoist sage Laozi, but this was still an age of great efflorescence in the Chinese Buddhist Church. Buddhism by this time was fully acculturated, and Chinese Buddhist thinkers expressed themselves in a Chinese idiom. For example, the legendary sage Hui Neng (d. 713) used the classical Daoist language of the Mirror Mind to capture the nature of nonattached Buddhist meditation characteristic of Zen (Chinese, Chan). The masses turned to savior figures like Amitabha and Maitreya, and one Tang empress circulated a scripture prophesying her rule as that of Maitreya incarnate.[14]

While Sui and Tang rulers patronized several religious communities, they restored and reformed the old Confucian system of civil service examinations to produce an educated but relatively independent cadre of state bureaucrats. When faced with financial pressures, certainly the wealthy Buddhist Church offered one tax-free target, and as Henry VIII would realize, the closing of monasteries would provide a large source of income. Criticized as "foreign" by Confucian officials, the Buddhist Church was crippled by a government confiscation of property and general persecution in the 840s that reportedly resulted in the destruction of several thousand monasteries and defrocking of over two hundred thousand monks.[15] Buddhism was never to recover as a religious institution in China; it survived largely as one strand in a complex of inarticulate folk-religious practices. This xenophobic persecution came after numerous less thorough repressions, and swept up Manichaeism as well. It occurred about a century after the bloody An Lushan uprising, named for a rebellious general of Persian descent. The persecution of Buddhism in the ninth century signaled the end of the period of dynamic pluralism in China, the period when silk brought wealth, and an ethnically diverse population of traders brought foreign religions, literature, and works of art. Confucianism was back as the ruling ideology of a less open society.

Meanwhile, the silk merchants were meeting and supplying the needs of a new power in the West. Arab armies conquered Persia in the seventh century, quickly advanced into Central Asia, and met Tang military forces with some success, but they could not bring China into the rapidly expanding Islamic Empire. As Arab power spread, China remained an important cultural counterweight as well as an important trading partner throughout the era of Islamic dominance.

Thus we see, in the Eurasian world of the fourth to sixth centuries, literate, cosmopolitan church institutions—Christian, Zoroastrian, Buddhist, and Manichaean—all seeking some advantageous relationship to imperial power. Minority religions like Judaism or Nestorian Christianity sought no more than a place to survive in a world where the majority community might, at best, tolerate them while reserving the right to really call the shots. Only in India did the old-fashioned pluralism that compares to Greco-Roman paganism survive under the aegis of a caste-based Hinduism; while Buddhism, with its universalist pretensions, ebbed away in the land of its birth, and flourished in China, only to fall prey to a Confucian revival. Perhaps of all these, Christianity came closest to fusing religion and politics into a single culture, a project entitled Constantinianism, after the emperor who established Christianity as the religion of the Roman Empire.

CONSTANTINE TO JUSTINIAN

After Constantine's conversion and his vigorous political patronage of Christianity, the stage seems to be set for a fully Christian Rome, the

Byzantine Empire, to oppose a Zoroastrian Persian Empire, Romans and Sasanians facing off against each other in Mesopotamia. Near ancient Babylon, where Cyrus and Alexander centered their great empires, there was now a political and military fault line. As we noted above, Alexander claimed, over three centuries before Christ, that Asia needed one king just as it needed one sun. The new claim seemed to be that there should be an homology of one God, one King, and one Empire.[16] Would Persians, or Romans, eventually triumph in Mesopotamia, and would one religion govern the crossroads of the world? Constantine fervently believed that he had the answer, that he was destined by God to prevail.

Such a binary obscures, however, a truer portrait of the borderlands of Persia and Rome in this period. As we have noted, the religious worlds of Rome and Iran were not fully comparable. Iran had turned away from the cosmopolitan, urban religion of Manichaeism to reformulate an ancient Zoroastrianism, a religion that had a distinctly Iranian character most attractive to rural nobles of the heartland. But unlike Christianity, it was not really exportable. In the cities and in the border regions, significant minorities still followed other religions, and even the Sasanian monarchs were not completely invulnerable to the claims of those traditions. In fact, since the Sasanian kings were city builders and often challenged by rural nobles, it is not surprising that they were often sympathetic to urban cultural traditions of the wider world. Besides the Jews who had lived in Persian lands since ancient times, groups of heterodox Christians, notably the Nestorians and Monophysites found shelter in Persia from the persecutions from the Chalcedonian Christians who were dominant in Byzantium. In contrast, Constantine followed a more fully universalist and missionary religion than his Persian counterpart, and he felt called upon not only to spread that religion throughout the world but to protect Christians outside as well as inside his realm. Moreover, his military ventures could not be fully distinguished from his religious goals. Constantine's ambition to found a world empire based on a single monotheistic faith was not realized until Arabs conquered the Middle East and Iran in the name of Islam in the seventh century, but such was the Roman Christian project, nonetheless. It was not matched by a similar Persian project to spread the faith of Zoroaster.

The universalism of Constantine's Christianity (and that of his successors) provided, in short, a legitimacy for his imperial ambition, a pretext to reach beyond his borders and claim Christian subjects who lived in Persian territories. Like it or not, those Persian Christians had a dual identity. On the one hand, they might enjoy the protection of Persian rule, a protection that allowed them doctrinal freedom. On the other hand, as Christians, they would always be a vulnerable and suspect minority, subject to persecution under any ruler who might choose to make Zoroastrianism the mark of the faithful Persian subject. And unlike Jews, whose religion allowed them to see their minority status as legitimate, Christian universalism made that a more difficult stance for its faithful.

The unifying effect of proclaiming a single religion for an expansive empire is a tempting project for any ambitious emperor. Similarly, the emperor would also want to claim a sacred legitimacy for his own rule, and sacral kingship has a long history. Though tolerating a religious pluralism, the Roman imperial system did insist on a sacred legitimacy for the emperor (as we have seen in the Augustan inscription, p. 50). It is noteworthy, however, that there is often a sort of separation of powers between priests and kings. In India, this was enshrined in the notion of two separate castes of men, one concerned with ritual and religious matters (the brahmins), who conferred blessings upon another endogamous group (the *kshatriyas*), who were concerned with politics and war. This is not to say that brahmins did not sometimes become kings, and there were many *kshatriyas* who became religious leaders, following a path similar to that of Gautama Buddha, who was born a prince. But the religious ideology conceived of the ideal world as governed in different ways by different sorts of people. In the European West, this division is expressed by the history of the often tense standoff between popes and kings, as popes became more royal and emperors became more religious, each eyeing the other's sources of power and charisma with envy. This tension is the ancestor of the modern binary of sacred and secular.

In the eastern parts of the Roman Empire, we see a greater unity of church and state. We should remind ourselves here that "the rise and fall of the Roman empire" is a phrase much more applicable to the West, where popes, bishops, and abbots reigned if not ruled over a politically chaotic Christendom after Rome's fall, while Constantinople, the New Rome, continued to flourish as the capital of the eastern Mediterranean empire, always the more wealthy, populous, and powerful half. This had profound consequences for the relationship of religion and political power in the two realms. The Byzantine emperor more fully inhabited the role of earthly representative of the Divine Monarch.[17]

At this juncture, we should note that the classical world historical narrative—the narrative still lodged in the minds of most western Europeans and Americans—which starts in the Fertile Crescent and Egypt, proceeds to Greece and Rome and from there to western Europe, is thus profoundly misleading. From Alexander to the Romans to the first Arab caliphs, all were pulled to Mesopotamia. For anyone interested in the centers of power and high culture, history did not proceed north and west from Rome, but repeatedly, turned back to the east. Constantine's founding of Constantinople was not the cause but the expression of this oriental gravitation. American students of world history tend to proceed directly from the late antique Roman world, the so-called "decline and fall of the Roman Empire," to medieval western Christendom, thus bypassing both the flourishing of the Byzantine world and the rise of the Islamic empires. We end up knowing a fair amount about the Egypt of the pyramids, and almost nothing of medieval Islamic Egypt.

So, as Rome fell, the New Rome arose in Constantinople. Like Ashoka, to whom he has been compared,[18] Constantine (d. 337 A.D.) wanted to claim authority in both sacred and secular realms. Christian writers had long seen in the fact that Christ and Augustus lived at the same time a sort of prelude to Christian empire, now realized under Constantine. Famously, Constantine had a consequential religious experience before battle, seeing a miraculous cross bearing the inscription "conquer by this sign" (*in hoc signo vinces*). He later styled himself a sort of bishop and apostle, convening the Council of Nicaea in 325 to settle questions of creedal orthodoxy (formulated as the Nicene Creed). His famous biographer, Eusebius, portrayed him in ecclesial terms; his palace was a church, and his speeches were homilies. "He would tell them [his governors] that God had given him the empire of all the world, and that, in imitation of God, he had himself given them portions of the empire to rule. But that everyone would have to render account of his deeds to the supreme God."[19]

To bring divine authority to the very human projects of political governance requires that the point of contact reflect the heavenly glory. Ramsay MacMullen has noted:

> When Constantine ... at the very center of his capital, the New Rome, placed his image portraying him as the Sun God, with rayed head and thunderbolt in hand, atop a huge red stone column, there receiving sacrifices and prayers exactly as Caesar's statue on *its* column in old Rome had once been the object of prayers and offerings, or again, when his smaller image was paraded about the hippodrome in the so-called Sun Chariot, among torches, and saluted ceremoniously from the royal box—by his successors, on their knees—no doubt ecclesiastical protest should have been instant.[20]

But it was not. Macmullen adds: "The bishops had learned the strength of their tremendous friend at Nicaea. . . . Accordingly, they kept quiet."[21]

By 400 A.D., perhaps half the Roman population was Christian, but paganism—what Macmullen calls that "spongy mass of tolerance and tradition"[22]—was surely not dead or even obviously doomed. Pagans and Christians lived side by side under Christian emperors for a long time, and certainly the Christianity that survived maintained much of what had constituted the pagan world. By this time, Christianity had become respectable, socially and intellectually, and was certainly no longer a religion of the urban proletariat, though many old aristocrats resented the social fluidity of middle-brow Christian culture. And one last emperor took their side and reverted to paganism, albeit a rather self-conscious version. Emperor Julian (r. 361–63), known by Christians as "the Apostate," after a childhood education under no less Christian a tutor than Eusebius, attempted to return Rome to the ways of the ancients. But he, too, recognized the need for a sort of religious universalism, though an inclusivist one. He felt it altogether appropriate that all the nations that made up the empire should reverence their respective local gods, but offered the Sun as a kind of singular father and divine king of all peoples. Ironically, he himself worshiped the sun as Mithras, a solar deity that had won the allegiance of so many Roman soldiers, but originally an Iranian god. His attack on Christianity was harsh, for after Constantine, its universalism was dangerously presumptuous; it not only spoke to all persons, but it also assumed the legitimate right to rule the world. It is noteworthy that while vehemently rejecting Christianity, Julian had no problems with Judaism, and even planned to rebuild Solomon's Temple, for Judaism was understood to be the religion of one people among the many peoples ruled by the emperor. It could be included because it was not a threat to the power and legitimacy of the emperor. Julian's use of the attractive universal symbol of the sun—already employed, as we have noted, by Constantine—suggests that his fight with Christianity had more to do with the specific groups who favored it than with its theology. But whatever his motives, Julian fought Christianity with a religious ideology that borrowed many of the institutions and structures present in his opponents' religion. Not only had Constantine already used solar imagery in his self-presentation as monarch, the liturgical year of Christianity was organized according to solar symbolism, with Christmas coinciding with the holiday of the Invincible Sun (*Sol Invictus*). In both cases, we have an expression of universalism giving political power absolute legitimacy.

Julian died in Ctesiphon, near Alexander's Mesopotamian capital, on campaign against the Persians. He had seen himself as a philosopher-king, a sort of reincarnation of Marcus Aurelius, but his brief reign of twenty months was the last example of a pagan Roman state. His successor quickly reinstated Christianity as the official state religion.[23]

But even after Christianity's political triumph, the old temples and institutions of Hellenism survived alongside the churches of the Mediterranean world, and Neoplatonism was embraced by Christian and non-Christian intellectuals alike. It is important to remember that the great Christian apologist of the West, St. Augustine (d. 430) did not live in a Christian world. He was surrounded by pagan philosophers and himself briefly lived as a Manichaean before accepting Christianity. He was turned from the gnostics' denunciation of matter by reading Plotinus's *On Beauty*, not by any Christian writer.[24] His contemporary, the famous philosopher Hypatia (d. 415), usually portrayed as a kind of tragic martyr for paganism, taught as many Christian students as pagans in her native Alexandria.

Hypatia's story may tell us a great deal about how religion and power are mixed up in surprising ways in a context of social change; it is not always a simple matter of two blocs standing off against one another in all-out conflict. Hypatia was an aristocratic philosopher and mathematician, well respected among the Greek-speaking intellectuals of Alexandria at the turn of the fifth century. But the destruction of the temple of the quintessentially syncretistic deity Serapis (the Serapeum) in 395 provides evidence of a growing group of Christians openly hostile to their non-Christian neighbors, and Hypatia's murder at the hands of monks loyal to the Alexandrian bishop Cyril seems to fit into a simple narrative of Christian-pagan conflict. Martin Bernal writes: "Twenty-five years later [after the destruction of the Serapis temple] the brilliant and beautiful philosopher and mathematician Hypatia was gruesomely murdered in the same city by a gang of monks instigated by St. Cyril. These two acts of violence mark the end of the Egypto-Paganism and the beginning of the Christian Dark Ages."[25] But, according to Maria Dzielska, such a story is complicated by the fact that much of what we know of Hypatia comes to us from the letters of her devoted student Synesius of Cyrene, who was a Christian and later became a bishop. Hypatia, it seems, was opposed by Cyril, but had many friends in high places, including Christian aristocrats with imperial connections in Constantinople, old elites who had supported Cyril's rival, Timothy, for the position of bishop. The struggle in which Hypatia was caught up and died was more a matter of class warfare, with her local bishop winning support of a class of Christians opposed to an old aristocracy. The bishop managed to portray her murder as the result of a Christian mob attacking a pagan witch, but it was more of a planned political assassination than that. It was but one battle, and not part of a grand war between pagans and Christians. As Dzielska points out, when the Arabs arrived two centuries later, the classical pagan traditions of Hypatia—Neoplatonism, mathematics, astronomy—were still flourishing in Alexandria.[26]

The primary imperial representative who was allied to Hypatia and her circle, Orestes, was himself a Christian, but as a political official was, perhaps not surprisingly, rather tolerant and pragmatic. But he was outflanked by the local bishop, a man who garnered power and influence by a certain rigid orthodoxy and in this case, a witch hunt. Throughout the fourth, fifth, and sixth centuries, important bishops often stirred the faithful by passionate sermons turning on precise points of doctrine.

Several of the well-known heresies of this period—Donatism, Arianism, Nestorianism, Monophysitism—not only threatened Christianity with schism but revealed the political fault lines in what was supposed to be a united Christendom. Alexandria in Egypt, Antioch in Syria, Caesarea in Anatolia, were all cities with powerful and sometimes rebellious bishops with whom the emperor at Constantinople had to contend—hence the repeated attempts at doctrinal compromise and agreement from Nicaea (325) to Chalcedon (451).

The case of Donatism suggests vividly how an imperial bureaucratic church had to respond to the challenge of purist groups. Simply put, the Donatists believed that for sacraments to be efficacious, the officiating priest had to be in a state of grace. In other words, although the priest might be an officially recognized, ordained minister of the church, his "magical powers" (so to speak) depended on the mysterious presence of the Holy Spirit, a presence that would be impossible if he were in a state of mortal sin. More specifically, Donatists could not easily overlook the backsliding of priests who had renounced Christianity under political pressure and violent persecution only to return to the church when the heat was off. The opponents of Donatism rightly saw that such a view might be consonant with the sort of social revolutionaries who had first followed the North African priest Donatus (d. 355), but that an organized, sustainable institution depended on the charisma of office. People could not be worrying about the particular moral state of their priests;

they had to believe that *his office,* and not his personal spirituality, made him an effective instrument of grace.

St. Augustine was an effective opponent of the Donatist position, for although he believed in the difference between the City of Man and the City of God and knew that no empire could be wholly good, he still thought it necessary to create the conditions for a Christian civilization. That is why he came to believe that insincere conversions could be a good thing.[27] If, for example, a man converted to Christianity only to please his Christian wife, and not through some profound change of heart, he nonetheless became a participant in Christian culture, contributing to Christian institutions, and doing his part to make sure that his children and grandchildren would grow up in a Christian world. If Christianity was to be taken for granted, the very basis of the entire culture, it had to rule through institutions, and those institutions must depend upon individuals who varied widely in matters of enthusiasm and sincerity.

Arius (d. 336), an Alexandrian priest, questioned the view that Christ was uncreated, a challenge that resembles the later Muslim controversy over whether the *Qur'an* was created (Mu'tazilism, see pp. 125–26). In both cases, the position that became orthodox was one affirming the fact that the point of mediation between the divine world and the human world (whether Christ or *Qur'an*) was indeed eternal and uncreated. One can see how those who challenged the ultimately victorious view felt that mainstream piety courted idolatry. But once again, we can see how Arianism might threaten the political health of the Christian religion as it began its alliance with empire. For if the transcendent God were known through a human mediator who was himself not fully divine, but a creature like us, God's will for the world would be mysterious, vague, and subject to multiple interpretations. (Of course that is always the case, but that is not the way the contestants here would see matters.) When the council of bishops at Nicaea rejected Arianism in Constantine's presence, they refused the idea that the source of absolute truth, the site where God made contact with the world, could be understood in any way other than God Himself being present. The Nicene Creed makes this abundantly clear: Jesus was "begotten *not made.*"[28]

But what sort of being could be wholly man and wholly God? If Jesus was fully God, how could he pray? Like Donatus, another purist, Nestorius (d. 451), a bishop in Constantinople, challenged the popular practice of referring to the Virgin Mary as Theotokos, "Bearer of God." He simply couldn't imagine *God* as a little *baby*—again, a problem of mediation. Nestorius was accused of denying Christ's divinity, but protested that he was simply challenging the popular understanding of how we might understand Christ as both divine and human. Whatever his actual beliefs, the powerful Cyril managed to portray him as claiming that Christ was, in effect, two persons, one divine and one human, whereas the orthodox view, affirmed at Ephesus in 431 and Chalcedon in 451, helpfully defined Christ as one person with two natures held in hypostatic union! The Nestorians who survived did so across the border, in Persia, where they wore their Nestorianism as a badge of their political independence from the Byzantine emperor, an important badge that often protected them from the Persian emperor's persecution.

Cyril had led the charge against Nestorius, once again reflecting a rivalry between Alexandria on one side and Constantinople and Antioch on the other. But although the council at Chalcedon banished Nestorius, its language of the incarnation was not entirely to Cyril's liking. He insisted that Christ's divinity issued "out of two natures" but not "in two natures," as defined at Chalcedon. Cyril's position, what came to be known as Monophysitism—a doctrine that Christ incarnate is not a hypostatic union of human and divine, but fully and perfectly divine—became the accepted theology in the churches of Egypt (the Coptic), Ethiopia, and Armenia, in other words in several regions on the periphery of Byzantine power. While all these places allied with Constantinople, forming what Garth Fowden terms the Byzantine Commonwealth, they all retained both a theological and political independence along the line of conflict between Persia and the New Rome.

Marshall Hodgson, following Max Weber, has argued that the rise of universalist monotheism in the center of Eurasia is a result of the rise of the merchant class, people who traded abroad, saw the world in cosmopolitan terms and for whom deals were based on justice.[29] This played out somewhat differently in Rome and Persia in the century before the rise of Islam. The long reigns of Khusraw I (r. 531–79),[30] and Justinian (r. 527–65), represent the rivalry for world dominion between the great empires of Romans and Persians in the sixth century. They were at war with each other for over twenty years and both had universalistic pretensions. Khusraw is said to have maintained three thrones at his palace in Ctesiphon, one for the emperor of the Romans, one for the emperor of the Chinese, and one for the king of the Khazars of the northern steppes between the Black and Caspian seas, just in case they were to visit, presumably as supplicants. Justinian famously codified Roman law, and built the magnificent church of Hagia Sophia, claiming to have outdone Solomon, and assuming thereby, to be a divinely appointed king with the divine mission of defending the faith and spreading it abroad.

We know less about Khusraw than about Justinian, but he was clearly successful as a reformer of taxation (copying a Roman model) and the military (where he developed a professional army less dependent on feudal levies, and included Arab soldiers among the others). In both these ways, his power rested less upon the strength of the rural aristocrats who had always supported a hierarchical society and the conservative Zoroastrianism that went with it. It is thus not surprising that the Persian-controlled Fertile Crescent, with its wealthy, mercantile, and cosmopolitan cities, continued to be the home for many followers of less provincial religions. Khusraw had resettled Roman populations from captured towns within his kingdom, and received Greek intellectuals from Athens after Justinian closed the "pagan" Academy of Plato, founding his own academy at Gundeshapur, where Greek and Indian traditions of philosophy, science and medicine met and flourished. There were many Jews with deep ties to the region, who had lived there since the exile a thousand years before. Indeed, Rabbinic Judaism came to rely upon the so-called Babylonian Talmud, the huge encyclopedic text of commentary finally completed and edited about 700 A.D. Most importantly, many of Khusraw's Mesopotamian officials were Nestorian Christians. It was never assumed that people whose traditions were not Iranian would convert to Zoroastrianism, or even adopt the middle Persian language. Many Mesopotamian Christian merchants and officials continued to speak a dialect of the language Jesus spoke (Syriac, a branch of Aramaic). Syriac-speaking Christians (Syro-Malabar or St. Thomas Christians) settled in faraway South India, but for centuries still looked to Iraq to supply them bishops.

Nonetheless, Khusraw's empire continued to be officially Zoroastrian. One of his earliest struggles as emperor was to crush a rebellious sect, followers of a prophet called Mazdak, who criticized the landed nobles and called for limits on their wealth and power. But since the Persian Empire was not an exclusivist Zoroastrian kingdom facing off against Christendom, but a multireligious state in which the progressive sectors of society often followed religious traditions other than the official religion of the monarch, Zoroastrianism was never exported beyond the Iranian zone, even to peoples living as integral parts of the Persian Empire.

By contrast, Justinian felt responsible not only for the Christians of his realm but for Christians living beyond Roman borders. Not only did he wage war with Khusraw, defending Christian cities along his Mesopotamian border, but he had to deal with heretic (Arian) barbarian kings who oppressed orthodox Christians in their North African, Italian, and Balkan kingdoms. Moreover, Egypt and Syria continued to be strongholds of Monophysitism.[31] In the first case, Justinian used military intervention to try to regain lost provinces or at least to mitigate the oppression of Chalcedonian Christians; in the second case, he used diplomacy to maintain alliances with societies that, if not orthodox, still followed the Christian religion. In an ideal world, the Christian monarch would rule a worldwide empire undivided by theological schism. Lacking that, he used whatever power he had to advance the interests of all Christians, whatever their particular theologies, at home and abroad.

During the momentous sixth century, when Byzantium and Persia were constantly at war, they drew two main Arab groups into their spheres of influence, unaware that a century later, Arabs would turn their borderlands into the centerpiece of their worldwide empire. The mercantile clans of the Ghassanids tended to ally with the Romans along the Syrian border, whereas the Lakhmids usually allied with Persia at the southern edges of Mesopotamia.[32] Arabs were increasingly drawn into the cosmopolitan ways of the wider world, as businessmen and soldiers, but also as followers of monotheistic religious movements—usually Nestorian or Monophysite Christianity, but Judaism, as well.[33] The central shrine at Mecca, the Ka'ba, was rebuilt in 600 A.D. along Ethiopian lines and may have housed an icon of the Virgin Mary alongside the pagan deities of pre-Islamic Arabia.[34]

Glen Bowersock writes of one Arab leader from the Yemen, Yusuf As'ar Yath'ar, (also known as Dhu Nuwas), who actively persecuted the Christians of Najran, a city not quite halfway between Mecca and Aden, carrying out a massacre (in 523 A.D.) in hopes of winning Lakhmid or Sasanian aid in his attempt to build up an expanded Jewish kingdom in southern Arabia. Failed in that, he instead provoked an Ethiopian invasion in 527 that resulted in his death and the Christianization of southern Arabia in the second half of the sixth century. At the time of this political crisis, one Lakhmid leader, Mundhir ibn Numan, received ambassadors from Byzantine, Persian, Nestorian, and Monophysite communities, all asking for his intervention on behalf of the Christians of Najran.[35] Yusuf's Jewish kingdom was thus finished, but meanwhile, Jewish tribes must have been settling in Medina, for when the prophet began his rule there in 622, they were well established.[36] The Byzantine-Sasanian proxy war suggests once again that monotheism, in its many guises, was a banner for empire building, in which Arabs were involved well before the birth of Muhammad.

War erupted once more between the Persians and Romans before both gave way to Arab power. Khusraw II (d. 628) invaded Byzantium and captured Antioch, Jerusalem, and Egypt by 620 A.D., but though he was suspicious of Chalcedonian Christians, he offered captured communities their choice of following either the Nestorian or the Monophysite faith; official Zoroastrianism was never even suggested as an option. (Perhaps this is why Arabs opposed to Rome might convert to Judaism as a sign of their alliance with Persia.) The Byzantine emperor Heraclius (r. 610–41) struck back in 627, recapturing these provinces along with the True Cross, which he hauled back to Constantinople. The seesaw of imperial competition might have continued its exhausting course, with both kings keeping an eye on each other and on their troublesome northern frontiers. But neither was to foresee the total transformation of the Mesopotamian frontier zone. This area, divided by military conflict, but united as a zone of economic and cultural vitality, was about to become the heartland of the Muslim empire that would extend from India to Spain only eighty years after Heraclius restored the True Cross to his capital. The crossroads of Eurasian trade, not politically united since Cyrus and Alexander, would once again be the center of a worldwide empire.[37] The Arabs would remember Alexander as Iskander, and see their rapid conquest of the world from Spain to India as outdoing him. And like Constantine, they would see their victory as a blessing of the One True God.

A whole host of changes had accompanied the shift from an imperial endorsement of paganism and polytheism to the patronage of monotheistic religion. Of these, one may note two especially: (1) a new emphasis on orthodoxy, creeds, and belief, replacing the previous emphasis on traditional practices; and (2) the replacement of inclusivism with exclusivism as the standard imperial approach to religious policy. The rise of Christianity disrupted the balance of inclusivist religion in the West and began the career of monotheism in which one religion would reign supreme, socially, culturally, and politically in ways ancient emperors could not have imagined. Muslims joined in this worldwide quest, with stunning success. This story, traced ably by Garth Fowden,[38] concerns the world's crossroads, from Constantinople to Iraq and the surrounding regions where Christianity arose. The ultimate rise of Islam was the last chapter in the history of imperial monotheism, and led to Arab control of the crossroads of worldwide trade.

Meanwhile, on the eastern edges of the Eurasian *oikoumene,* Buddhism flourished as an inclusivist but nonetheless universalist confessional religion, spreading from India to Central Asia to China. But nowhere was it to become a lasting and dominant religion patronized by a major imperial power, despite the great promise it had in the East during the age of Constantine. During the age to follow, when Islam became the religious banner of great empire builders, Buddhism became a religion favored by regimes only on the edges (Tibet, Japan, Sri Lanka), losing most if not all its political influence in India and China.

CHAPTER 5

The Rise of Islam and the Early Caliphate, 622–711 A.D.

Successful indeed are the Believers.

—*Qur'an* 23.1

No Believer will help an un-Believer against a Believer.

—Constitution of Medina

It is often assumed that religions arise as the result of intense personal experience, and are appropriately the concern of sincere individuals in their quest for truth. This rather protestant bias assumes that the wedding of religion to politics is an illegitimate one, even though Protestantism itself arose as a very political movement. A bias of this sort, along with the historiographical bias mentioned above, namely that the world of late antiquity concludes with the beginning of medieval Christendom in western Europe, has pushed the history of the rise of Islam to the margins of both religious and historical discourse in European and American circles.

The corrective to the historiographical bias is rather straightforward. However much Americans and Europeans see the survival of Christianity in the monasteries of western Europe's Dark Ages as a chapter in *their* history, the world of medieval western Christendom was frontier territory to the real centers of power, wealth, and culture during those centuries. In world-historical terms, Muslim power was to be ascendant from the eighth to the seventeenth century. This is undeniable, but what I am calling a religious bias here is a more controversial and contestable point, is central to the argument of this entire book, and the rise of Islam almost simultaneously as a religion and as an empire brings this issue into sharp focus.

After Constantine, Christianity becomes the ruling ideology of the empire and we can speak of Christen*dom,* a Christian empire, a society in which Christian values become the taken-for-granted values of the realm, and the sort of inclusivist absorption of cults assumed by Roman imperial paganism—a pattern that survives in India throughout the period in which it dies out in the central regions of the Afro-Eurasian *oikoumene*—gives way to exclusivism, the operating assumption that there is one truth available to all persons and it is on the basis of that truth that the entire political enterprise should be undertaken. For modern secularists, these sorts of claims seem to be the height of hubris, and they often call for a sort of multi-cultural tolerance to replace the intolerance they see operative in medieval times. Indeed, the word *medieval* itself is often used as synonymous with the word intolerant, as when the Taliban of modern Afghanistan are characterized as "medieval" in their approach to matters of religion, culture, and governance. Of course, as I have tried to show, however attractive a broad religious inclusivism first appears, it usually operates at the level of politics as a system which accords some sort of meta-religion, some taken-for-granted notion of the reasonable and civilized the right to rule while organizing and controlling a host of cults. Thus viewed from the angle of politics, the differences in inclusivism and exclusivism may not be so great after all. Moreover, as Garth Fowden has argued, the very quest for doctrinal orthodoxy, a central feature of monotheism, itself provokes a series of arguments that proves politically fractious.[1]

Nonetheless, the dream of a universal empire ruled by one great emperor, reflecting on earth the glory of the one true God in heaven, was characteristic of the confessional empires that preceded the rise of Islam. Marshall Hodgson has characterized them thus:

> By the early centuries of the Christian era were thus established, all across the citied zone of the Afro-Eurasian Oikoumene, organized religious traditions which, in contrast to most of the previous religious traditions, made not tribal or civic, but primarily personal demands. They looked to *individual* personal adherence to ("confession" of) an explicit and often self-sufficient body of moral and cosmological *belief* (and sometimes adherence to the lay *community* formed of such believers); belief which was embodied in a corpus of sacred scriptures, claiming universal validity for all men and promising a comprehensive solution of human problems in terms which involved a *world beyond death.*[2]

The Islamic religion would have all these characteristics, and would reshape the political world in a few short decades after Muhammad's

MAP 5. Arabia, ca. 600 A.D.

death, but at the time the first revelations came to Muhammad, Arabia was largely pagan and at the margins of the confessional empires it would soon successfully challenge. In that sense, while the Roman world evolved over the centuries from an inclusivist paganism to an exclusivist Christianity, over a few short decades Arabia went through a parallel transformation.[3]

Arabs were aware of the confessional empires, Rome and Persia, on their borders, and though pre-Islamic Arabs were tribal, those Arabs, who, like Muhammad, were engaged in long-distance trade, had commercial interests that put them into contact with Persians and Romans to the north as well as with the Ethiopians and Yemenis on their southern and western borders. These traders were middlemen, overseeing east-west caravans that brought goods from India to Rome without crossing Persian territories, and more importantly, leading north-south caravans from the Yemen to Roman Syria. At the edges of the Fertile Crescent and Syria, Arab clans allied with the imperial powers, served as mercenaries in their armies, and often converted to their religions; both Lakhmids and Ghassanids were largely Christian. Mecca remained politically and religiously neutral and had developed, in the generation before Muhammad, a system that served to organize the feuding tribes of Arabia into a loosely cooperative economic system. The dominant clan at Mecca, the Quraysh, organized trade in Mecca by instituting periods of truce, coinciding with a religious pilgrimage to the holy Ka'ba, a shrine that housed icons of all the tribes. Here we see pagan inclusivism par excellence. Just as the Romans happily established temples in Rome to the foreign gods of the peoples they had conquered, the Quraysh invited into their cult the images of all the gods of the various tribes they dominated. Even Christian Arabs worshiped there the One True God (whom they called Allah, using the Arab word for God that other pagan Arabs also used to describe a rather vague, abstract deity that stood behind or above, as it were, the local manifestations of divine power), and, as noted above, may have installed in the Ka'ba an Ethiopian image of the Virgin Mary.[4]

For over a decade (ca. 610–20), Muhammad received revelations that would form part of the *Qur'an*, but failed to win much of a following for his new teaching. One can easily imagine that his monotheistic preaching might never have won more than a few followers or had much of a political impact. Certainly in the decade after his first revelation, that would have appeared to be the likeliest outcome. Muhammad's version of monotheism would have been but one of several versions that contested popular paganism. Besides the Christians and Jews of Arabia, there were also individuals called *hanif*s who espoused monotheism as a personal choice; Muhammad, at first, would have been seen to be a member of such an apolitical club. Early on, his commitment to monotheism might have been seen as rather like a modern American's espousal of vegetarianism or a belief in reincarnation—personal beliefs without obvious political significance. Surely in the early years Muhammad could never have imagined that his mission would totally transform the religious world of Arabia and ultimately, the world. He might have been quite content with a moderately successful movement, but at first, he was denied even that. He was largely ridiculed in Mecca, and though protected by his clansmen, most of them also rejected his religious message as disruptive to the system of Meccan trade. When his beloved wife and strongest supporter, Khadija, and his

FIGURE 13. The Ka'ba. Getty Images, photograph courtesy of iStockphoto.

powerful uncle Abu Talib both died, he was endangered and vulnerable to attack. During this crucial period, Muhammad negotiated with leaders of the town of Medina, an oasis north of Mecca but on the same trade route with Syria, to become a judge-arbiter (*hakam*) among the various clans there. He migrated there with his band of followers and began to establish an effective political base for his community. Muslims note the year of that migration (the *hijra*, 622) as the beginning of their calendar.

We do not really know why the leaders of Medina turned to Muhammad to take a primary political role at that time, but his ten years in Medina (622–32) resulted in an extraordinary transformation of Arabian society and became the basis for what would become Islamic civilization. It is noteworthy that with some notable exceptions, Muhammad did not primarily convert individuals to his religious views, and then build a political structure based on shared religious commitment; rather, he first won *groups* of people committed to his political project.

For example, an entire tribe of Bedouins would accept his leadership and become a part of the movement. In that sense, Islam-as-religion evolved as the ruling ideology of a total social experiment.

When Muhammad first came to Medina, the town was politically divided. Among the feuding clans, some were pagan and some Jewish. All were expected to accept the Prophet's leadership, and it seems that he first assumed the Jews there to recognize his authentic prophethood. In the beginning, the religious practices he urged were largely consistent with Jewish practice, and regular prayer was directed toward Jerusalem. Fred Donner argues that at first, clear boundaries were not drawn between Muhammad's movement and the followers of other monotheistic traditions.[5] Only after it became clear to Muhammad that neither Jews nor Christians would accept his prophetic pronouncements as the culmination of their long history of monotheism did he begin to differentiate Islam as a distinct religion, and redirect the daily prayers toward Mecca. Muslims continued to see their nascent religion as superseding and fulfilling other forms of monotheism, but not denying them. In pragmatic terms, Christians and Jews were accepted as fellow monotheists, and Christian Arabs fought along Muslim Arabs in early conquests. Muhammad's relationships with the Jewish clans of Medina, however, quickly soured. As he carried out early military ventures, several of these tribes proved disloyal and were exiled, and in one case, all its male members executed as traitors. In establishing his new authority, it is clear that Muhammad had to be decisive and sometimes harsh.

The biggest transformation to Arabian life that Muhammad wrought was his work in replacing the old tribal and clan society with a new community based upon membership in his religious movement. When he first came to Medina, he brought with him a band of followers who had cut themselves off from previous clan relationships. Their economic survival depended on the raiding of caravans coming from Mecca, further alienating them from old allies. Whereas the Quraysh clan prospered by organizing existing tribes, Muhammad challenged the very system of tribes, and thus, most directly, the Quraysh. To join the Muslim community (the *ummah*) was to be a member of a brotherhood that superseded all other affiliations, and to accept a universalistic ethic that abrogated a narrow ethic of revenge, clan pride, and blind loyalties. In the last years of his life, Muhammad successfully won over tribes all over Arabia, eradicating the balance of power in the Quraysh system of alliances. Having left Mecca by night in 622, followed by perhaps a hundred followers, he returned in 630 with ten thousand soldiers.

Accepting the inevitable, even the Quraysh capitulated, accepting Muhammad as the leader of all Arabs. Subsequently, many Qurayshis were to become important leaders and soldiers in the new movement.

As a final symbolic gesture of the new regime, Muhammad reformed the old pilgrimage to Mecca, cleansing the Ka'ba of all signs of idolatry. What once was a shrine in which all the local gods of Arabia gathered, just as all the semi-independent tribes themselves gathered, now became a shrine to the One God, nullifying all previous practices and bringing all Arabs as individuals before Allah. Inclusivism abruptly gave way to exclusivism. As Salman Rushdie's controversial novel, *The Satanic Verses*, brought to light, the Prophet might have been tempted to include three goddesses in his Ka'ba cult, a last remnant of the old sort of tolerant inclusivism, but a Quranic revelation made it clear that the monotheism of Islam had to be absolute and exclusive.[6] Often lost in the heat of controversy was any thought as to why Rushdie might have brought to light this incident, but it seems clear from the whole framework of his ideology that as a man committed to the modern secular values of tolerance, pluralism, and feminism, he was embracing a kind of Indian inclusivism that monotheists of Constantinople and Medina rejected.

Muhammad's success in transforming a polytheistic and fractious Arab society into one community united in worship of one God came just before he died in 632. His religious and political venture was but ten years old. Many tribes that had sworn allegiance to Muhammad now assumed that they would revert to their former independence from Medina and Mecca. New prophets arose in the desert, and only the concerted efforts of the Prophet's inner circle prevented the new polity from splintering.

Whatever the Prophet's own dreams for his community, it was the work of his followers that resulted in a permanent state and, ultimately, a new civilization. When the Prophet was alive, he was the recipient of God's revelations, and accepted as final authority for all community matters, religious, political, or military. With his death, no one could continue to claim his religious authority, but when his military lieutenant, Abu Bakr, asserted authority as his political successor (an office entitled caliph), the foundations for an enduring Muslim state were established. The simple assertion of their authority did not, however, go unchallenged. Tribes that broke away from Medina's authority had to be subdued militarily in a series of battles referred to as the Riddah ("Apostasy") wars. And there were those who supported the prophet's son-in-law Ali and felt he was the obvious successor.

We can imagine that things might have turned out rather differently. Islam might have fragmented into a number of variant versions, as other prophets claimed authority to speak for God. That option was ruled out as the Medinese asserted a new doctrine, not found in the *Qur'an,* which declared Muhammad the "seal of the prophets," the last and definitive prophet for all time, a claim embedded in the simple declaration of Muslim faith, "There is no god but God and Muhammad is His Prophet." The first half of the declaration could be the declaration of a very vague and abstract Unitarianism, but it is the latter half that is the basis of a unified community and a grand political venture. And from the beginning, the leaders assumed that the Islamic movement would be realized as a singular political community.

Along with the declaration of faith, Muslims early on developed a set of four other "pillars" that define their praxis: pilgrimage to Mecca; prayers five times a day; fasting during the month of Ramadan; paying *zakat,* or alms. Again, we often interpret these practices in an individualistic way; we imagine individual *hanif*s choosing to observe these tenets. And, of course, there has been very wide variance in the degree to which individual Muslims are observant. To take one example, if we look, however, at the way Muhammad and his successors at Medina understood *zakat,* we see how the communal political and military venture preceded the project of inculcating personal piety. In two statements of Ira Lapidus, we see the two ways *zakat* might be understood, first as a personal virtue: "Almsgiving [the pillar of *zakat*] was a symbol of the renunciation of selfish greed and acceptance of responsibility for all members of the community of faith."[7] And then, as a tax, levied upon the willing and unwilling to support the cause:

> The victory over Mecca was also the culmination of Muhammad's tribal policy. Throughout the eight-year struggle [622–30], Muhammad had tried to gain control of the tribes in order to subdue Mecca. Missionaries and embassies were sent throughout Arabia, factions loyal to Muhammad were supported, and tribes were raided to compel them to pay allegiance and zakat, the alms tax, to Muhammad. He regarded the tax as a sign of membership in the Muslim community and acceptance of himself as Prophet. The Bedouins looked on it as a tribute plain and simple, and conspired to evade it as soon as they could.[8]

During the Riddah wars, tribes were once again compelled to pay *zakat* as a sign of their membership in a unified Muslim state based at Medina. This fact is one of the clearest signs that with the establishment of the caliphate under Muhammad's associates, especially under Abu

Bakr (632–34) and Umar (634–44), the venture of Islam, to invoke Hodgson, was to be communal, unified, political, and military. The option of promoting Islam simply as a religious movement with a specific creed and set of practices, freely chosen by individuals to follow more or less privately, was the road not taken.

The second caliph Umar (r. 634–44), called "Commander of the Faithful," led armies in conquest of many of the great ancient cities of the Middle East: Damascus (635), Ctesiphon (637), Jerusalem (638), Alexandria (642). More importantly, he was a pious and ascetic man who not only formed raiding bands into a unified, efficient army of conquest, but settled Arabs in garrison towns where they cultivated their distinct religious life, and he distributed tribute and taxation in such a way that all Arabs could feel a part of this dramatic, world-altering movement.

The Arabs made use of the administrative machinery of conquered Roman and Persian cities and agricultural lands, but they claimed for themselves the right to rule at the highest levels according to an increasingly elaborated Islamic set of principles. Astonishing wealth flowed to this community of Arab conquerors. It is a testament to Umar's strong leadership that the age of conquest remained so unified and disciplined, and that fractious bands of nomad Arab soldiers did not assert their independence and begin an orgy of looting. The leadership of Umar in careful administration of taxation and a growing Muslim piety made the Arab conquest something more than a military victory. The soldiers and merchants pouring out of Arabia into Syria, Iraq, and Egypt laid the very foundations of a new civilization that was to endure until modern times.

In the early period, Arabs assumed the role of the ruling elite class and assumed that their religion was a superior basis for legitimate rule of the Christians, Jews, and Zoroastrians they conquered. Initially, they had no interest in converting these subject peoples to their faith. Those Christian Arab tribes fighting alongside their Muslim allies were not subject to the usual tax (*jizyah*) levied on all other non-Muslims; their identity as Arabs was more important than their identity as Christians. In general, "Islam" was the badge of a new, supratribal Arab solidarity. In time, of course, many non-Arabs would convert to Islam, but this did not occur in the first century, nor was it associated with military conquest. The idea that Arab conquest was a military effort undertaken to force subject peoples to convert to Islam is a fantasy without historical basis.

If we consider the caliphate from the time of Umar (634–44), to Mu'awiyah (r. 661–80), and Abd al-Malik (r. 692–705), we cover the majority of the early period of great conquests, and the internal developments that led to the development of an Islamic religion that ceased to be a purely Arab phenomenon, and a religious tradition of great intellectual and spiritual diversity, with many Muslims raising profound questions about the tension between the quest of wealth and power as central to the Arab Muslim imperial project, and the goal of creating a godly society committed to the Islamic ideals of justice and piety. Pious opposition to royal power becomes a central and persistent feature of the Islamic world and leads to a series of attempts to work out an appropriate relationship between religious idealism and the practical requirements of political life. On the one hand, without the effective exercise of dominant political power, Muslims would be unable to create a society whose institutions would be Islamic. On the other hand, if the quest for power was too emphasized, those institutions would be managed by individuals without deep commitment to Islamic ideals.

During the rule of Mu'awiyah, which began less than three decades after the death of the Prophet, we see the development of strong caliphal rule, in the name of preserving the unity of the Islamic community and continued military success, but with an acceptance, for the first time, that the caliph might not be a moral exemplar. Those unwilling to accept this worldly compromise formed a wide range of responses, so that a century later we have Muslim legal scholars (the *ulama*) developing an elaborate code of personal conduct for committed orthoprax Muslims to follow as individuals, whatever the moral failings of the royalty. We also have the beginnings of an ascetic tradition of Sufis reminiscent of the god-fearing monks of Syria and Egypt, involving the cultivation of an intense spirituality of fasting, withdrawal, and contemplation We have zealous war bands (the Kharijites) committed to following no one but *their* choice of the truly Muslim leader, rebelling against the corrupt status quo. And we have the historical basis for an elaborate ideology of critique of the worldly compromise, the belief that the Prophet's own relatives, beginning with his son-in-law Ali and his grandson Husayn, were God's choices to rule, but passed over by those who saw military success and wealth and power as more important than the goal of finding a righteous leader to build a righteous society. That ideology (Shi'ism), whatever its particular form, looks back to Mu'awiyah's rivalry with Ali as the basis for a Muslim imperial tradition that favors successful and powerful leaders over pious and just ones.

Mu'awiyah, the son of a Meccan general who had opposed the Prophet, was himself a successful general and the basis of his power was his large and dedicated Syrian army. With the very foundation of his power in Syria, the capital of the empire was shifted to Damascus, where it remained until 750. Rivalries between the old families of Mecca and those of Medina, and the old tribal blocs of Arabs now living throughout the empire, always were a source of unrest, and unpopular caliphs had to contend with revolts led by fellow Muslims who challenged their legitimacy, often in the language of what became Shi'sm. Dissidents often argued that if only a descendant of the Prophet ruled, a guardian of the traditions the Prophet supported, the unjust rule of the corrupt caliph at Damascus could be overturned.

One such rebellion, led by Ali's son Husayn in Iraq, ended with Husayn's martyrdom at the hands of Mu'awiyah's son, Yazid. Yazid, the first caliph to succeed his father (thus following a traditional pattern of royal succession not sanctioned by Islam), was thought to be a cruel, intemperate, and bibulous ruler by the followers of Ali's son, and the death of their leader at Karbala still forms the core of the Shi'i mythology of Iranian and Iraqi Shi'ites. Their tale becomes a tragic morality tale, a narrative rumination on the fact that the righteous may not win, and that winners are often not righteous. For them, the imperial grandeur of the caliph's court was not a sign that God smiled upon the Islamic community, and blessed its obvious successes. It was a sign of corruption.

INCLUSIVISM, EXCLUSIVISM, AND THE RELIGIOUS POLICIES OF THE EMPIRES OF THE ANCIENT WORLD

A thousand years after the death of Alexander the Great, with the rise of an almost worldwide Islamic Empire, a dominion that pushed up against Byzantium (their important predecessors in faith and politics), as well as to the boundaries of the distant Tang Empire of China, and thus dominating the mercantile crossroads of the world, Muslim caliphs seemed to realize an even more thorough exercise of imperial power than Alexander had ever dreamed. If Alexander could proclaim that Asia deserved one king just as she had one sun, and if the Sun King Constantine could hope for a world under one God, one religion, and one king, the Arab caliphs seemed far closer to realizing such an ambition in the eighth century. Their power was exercised in military, political, and economic arenas from the western Mediterranean to the edges of India and China, and they might look forward to realizing worldwide dominance, a dominance that seemed guaranteed by their role as the representatives of God, those truly obedient to His final revelation.

Muslims, like Christians, largely lived with that confidence, that their religion was the final, and, in a sense, *only* real answer; that they bore a universal truth for all people in all places, now and forever. Unlike Alexander, who could more readily imagine the spread of Greek as a universal language than Greek religion as a universal cult, the caliphs of Baghdad might confidently predict a day when Muslims ruled all the earth, and all people accepted Islam. This confidence might be termed a final and completely universal exclusivism, a religious state of affairs in which the One True Faith had eclipsed all others and made them obsolete.

But before Muslims might dream of such a world, they felt compelled to maintain vestiges of the old imperial style of inclusivism, the notion that different peoples, proclaiming different truths, different religions, could be included within a religious system overseen by Islam. Of course, even before Islam was fully reified or even named as a distinct religion, Muhammad's revelation was considered simply the last chapter in the history of monotheism, and thus Jews and Christians were already "believers." The acceptance of these people as fellow monotheists, People of the Book, and the presumption that they would *not* convert, meant a governing policy of favoring Arab Muslims as the overseers of a society in which non-Arab monotheists might also have prominent, if subservient roles. Aspects of such a view have continued throughout the history of Islam. But by the eighth century, some Muslims limited such a policy of inclusivism. Those who actively supported the conversion of non-Arabs to Islam more forcefully declared their religion's universalism and exclusive claims to final truth.

For most of antiquity, great kings had ambitions of extending their rule to distant realms, receiving tribute and honor from the kings they conquered. But that ambition did not often extend to the hope of having all their subjects participate in a common religious culture, a universal and exclusive religion transcending all the world's many local folkways. As we have seen, they often sought to establish a sort of meta-religion, which could supersede the many local cults and provide a framework for adjudicating between them and providing criteria for judging their practices. But meta-religious inclusivism assumes that each local culture and religion has its legitimacy. There are many today who see such inclusivism as an enlightened policy of tolerance and respect, and it may indeed have its laudable merits. The policy of inclusivism in the ancient world must be seen, however, as primarily a political policy, a policy favored by kings who saw in it the most effective way of governing diverse peoples.

Some aspects of inclusivism survive the ancient period, and inclusivism has always been one possibility for rulers of religiously diverse polities. Even those who theoretically embrace a religious policy of exclusivism, who reign as defenders of a single true faith, have often had to accept pragmatically the necessity of some degree of toleration. A ruler committed to universalist exclusivism may adopt tolerant and inclusivist policies, if only as a temporary solution to practical problems. He looks forward to the final triumph of the one true faith, however remote that hope might seem.

Thus it was that in the late antique world, with the rise of Constantine's Byzantine Empire and finally the Arab caliphate, kings begin to imagine a world in which their kingdom might overspread the world, and their subjects proclaim them as the one true king and representative of the One True God and the one true religion He enjoins. Such a religious and political imaginary characterizes much of Eurasia in the medieval world. From England to India such views held sway, and since Muslims controlled the central zones of this world, we shall term this era the "Islamic Millennium." To it, we now turn.

PART TWO

The Islamic Millennium

700–1700 A.D.

As luck would have it, it was Islam that from the seventh century became the unifying force of the Ancient World. Between the densely populated landmasses, Europe in the largest sense, Black Africa, and the Far East, it held the critical passes and thrived because of its profitable function as an intermediary. Without its consent or will, nothing could pass through. Within this solid world whose center lacked the flexibility of shipping routes, Islam was what Europe triumphant was later to become on a world scale, a dominant economy and civilization.

—Fernand Braudel[1]

762	Founding of Baghdad, capital of the Abbasid Caliphate
800	Charlemagne crowned Holy Roman Emperor
842	Great Persecution of Buddhism in China
922	Death of al-Hallaj
750–1258	Abbassid Caliphate
1021	Death of al-Hakim, Fatimid ruler of Egypt
909–1171	Fatimid Caliphate
1111	Death of al-Ghazali
1147	Beginning of Second Crusade
1192	Death of Saladin
1204	Death of Maimonides

1227	Death of Genghis Khan
1272–1368	Yuan (Mongol) Dynasty in China
1253	Death of Dogen
1258	Mongols sack Baghdad
1263	Death of Shinran
1185–1333	Kamakura Period (Japan)
1273	Death of Rumi
1274	Death of Thomas Aquinas
1316	Death of Alauddin Khilji
1448	Death of Kabir

"Gunpowder empires"

1299–1923	Ottoman
1501–1736	Safavid
1526–1857	Mughal

1492	Columbus discovers America; Jews expelled from Spain
1524	Death of Ismail I
1566	Death of Suleyman the Magnificent
1605	Death of Akbar
1707	Death of Aurangzeb, last great Mughal

CHAPTER 6

Imperial Islam, 690–1500 A.D.

In the century following the foundation of Baghdad, especially in the reign of Harun al-Rashid (788–809) and his
successors, a world that never lost touch with its Late
Antique roots enjoyed a final efflorescence in its last, Muslim
and Arabic-speaking transformation.

—Peter Brown[1]

Just sixty years after the death of the Prophet, caliphs ruled not as tribal
chieftains but as absolute monarchs in the Persian style. Indeed, by the
time of Abd al-Malik (r. 685–705), caliphal rule could only be preserved
only by ruthless absolutism. He was never reluctant to use brutal force
to subdue fellow Muslims who resisted his authority. One of his generals even bombarded the Ka'ba in quashing rebellion in Mecca, and like
Mu'awiyah, he policed Iraq with Syrian troops.[2] If as caliph he inherited
the political role of the Prophet as military commander of the faithful,
there was no way that he partook of his religious role. He was a king,
like other Middle Eastern kings, and most of the caliphs that followed
him were similarly men of splendor and pomp but not possessed of
saintly virtues.

Abd al-Malik nonetheless took his public role as defender of the faith
seriously. He oversaw the construction of the Dome of the Rock in Jerusalem in 692, sixty years after the prophet's death. The Dome was built
at the site of Solomon's ancient temple, and on its base was inscribed a
Qur'anic verse that critiqued Trinitarian Christianity:

> O ye People of the Book, overstep not bounds in your religion; and of God
> speak only truth. The Messiah, Jesus, son of Mary, is only an apostle of God,
> and His Word which he conveyed into Mary, and a Spirit proceeding from
> Him. Believe therefore in God and His apostles and say not "Three." It will
> be better for you. God is only one God. Far be it from His glory that He

FIGURE 14. Dome of the Rock, Jerusalem. Askii, photograph
courtesy of Creative Commons.

should have a son. His is whatever is in the heavens, and whatever is on the
earth. . . . God witnesses that there is no God but He: and the angels, and men
endowed with knowledge, established in righteousness, proclaim that there is
no God but He, the Mighty, the Wise. The true religion with God is Islam.[3]

Despite the fact that few people encouraged non-Arab conversion to
Islam in Abd al-Malik's time, and of course very few non-Arab Christians could read the inscription, the Dome of the Rock stands as a mon-
ument to Islamic assertion of supersession. Islam completes, corrects
and eclipses the prophetic monotheism of Christianity, or, in Islamic
terms, it returns all monotheisms to their roots, the pure monotheism of
Abraham. But in addition to their many Christian and Jewish subjects,
the caliphs of Damascus had many non-Muslim courtiers. For example,
Abd al-Malik's own panegyrist was the Christian Arab al-Akhtal, and
St. John of Damascus (d. 749), whose father had also served Abd al-
Malik, served as a chief administrator in the court of Abd Al-Malik's
successors, all the while composing Christian hymns and theological
treatises, where he referred to Islam as an "Ishmaelite heresy." How are
we to square what seems to be a public proclamation of Islamic superiority with what appears to be a pragmatic disinterest in spreading the
faith to non-Arabs, even those working at the highest levels of government? One can only surmise that for a caliph like Abd al-Malik there
was something of a disconnect between a lofty universalist theology and
a down-to-earth view of the world, in which military, political, and economic policies dictated an acceptance of a legitimate role for the non-
Muslim subjects of the realm. At the least, Abd al-Malik would want his
Arab Muslim subjects to see in the Dome of the Rock an expression of
Islam's superiority, overshadowing the great shrines of the other religions in Jerusalem.

The eighth century was, then, a time in which the foundations of an Islamic civilization were being laid, during which Arabs ruled a vast, but still internally diverse empire. Administrative documents were being translated into Arabic, and Arabs were a ruling class, but their close associates were still often speakers of indigenous languages and followers of different faiths. Arabs were no longer an occupying army living in suburban garrisons. They were a landlord class, living alongside and working closely with native bureaucrats throughout the Middle East and beyond. Those non-Arab associates participated fully in the building of Islamic civilization, even while resisting conversion for generations.

Early on, those few who did convert did so as "clients" of particular tribes, a sign that we have not reached the state when one thinks of Islam as a vast cosmopolitan society in which individuals came to the faith; it is a movement still governed by the tribal politics it theoretically rejected. The transformation of this society, from one made up of Arabs who happened to be largely Muslim to a society of Muslims who happened to speak Arabic, is far from complete.[4] But it is underway. Just twenty years later, the caliph Umar II (r. 717–20), took up an explicit policy of actively promoting the conversion of non-Arabs to Islam. Muslims would remain, however, a minority population throughout their empire for centuries to come.[5]

The political transformation of the political world from Spain to the Indus River, and the creation of a vast Arabic-speaking zone in which Islamic culture struck deep roots and was assumed to be paramount, should not obscure the fact that Arabs too had to adjust to their new role as empire builders, learning administrative systems from the people they conquered. And perhaps most strikingly, we see the subtle "conquering of the conqueror" in the ways in which the caliph's court became a version of the Persian court of the king of kings.

The establishment of an imperial capital at Baghdad, ushering in a golden age of wealth and sophistication—not without its exceedingly bloody confrontations—brings us back where we started: to the Mesopotamian site of so many imperial projects in the ancient world. It was situated not only near to ancient Babylon and the Persian capital of Ctesiphon, but was thought to be nearby to the lost Garden of Eden. Here, the peak of the Arab caliphal power and cultural influence, culminating in the storied reign of Harun al-Rashid (d. 809), represents a certain final chapter to late antiquity.[6] It is not a break from the classical world, but is in many ways its fulfillment. Certainly the massive intellectual project of translating Greek and even Sanskrit masterpieces at

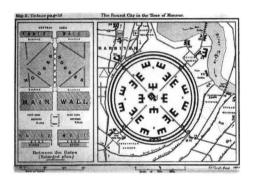

FIGURE 15. Eighth-century map of Baghdad's round city. Guy Le Strange, image courtesy of Creative Commons.

the court of the caliph suggests this sort of closure, as Arab aristocrats saw themselves as at the center of both world history and geography.[7] The Abbasid caliphs reigned in Baghdad from 750 to 1258, though their actual power waned considerably after the middle of the ninth century. They nonetheless represented a continued longing for a unified Islamic polity long after it effectively disappeared. Political disunity did not mean, however, that Islamic culture did not continue to thrive and flower; it did, in Turkey, Iran, and India until early modern times (see chapter 7), and Muslims confidently thought of themselves as the heirs of the world's supreme culture and civilization until they were rudely discomfited in the age of European colonialism. In the later centuries of the Islamic Millennium, a cosmopolitan Muslim could travel from Morocco to Indonesia and always expect to find cultured men who spoke poetic Persian and could recite the *Qur'an* by heart.[8]

However, the sophisticated and cosmopolitan culture of the caliph's court at Baghdad was to some extent at odds with the more truly religious aspirations of many Muslims of humbler station and means. In tracing the story of religion and power to this point, the issue is not just the triumph of the Arabs, bringing Greek and Persian cultures together under the aegis of Islam. With Arabs in undisputed control of the world's crossroads (rivaled politically and economically only by the distant Tang Empire in China), Islam was taken for granted as the ruling ideology just as the Arabic language was assumed to be the language of culture and governance. But just what constituted "Islam"? There were many answers, and thus disagreements among Muslims whose different camps contested for power and influence.

Seventh-century Damascus had become the capital of the expansionist Muslim state because it was closer to the populous centers of wealth

Arab soldiers were capturing. But the caliphs there also depended on Syrian troops to man their large armies. When the Abbasids took power and shifted the capital once again, to Baghdad, they did so with another source of troops, the Khurasani highlands of Iran, while also remaining close to the world's most important trade routes. Iraq had been the hotbed of rebellion during the rule of the Damascus caliphs, but was undeniably a wealthy province. The rebels who brought the Abbasids to power drew upon the old discontent of Shi'i critics, but their enduring success depended on a ready supply of soldiers and the willingness to use them in brutal assertions of authority and power.

Reading about the bloodbath that brought the Abbasids to power, and the fairly bloody revolutionary struggles at times of imperial succession, it is easy to forget that, despite these episodes, for the average person living in Abbasid times it was a relatively peaceful and prosperous world in which the strong central power insured order and security, and thus the conditions for prosperity. Thus *relative* peace and prosperity, accompanied by a yearning for a unified Islam, in time brought the Abbasids broad support, but there were always several sources of contention and contest. While modern people—fundamentalists, romanticists, or otherwise—may look back to the golden age of the *Arabian Nights* and assume a world where everyone shared a "traditional" and conservative Islamic worldview, in fact, while "Islam" ruled supreme, *islam* was never a settled matter, but a rich cultural dialogue and debate, with numerous parties using persuasion, and far blunter instruments of power, to influence the course of their religion and civilization.

Theological controversy did not have the same political importance in the Islamic world as it did in the Christian, but while Muslim intellectuals largely concerned themselves with matters of *shari'ah,* some thinkers did turn to theology and its sister discipline, philosophy, where old Greek traditions of reasoned analysis were brought to bear. One Greek-influenced group, the Mu'tazila, won for a while the caliph's support for their theological opinion that anthropomorphic descriptions of God in the *Qur'an* required that such passages be interpreted as symbolic rather than literal. Moreover, they held that the *Qur'an* itself was created in time, and was not eternal. In their view, to claim eternal status for the *Qur'an* would be a kind of idolatry. In the end, however, such a view was rejected. Muslims, like Christians, accepted that the Word of God, the site where God made contact with His world, was eternal and of His essence. Despite the danger of idolatry, to say otherwise seems to court an even greater danger, the embrace of monotheistic faith without specificity and concreteness.

The Mu'tazila were sometimes called "the people of unity and justice" because they believed God acted in a necessarily just manner, while the more orthodox (i.e., those ultimately declared orthodox, the followers of al-Ashari, d. 936) argued that *whatever* God did was just; He was not subject to human reason's ideas of justice. In other words, God's absolute sovereignty requires that His actions not be limited to those the philosopher might feel were ethical.

We can readily see how the Mu'tazila view would make God more remote, as the one worldly link to the mind of God, the *Qur'an,* would be subject to human interpretation and less of an absolute incarnation of divinity. Moreover, the Mu'tazila requirement that God's actions be just would limit the divine's absolute nature. It would be tempting to say that any limit on the absolute authority of God might also limit religious and even human authority in general. Without a supremely divine *Qur'an,* there would be no basis for any claim to rule with divine sanction and authority.

Thinking about the legitimacy of the caliph involved a tangle of half-formed arguments and biases. The emerging Shi'i view was that the Prophet's son-in-law Ali should have been his successor, from the beginning. Like the Prophet himself, he was a pious exemplar, but was pushed aside by more ambitious and worldly men. From the perspective of the partisans of Ali, the third caliph, Uthman, though himself married to one of the Prophet's daughters, was from a Meccan clan, the Umayyads, who became Muslims only when the writing was on the wall. So there persisted a sense that true Islam was born in Medina, among those who followed the Prophet even in a time of danger and persecution, whereas the old aristocrats of Mecca joined the cause only when they saw the tide turn in favor the Medinans. Uthman was also criticized for favoring his Meccan relatives in a nepotistic way. Thus there emerged a certain distrust of the Umayyads, successors of Uthman, who ruled as caliphs in Damascus from 661 to 750.

The revolutionaries who overthrew the Umayyads came to power with the backing of those who held Shi'i views. Their leader could claim a lineage, however, that only led back to the Prophet's uncle Abbas, a man who like Ali's father, Abu Taleb, never became a Muslim. And in the end, once in power, the Abbasid caliphs embraced not the purist sensibilities of Shi'ism but rather a mainstream Sunni ideology. As a worldview, Shi'sm remained a banner for those harboring a smoldering resentment of Abbasid rule, and in time would produce rival kingdoms (e.g., Fatimid Egypt, 909–1171 A.D.). In the heyday of Abbasid rule, persecuted and discontented Shi'is nurtured secret dreams of a descendent of the Prophet assuming the throne and bringing about a final revolution. Such dreams took on an increasingly cosmic and mythological coloring, finally resulting in a full-fledged messianic apocalypticism. Shi'is began to believe that however much the winners seemed to be corrupt accommodationists, one day the hidden Imam, the Mahdi, would return to earth to bring about a true reversal of the fortunes of the just and unjust. The fervor of the Ayatollah Khomeini's revolutionaries in Iran in 1979 attests to the durability of the Shi'i dream.

The Sunnis, those who accepted the early caliphs and built a way of life based on the model of life in Medina under the Prophet's leadership, also had their critics of the Abbasid regime. They accepted the necessity of strong, monarchical rule but still sought to build a godly society governed, not by the aristocratic ideals of a powerful and wealthy elite, but according to populist ideals of tribal and mercantile society. These critics supported the intellectual project of developing a code of personal conduct—what today we might call orthopraxy—that corresponds to the sort of laws of the observant Jew. This code, the *shari'ah,* was the product of legal reasoning designed to understand a person's life, in all its detailed complexity, as a conscious response to the will of God. Discerning the will of God was an enterprise that led to careful study of the *Qur'an,* a powerful and evocative text demanding awe, devotion, and obedience, and setting forth principles of justice but lacking any comprehensive code of conduct. Pious scholars thus sought further "knowledge" (*ilm*), and finding it in the received body of traditions (*hadith*) about the Prophet's behavior, these "knowledgeable ones" (the *ulama*) formed schools of legal reasoning that developed the *shari'ah* into a vast and complex set of observations on the way a good Muslim should live his or her life, in all its particulars. In theory, knowledge of the path of righteous living, *shari'ah,* would allow one to discern God's will, in matters of ritual practice, diet, sex, dress, etiquette, inheritance, and so on. At any given moment, the pious Muslim could be assured of living a life in accordance with God's will, and in that observance, express an attitude of obedience.

By the middle of the ninth century, the grand enterprise of the *ulama* produced all the major schools of legal reasoning that exist today. But this was more than an intellectual and religious exercise. The claim of the *ulama* to have definitive knowledge of God's will gave them a following, and gave them an authority that caliphs could not ignore. Caliphs themselves did not, by and large, live their lives in conformity with the dictates of *shari'ah*. Their personal lives were most often lives of excess. They indulged in wine, women, and song in ways strictly prohibited by *shari'ah* law. More importantly, they clung to royal power by means of ruthless, cruel, and murderous methods. But they could not publicly ignore the claims of the *ulama* without endangering their own legitimacy as Muslim rulers. The schools of Islamic law became the most important centers of Islamic intellectual life, and the scholars there, while not strictly speaking clergy, nonetheless exercised great influence over the lives of a large portion of the pious Muslim populace. We often hear today that the Muslim world cannot separate church and state, that politics is a matter of religion. That may be true in some limited sense, but in the period of Muslim ascendance as a world power, from the eighth to the seventeenth centuries, there were distinct domains in Muslim culture, realms where powerful kings ruled from courts where not that much thought was given to the pious concerns of religious folk, but other spaces where the religiously inclined challenged the society to live up to its Islamic ideals.

Besides the observant folk searching the *hadith* for clues to the ideal life, others cultivated lives of prayer and asceticism. For them, the *Qur'an* issued a challenge to deepen one's awareness of God's majesty and beauty. Perhaps drawing on some of the ways of the Christian ascetic monks of the desert, these seekers, called Sufis (after their distinctive rough woolen cloaks), saw the Prophet not primarily as a political leader but as a mystic and man of intense devotion. Sufism is hard to characterize, but it is perhaps best to describe it as a series of experiments in the cultivation of the spirit. For some, the ascetic quest of all-night vigils, weeping for one's sins, meditation, and fasting made proper Islamic observance only the first step in a life of progressively higher steps toward a full awareness of God's presence. For others, the Sufi path was superior to the path of observance, and made obedience to rules superfluous and even self-defeating. In later centuries, Sufi saints become the founders of lineages, and they and their successors are seen as leaders (*sheikhs* or *pirs*) of organizations with distinctive religious practices, but men with important political power as well.

At the close of the golden age, the great emperors of the Islamic world saw themselves as the heirs and patrons of the legacies of human civilization. Baghdad was to be the center not just of the Islamic world but of the entire world, and though Islam was honored above all, there was room for the cultural heritage of the Greeks, the Persians, and even the Indians. That rich heritage properly *belonged* to them, just as the nineteenth-century British imperialist might similarly assume rightful ownership of the artifacts of the ancient world.[9]

Not everyone shared the worldly values of the caliph's court, and the other centers of power, whether schools of pious and observant *ulama,* Shi'i revolutionary circles, or the lodges of Sufi ascetics, were places where worldly success might suggest a lamentable loss of true piety. But until the age of European colonialism, and with it, the radical transformation of geopolitical power, most Muslims, whether devout or lax, could quite confidently presume their civilization and religion to be at the center of world history and cosmopolitan culture. Even after the challenge of the thirteenth-century Mongol invasions, and long after the dream of restoring the Baghdad caliphate had died, the age of the so-called gunpowder empires (the Ottoman Empire, the Safavid Empire, and the Mughals in the sixteenth and seventeenth centuries) saw the greatest global expansion of Muslim power and cultural influence.

The wealth of great Islamic empires and the splendor of their royal courts might reassure many Muslims that God was on their side, but for some Muslims, the same wealth and power could be the cause of a disquieting reflection on the failures of Islam-as-religion. Such persons could not square their view that Islam was a call for social justice or prayerful austerity with the harsh realities of ambitious empire building. But whatever the moral failings of their rulers, these empires were confidently established at the center of world power, despite the repeated shocks of political fragmentation after the tenth century and the eventual fall of Baghdad to the Mongol invaders in 1258. Repeated political and military crises could not dislodge the confident sense among the majority of Muslims that their religion was properly at the center of world history and that they were meant to lead. That sense of superiority and entitlement did not usually translate, however, into rigid intolerance of other religions. Quite the contrary. The wealthy and powerful Islamic world of premodern times was not an intolerant one. The intolerant Islam of al-Qaida or the Taliban is the product of postcolonial weakness, desperation, shame, and despair, not the arrogance of imperial majesty. From the tenth century on, as more and more non-Arabs embraced Islam, centers of Muslim high culture far from Baghdad arose where a great variety of religious and cultural styles could be cultivated.

Rivaled only by distant China in terms of wealth and cultural sophistication, Muslims controlled many of the world's economic and political centers, and were bearers of an enormously expansive and culturally rich civilization that incorporated first Iranians, then Turks as well as

Mongols, Hindus, and Christians into their cosmopolitan world, blending a range of royal traditions with a core of Arabic Islam. Beyond Baghdad, numerous royal courts competed for preeminence from Spain to Afghanistan, India, and Southeast Asia, while Muslims still felt themselves to be part of a single Islamic world.

In most complex societies, we find a tension between religious ideals and the political, military, and economic aspirations of elite rulers. Some sort of compromise must be struck, however uneasily, between the sacred and the secular. In medieval Europe, kings were "protectors" of the Church, even while squabbling with the pope over the right to appoint bishops to head the dioceses of their realms, just as the popes held not only the final authority to excommunicate rebellious kings, but began to oversee military conquests and take on all the regalia of worldly monarchs.[10] For Muslims, the early growth in wealth, power, and prestige of the expansive Islamic world was accompanied by the growth in royal power and prestige at Baghdad. What does it really mean to say that Muslims do not recognize a distinction between the sacred and profane (or church and state)? Such claims usually rest upon a reading of religious doctrine, and an incomplete and misleading reading of the actual *history* of the Islamic world. Whether they made challenges as Shi'is, Sufis, or scholars of *shari'ah* (the *ulama*) to the pretensions of the caliph's court, many pious Muslims took religious stances that tested the legitimacy of the royalty. Meanwhile the caliphs and sultans pushed back, seeking a certain kind of religious legitimacy for their rule, largely by refashioning ancient Persian ideologies of sacral kingship (in the face of the fact that the Prophet Muhammad had clearly *not* ruled as a king). In the courts of the regional sultans ruling after Baghdad's decline and fall, religiously based legitimacy was won in one of several ways: either by (1) the assertion of old Shi'i claims that political power rightly rested with a descendent of the Prophet's holy family; or by (2) winning the blessings of a powerful saint; or by (3) a reading of world history that made kingship a part of God's plans, from the beginning of human history to the present; or by (4) some combination of these. But religious virtuosi contested all such claims, and there were always pious and thoughtful Muslims suspicious of worldly power. The so-called "medieval" political culture of the Taliban today is a style of religious governance unimaginable in the medieval and early modern Islamic world, which always had a range of sacred and secular domains.

The lack of any *obvious* religious basis for the legitimacy of the king, and the violent struggles that troubled succession, meant that caliphs and later sultans were always plagued by the need to strengthen whatever religious reasons they could claim for their right to rule. If in some sense all Muslims should be equal subjects of God, requiring some Muslims to bow down before the monarch would seem to be improper and un-Islamic, if not downright sinful. Yet caliphs, and later on sultans and shahs, often claimed titles like the "shadow of God on earth," men before whom all others must, quite literally, bow down. In the grand style of Persian absolutism, these kings claimed ever more exalted status and exercised ever greater authority, all in the name, presumably, of an expansive and successful realm in which Muslims were supreme and Islam the unquestioned creed.

But the exact nature of the emperor's authority was never beyond discussion and dispute. Just as the Abbasids had first come to power in the eighth century with the support of Shi'is, large parts of their empire were carved off in the tenth century by Shi'i partisans and others who established rival kingdoms—semi-independent or fully independent—in Spain, North Africa, Iran, and Central Asia. Perhaps the most interesting of these breakaways was the Fatimid Caliphate, a Shi'i kingdom centered in Egypt that was to last over two centuries (909–1171 A.D.). The Fatimids (claiming descent from Fatima, daughter of the Prophet and wife of Ali) called themselves the true caliphs, largely on Shi'i grounds, and backed it up by building the great city of Cairo, a cosmopolitan center of trade and scholarship, the rival of Baghdad.

Despite their Shi'i ideological commitments, most of the Fatimid rulers pursued a broadly ecumenical policy, and pragmatically employed Sunnis, Christians, and Jews based on their merits, but the dynasty is often associated with one eccentric ruler, the autocrat al-Hakim (d. 1021). Al-Hakim, whose religious policies fluctuated wildly, is remembered for peculiar decrees, such as the rather bizarre command that Cairo's shops stay open at night and citizens sleep during the day, and like many unstable rulers drunk on power, he claimed for himself a supreme authority in matters of religion. Tales are told of al-Hakim, offering his subjects the chance to play a sort of Russian roulette, the prize being either vast wealth or immediate execution; in this, he saw himself as taking on the divine role of arbiter of fate. He even toyed with the idea of announcing a new revelation to supersede the *Qur'an*, and some subjects began to believe in al-Hakim's divinity, a claim the Druze sect (a small breakaway group in Israel and Lebanon) upholds to this very day. The Druze religion is thought to be derived from gnostic, esotericist Shi'ism, but the Druze simply proclaim themselves "people of unity" (*ahl al-tawhid*), thus Muslims in the truest (or most abstract) sense, transcending all parochialism. Perhaps al-Hakim saw himself in a similar light. Copying the Baghdad caliphs, he too established a House of Wisdom (*Dar al-Hikma*) as a site of religious dialogue in his palace. This strategy of universalism, which al-Hakim seemed to embrace, will recur in the inclusivism of the Mughal emperor Akbar, to whom will turn in the next chapter.

Certainly it would be wrong to evaluate the Fatimids based on the rule of al-Hakim, but his reign is nonetheless telling for at least two reasons. First, it reveals the degree to which the ruler, no doubt intoxicated with his own absolute power, would be tempted to assert a religious authority to complement his political power. Second, al-Hakim's ability to rule without facing serious rebellion suggests the degree to which power and splendor become the very basis for legitimacy. Might, it seems, makes right, despite the ruler's apparent heresies.

Of course, what starts out sounding orthodox can end up sounding heretical, and what starts out heretical can end up sounding orthodox. Al-Hakim's rough contemporary, the ecstatic Persian mystic al-Hallaj (d. 922) was executed for what seemed to be his claim of divinity: "I am the Truth!" (truth, *al-haqq*, being one of the ninety-nine names or attributes of God). The famous Sufi poet Rumi discussed al-Hallaj's ecstatic pronouncement three centuries later, exonerating him of the charge of disbelief: "Take the famous utterance 'I am the Divine Truth.' Some people consider it a great pretension. But '*ana al-haqq*' is in fact great humility. . . . He has annihilated himself and given to the winds. He says, 'I am the Divine Truth,' that is, 'I am not, He is all, nothing exists but God, I am pure not-being, I am nothing.'"[11] Anecdotes of al-Hallaj's travels give a sense of the expansive, culturally diverse Islamic world of the tenth century. He traveled widely, to India and Turfan, where the caliph no longer exercised real political power and where Arabic was no longer the only language of culture.[12]

Five centuries after the Prophet, another Persian, Abu Hamid al-Ghazali (d. 1111), gained prominence as the "reviver of Islam." The great scholar found a patron in the vizier of the Seljuk rulers, Nizamulmulk. With Baghdad's decline, Turkish rulers like the Seljuks represented the best chance at reunifying a splintered Islamic world, and Ghazali perhaps represented the intellectual aspiration to synthesize the learning of various Islamic disciplines into a single orthodoxy. His first target was Shi'ism, the ideology that supported the political fracturing of the Islamic world. Writing in Arabic and Persian, he also challenged those philosophers who felt their rationalism put them above orthodox teaching. His last project was to challenge men like himself, the scholars of *shari'ah*, to deepen their piety by embracing the mystical path. According to his autobiography, he resolved both his own philosophical doubts and his personal struggles by walking away from his prestigious position as a professor in Baghdad to seek out Sufi teachers in Jerusalem. Enormously influential as an intellectual, Ghazali's primary importance lies in his ability to give a firm foundation to theology, law, and Sufi disciplines while limiting the scope of Greek philosophy.

After the fall of Ghazali's Shi'i nemesis, the Fatimid Caliphate, the legendary Saladin (d. 1192) came to power, bringing Egypt as well as Jerusalem, Syria, Mecca, and the Yemen under his sway, and ruled as a Sunni military commander, nominally in service of the Abbassids. A Kurd, Saladin was born in Iraq (in Tikrit, Saddam Hussein's hometown), and became famous in medieval legend for his chivalrous exchanges with Richard the Lionheart, commander of the Third Crusade. Once in Saladin's captivity, Richard received the attention of Saladin's personal physician, the Jewish philosopher Maimonides. Here we have an anti-Semitic crusader treated by a Jewish physician, who was born in Spain and because of religious persecution, migrated to Egypt to work for a Muslim prince. Maimonides is a sort of Jewish successor to Philo of Alexandria, an intellectual famous for his knowledge of Greek learning (now through Arabic translations). He succeeded in his efforts to participate fully in a cosmopolitan world (this time a Muslim one) by interpreting Judaism in universalistic and rational terms. His famous treatise on the thirteen essentials of Judaism effectively condenses Judaism into a system of belief,[13] and his philosophical treatises on the nature of God, argued from an Aristotelian perspective, were read by Muslim thinkers as well as by the great Catholic theologian Thomas Aquinas. The point here is that the Islamic world had a place for a thinker like Maimonides, and a cosmopolitan Jew like him could imagine his religion as a creed rather than as a whole set of culture-defining practices that would serve to ghettoize his community. The attraction of such a move, as with Philo, was full participation in the broader culture; the danger would be that Jewish identity is so compromised that it ceases to be a distinctive way of life.[14]

Culturally and religiously, the Muslims of the Middle East, however much they were divided politically, were still part of a confident, dominant culture, a culture that could afford to be rather open and flexible. In thinking about religion and power in the medieval Islamic world, it is important to consider the social totality of that world rather than considering the religion of "good" Muslims in isolation from the seemingly eccentric policies of a ruler like al-Hakim. The very fact that a ruler like al-Hakim could thrive is testimony to the fluid nature of religion and politics in this world. Intellectuals could debate with precision the theological subtleties of Islamic theology, but the blasphemous arrogance of an al-Hakim suggests the profound degree to which the status of the ruler was ambiguous. For the *ulama* or the theologians, alert to the dangers of idolatry, any royal claim of divinity was suspect. But the king, surrounded by a quasi-religious aura of awesome power, could plausibly claim an ever-higher status, as the representative of God on earth, or even, it seems in the case of al-Hakim, as a divine incarnation.

At the other end of the Islamic world, in the wake of the rise of Mongol power, another king was rashly tempted to claim a supreme religious authority to match his secular powers. Alauddin Khilji (d. 1316), one of the great Turkish sultans of Delhi, like all the kings of his dynasty, exhibited great royal pretensions derived from the revived tradition of Persian kingship, dating from Firdawsi's famous and massive epic, the *Shah Nama* or "Book of Kings," a text widely copied and revered by sultans across the Islamic world. Firdawsi portrayed kingship as a central part of God's plan. He imagined a sort of halo emanating from truly royal leaders, beginning with the first man and continuing to the great Sasanian kings of pre-Islamic Persia. The Indian courtier Ziya al-Din Barani (d. 1351) followed in this tradition, declaring "religion and kingship are twins" and tracing kingship and prophethood back to Adam's two sons.[15] In a sense, Barani engages the problem we first saw with Ashoka. The tales of Ashoka reflect a tension between what Buddhists call the "two wheels of *dharma*," that is, the necessity of having a society in which monks pursue enlightenment, in monasteries protected by kings who make possible peace, prosperity, and monastic institutions. We may admire the monks as truer to the religious ideal, but their very existence depends on the king who may have to exercise military power to fulfill his role. A similar inner conflict is inherent in medieval Islam. As Carl Ernst has written:

> Barani attempts to resolve the apparent contradictions between kingship and Islam by stating that kingship is the reflection of divinity on earth, and thus is superior to prophecy in this respect. Prophecy is the perfection of religiousness and kingship the perfection of the world, but they are contradictory perfections. Religiousness is servantship, which is characterized by weakness, poverty and need, while worldly kingship has the qualities of lordship,

such as power, greatness and bounty. The qualities of kingship are thus more properly divine attributes than those of prophecy.[16]

Barani thus expressed the rather extreme Sunni view that the king was allowed to transgress particulars of *shari'ah*, when his ultimate aim was the support of Islam as the religion of the realm, and held that prostration before an emperor was not idolatrous because the king was the shadow of God on earth. Thus, though Barani disapproved of the most arrogant claims and policies of Alauddin, he should not have been surprised at the king's presumptions. He records a conversation between the king and his chief counselor and drinking companion, in which Alauddin not only plans to undertake world conquest (he had already claimed the title of Second Alexander on his coins), but to emulate the Prophet himself in founding a new religion (*din*) and teaching (*mazhab*, or *madhhab*). His counselor talked him out of both of these impractical ambitions, noting wisely that even the great Mongol armies spread their political dominion but ended up converting to the religion of those they conquered.[17] Alauddin himself had faced off against the Mongols, and did conquer large portions of northern India, so he was more than a man of drunken boasts. But like many of the great kings influenced by Persian ideas of royal kingship, he stopped just short of claiming absolute divinity—at least when he was sober.

Some fervent souls so thirst for God that they challenge the legitimacy of any intermediary, of religion itself. A mystic poet like the northern Indian Kabir (d. ca. 1448), born into a Muslim weaving caste but given to using a Hindu name for God (Ram), did not so much *include* both faiths in a tolerant universalism (which is how he is often portrayed), as iconoclastically reject both as idolatrous obstructions blocking the way to an unmediated experience of God.

> Saints, I see the world is mad.
> If I tell the truth they rush to beat me,
> if I lie they trust me.
> I've seen the pious Hindus, rule-followers,
> early morning bath-takers—
> killing souls, they worship rocks.
> They know nothing.
> I've seen plenty of Muslim teachers, holy men,
> reading their holy books
> and teaching their pupils techniques.
> They know just as much.
> And posturing yogis, hypocrites,
> hearts crammed with pride,

praying to brass, to stones, reeling
with pride in their pilgrimage,
fixing their caps and prayer-beads,
painting their brow-marks and arm-marks,
braying their hymns and their couplets,
reeling. They never heard of soul.
The Hindu says Ram is the Beloved,
The Turk says Rahim.
Then they kill each other.
No one knows the secret.
They buzz their mantras from house to house,
puffed with pride.
The pupils drown along with their gurus.
In the end they're sorry.
Kabir says, listen saints:
they're all deluded!
Whatever I say, nobody gets it.
It's too simple.[18]

Qazi, what are you lecturing on?
Yak yak yak, day and night.
You never had an original thought.
Feeling your power, you circumcise—
I can't go along with that, brother.
If God favored circumcision,
why didn't you come out cut?
If circumcision makes you a Muslim,
what do you call your women?
Since women are called man's other half,
you might as well be Hindus.
If putting on the thread makes you Brahmin,
what does the wife put on?
That Shudra is touching your food, pandit!
How can you eat it?
Hindu, Muslim—where did they come from?
Who started this road?
Look into your heart, send out scouts: where is heaven?
Now you get your way by force,
but when its time for dying,
without Ram's refuge, says Kabir,
brother, you'll go out crying.[19]

Kabir's rejection of institutional religion was consistent with a general attitude of rejecting the external and formal in favor of the interior path. From the thirteenth century onward, a movement of devotionally minded Indians flourished under the leadership of *sants*, holy poet-saints who won their followers by a direct appeal to the heart.[20] De-emphasizing caste and ritual propriety, some of these teachers further emphasized an iconoclastic view of God as One beyond description (*nirguna,* "without qualities") and thus unable to be imagined or depicted in concrete form. The founder of the Sikhs, Guru Nanak (d. 1539), was completely in agreement with this view. In the end, however, both men inspired followers who were to resort to some external, institutional structures just to survive and maintain the legacy of their teachers. Somewhat ironically, the preservation of the Sikh teaching in a later era of persecution first led to the establishment of a doctrine of leadership that asserted the community leader's authority not only in the realm of spiritual matters but in political matters as well. The sixth Guru, Hargobind (d. 1644), assumed a throne with two swords representing *piri* (saintly authority) and *miri* (political authority),[21] using Persian terms that also recall the ancient Buddhist notion of two wheels of *dharma.* The appeal of saints who claim to pare away cultural particulars as inessential would seem obvious in a religiously pluralistic setting like late-medieval India. Many humble individuals still clung, however, to reassuring traditions and authorities, while persons of prominence held fast to those caste privileges or high offices associated with traditional religious orthodoxy and orthopraxy. Conversions to Sikhism and Islam took place in the Punjab, and to Islam in Bengal, both regions far from the capital and among groups more marginal to the high Sanskritic traditions.[22] And, as we see from the history of Sikhism, what begins as a universalism that dissolves old allegiances in the name of something transcendent can end up as just one more particularist tradition. A cultural experiment that posits a truth that relativizes the claims of a plurality of religions in a place like fifteenth-century India would need real power and authority to have much effect.

RELIGION AND POWER IN THE THIRTEENTH CENTURY: FROM SPAIN TO JAPAN

In world-historical terms, the spread of Mongol power across the globe was the most significant political fact of the thirteenth century. The Abbasid Caliphate fell to Mongol armies in 1258, and Mongols established the Yuan Dynasty in China in 1272. But Europe escaped Mongol conquest, and in both China and the Middle East, older religious and cultural patterns were soon restored under Mongol rule. Islamic religious and cultural dominance continued in the central zones of Eurasia and would continue to spread until the eighteenth century.

Thus the Far East continued to be largely untouched by the cosmopolitan culture of Islam. Once in power as emperor of China, the Mongol emperor became a supporter of Buddhism and employed Tibetan lamas as court advisors. The Daoist Church had grown wealthy by taking over Buddhist temples after the great persecution, but its fortunes declined under Khublai Khan, who returned temples to Buddhist ownership and destroyed Daoist texts. In Japan, military rulers (the shoguns) supported Buddhism as a way of deemphasizing the role of the Japanese emperor as a Shinto deity. Though under Chinese influence, creative Japanese Buddhist leaders established important new sects in this period. The most notable were Dogen (d. 1253), founder of the Soto Zen sect; Shinran (d. 1263), founder of the True Pure Land sect; and Nichiren (d. 1282), founder of a militant evangelical sect of Buddhism that, unlike most Buddhist schools, rejects all other forms of Buddhism as heretical. As in China, the government sought to control religion and harness it for its political aims, but considering the *longue durée,* Japanese church and sect organizations tended to have greater independence, and generally, greater vitality and creativity than their Chinese equivalents.[23]

Centuries before Luther, Shinran embraced a form of Buddhism that taught that Gautama Buddha spoke to a less corrupt age, when individuals could realistically pursue enlightenment by diligently practicing meditation. Shinran felt that his age demanded a Buddhism of grace, not works, when individuals could rely on the merits of another. He urged reliance upon a celestial Buddha, Amida Buddha, who had established a heavenly Pure Land for all those who cried out to him with faith. Shinran went even farther in emphasizing the importance of faith and grace. For Shinran, any attempt to win one's own salvation (through celibacy, meditation, even prayer) only made one's egoism worse and thus enlightenment more remote. Only by relying on the help of Amida could one find salvation, now understood not as *nirvana,* but as rebirth in the Pure Land. Theoretically, once reborn in the Pure Land, the road to final *nirvana* was easy, but little attention was given to such doctrines. In actual practice, Pure Land teachings created a religion of grace that turned away from meditation, monasticism, and virtually all the teachings of Gautama. Similarly, Nichiren emphasized the "degenerate age" and offered a Buddhism with neither meditation nor monks. He was, however, a militant nationalist, and saw Japan and himself as central in the effort to bring about a timely new Buddhism based on the *Lotus Sutra.* Chanting just the name of the *Lotus Sutra* became the central pious act for Nichiren Buddhists while surprisingly, they ignored its inclusivist spirit in favor of a kind of militant fundamentalism.

In contrast to the new lay emphasis of teachers like Shinran and Nichiren, Dogen cultivated a tradition completely focused upon meditation, since the word *Zen* can be translated as "meditation." This was to be a sect of serious practitioners, monks cultivating the simple practice of "just sitting" and being in the present. But like his contemporaries, Dogen seemed to be eager to simplify Buddhism, reduce it to its essentials, and jettison some of the baroque complexity of the Buddhism of the previous age. Perhaps the threat of Mongol invasion, and the political and military turbulence of thirteenth-century Japan, produced thinkers more sharply attentive to the central question of salvation.

About the time Dogen was teaching an austere practice of sitting meditation and Shinran was offering a religion of salvation through the grace of Amida Buddha, at the other end of the Eurasian world, St. Francis (d. 1226) sought to reform the church by offering a simple gospel of love and charity to the poor. His story is well known, but it is often not set in the context of the Crusades. Francis himself once accompanied a Christian army to Egypt and obtained an audience with the sultan, a nephew of Saladin. He failed to convert the sultan, his aim, but Franciscans were allowed to carry out missions in Jerusalem. They are still there.

As noted above, the thirteenth century was a period when Christendom was on the edges of a wealthy, powerful, more culturally advanced Islamic world. In that day, most European Christians may have dismissed their Muslim rivals simply as heretics, despite the fact that a scholar like Thomas Aquinas (d. 1274) recognized Muslim philosophers as authoritative and edifying interpreters of Aristotle. It is interesting to note that Thomas may have first encountered Arab thinkers while studying at the University of Naples, soon after it was established by Frederick II. Frederick (d. 1250), claiming the title of Holy Roman Emperor, saw himself as a successor of the great Roman and Byzantine emperors, but ruled largely from Sicily as a determined enemy of the pope, who more than once excommunicated him. Despite his role as a crusader, he won Jerusalem through negotiation, and, at least to his enemies, was less interested in spreading Christianity than in spreading his own influence. He spoke Arabic, along with five other languages, and is said to have dismissed Moses, Jesus, and Muhammad as frauds. That may be an exaggeration, the charge of his enemies, but he was clearly a cosmopolitan freethinker who continued to allow mosques to stand and function in his Sicilian capital. He also employed the mathematician Michael Scot as an Arabic translator of the very texts Thomas Aquinas would soon read. So, while Muslim and Christian armies fought over the Holy Land, we see the ways a common intellectual heritage (with ancient Greek texts preserved in Arabic now translated into Hebrew and Latin), was being nourished, and perhaps, for a few persons, becoming a vision of truth that transcended the absolutist commitments of most Muslims and Christians. Meanwhile, proud absolutist monarchs like Alauddin and Frederick II often presumed to stand above the multiple religions of their realms.

Meanwhile, in the wake of crusaders, Italian merchants were opening up markets in the Middle East, and one, Marco Polo, would make it to China. In the coming centuries western European Christians were to catch up with Muslims in learning about the rest of the world, and would have to come to terms with the great religious diversity of that world, just as their own religious unity was fractured by the rise of Protestantism. It is important to note that during the age of the Renaissance and Reformation, during the Age of Discovery, Muslim rulers still exercised political and economic dominance throughout much of the world. Before we turn too quickly to the story of Europe's rise, we must first attend to the great Islamic empires of the early modern world.

CHAPTER 7

The Great Islamic Empires of the Early Modern Era, ca. 1500–1700

He was Adam's heir, not Muhammad's or the Caliphs', Abul Fazl told him; his legitimacy and authority sprang from his descent from the First Man, the father of all men. No single faith could contain him, nor any geographical territory. Greater than the king of kings who ruled Persia before the Muslims came, superior to the ancient Hindu notion of the Chakravartin—the king whose chariot wheels could roll everywhere, whose movements could not be obstructed—he was the Universal Ruler, king of the world without frontiers or ideological limitations. . . . He, Akbar, the perfect man, was the engine of time.

—Salman Rushdie[1]

This Sophy is loved and reverenced by his people as God, and especially by his soldiers many of whom enter into battle without armour, expecting their master Ismael to watch over them in the fight.

—A Venetian traveler (1518)[2]

As the West banished its Jews, enclosed them in small and filthy ghettos, burned their heretics, unleashed its inquisitors among its own people, and tore apart the fabric of society in religious wars, the realms of the Ottomans were mostly peaceful, accepted diversity, and pursued policies of accommodation (*istimalet*).

—Karen Barkey[3]

FIGURE 16. Taj Mahal, Agra, India. EriN, photograph courtesy of Creative Commons.

In the sixteenth and seventeenth centuries, three great Muslim empires—the Mughal in India; the Safavid in Persia; and the Ottoman in Turkey, the Balkans, and the Middle East—were held in a balance of power that checked their individual ambitions, and strained but did not break the unity of Islamic civilization. In all three, emperors ruled who had Turkish bloodlines and whose legitimacy was buttressed by the royal traditions of Persia and the charisma of Sufi saints. Their rivalry with each other was of greater import to them than their rivalry with other civilizations on their borders. Only at the end of this period, at a time when Muslims were politically, and often culturally and religiously, dominant in regions far from their Middle Eastern heartlands—in southeastern Europe, Africa, central Asia, India, and Indonesia—would a few Muslim thinkers begin to be aware of a serious European challenge to their worldwide primacy. But for the most part, Muslim rulers from Istanbul to Delhi could admire Italian painters and purchase European guns without really considering Europeans their cultural or military equals. When the Mughal emperor Shah Jahan (r. 1628–58) was building the magnificent Taj Mahal in northern India, the very emblem of Islamicate splendor, he was also negotiating with the adventurous Portuguese who had established small trading colonies on India's western coast. But surely no one at his court saw the presence of these

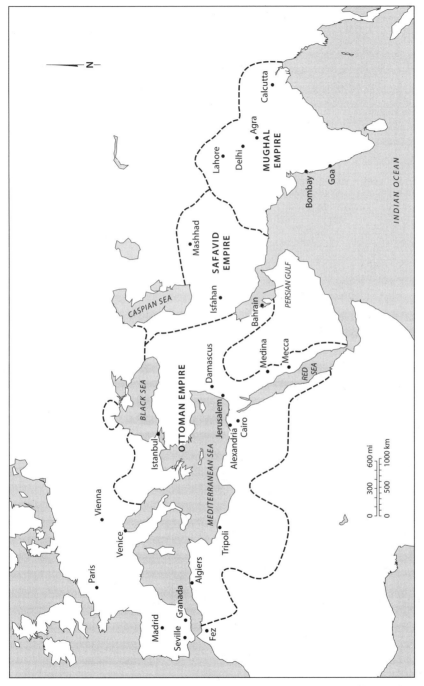

MAP 6. The "gunpowder empires": Ottoman, Safavid, and Mughal, ca. 1500–1700.

Europeans as the first signs of the total transformation of the world's political balance.[4]

While assuming the preeminence of Muslim civilization, some powerful Muslims nonetheless adopted an inclusivist view of religion in ways reminiscent of the pluralistic policies of ancient pagan kings. The Turks, who saw themselves as heirs to a classical Greek and Christian civilization, now governed a large Christian population in the Balkans as well as in Anatolia. In India, inclusivism had particular salience, since the majority of Indian subjects never embraced the Islamic faith of their emperors. In such religiously complex contexts, perhaps the last court of appeal, the apex of power and authority, needed an intellectually and spiritually legitimate way to adjudicate between, and stand above, the several particular traditions of the realm. In the reign of the great Mughal emperor Akbar (r. 1556–1605), we see the clearest example of just such an experiment, one not altogether successful, but fascinating in its scope and lasting in its effects.

Often portrayed anachronistically by modern Indian patriots as the wise and tolerant ruler who put nation before religion, in his own time, Akbar pursued his policies not so much out of a high-minded tolerance or a nationalistic patriotism but out of a desire to buttress his authority as emperor. The one constant factor in his imperial policies is his quest to extend his power, out on the frontiers and within the palace. Akbar came to the throne as a boy but did not long remain the courtiers' pawn, as he forcefully took the reins of government at the age of eighteen. He was heir to at least two traditions of kingship, one Persian and one Mongol, both of which were articulated by his courtier Abul Fazl. In Abul Fazl's great work, the *Akbar Nama,* we find a detailed account of his reign, everything from the emperor's interest in weaponry and perfumes and architecture to his religious and dietary concerns. It is a portrait of a hands-on ruler. Akbar allowed the office of vizier (chief minister) to lapse, and energetically immersed himself in every detail of his empire's governance.

Abul Fazl attributes Akbar's greatness to bloodlines that have carried a halo of royalty from the first man, Adam, to the biblical prophets Enoch and Joseph, seen as the heroic ancestors of the Turkish and Mongol (Mughal) peoples. Taking Firdawsi's notion of a sacred kingship preceding Muhammad, but rooted in God's plan for human history, he relates this heritage both to the stories of the great pre-Islamic Persian kings and to the Mongol myth of Genghis Khan's ancestress Alanquwa. In Abul Fazl's telling, Alanquwa conceived a child immaculately by divine illumination: "One night this divinely radiant one [Alanquwa = 'immaculate woman'] was reposing on her bed when suddenly a glorious light cast a ray into the tent and entered the mouth and throat of that fount of spiritual knowledge and chastity. The cupola of chastity became pregnant by that light in the same way as did Hazrat Miryam [the Virgin Mary], the daughter of 'Imran [Joachim].'"[5] For Abul Fazl, this not unprecedented event of radiant divine paternity is understood within a timeless Neoplatonic doctrine, known in its Persian form as illuminationism.

To supplement his theories of Mongol divine royalty with illuminationist (*ishraqi*) thought,[6] Abul Fazl drew upon the thought of Suhrawardi (d. 1191), a Persian mystic and philosopher. John Richards summarizes Suhrawardi's theosophical doctrine of light thusly: "All life, all 'reality' in the world . . . is light given existence by the constant blinding illumination of the Light of lights (*nur al-anwar*), or God. The degree of luminosity each being or object possesses is a measure of its ontological reality and also an expression of its self-awareness."[7] Among human beings, there are varying degrees of illumination, with a figure like Plato residing in the category of the highly enlightened. In Abul Fazl's reading of Suhrawardi, Akbar is similarly illumined, perhaps uniquely effulgent, a sort of Platonic ideal of humanity. Other Muslim philosophers had identified the prophet Muhammad as the Perfect Man,[8] and Akbar, in Abul Fazl's estimation, belongs in such company, a microcosmic reflection of the universe itself. Akbar's critic Badauni, speaking for the more orthodox religious scholars, accused him of planning to substitute for the universal Muslim declaration of faith ("There is no god but God, and Muhammad is his Prophet") the statement: "There is no god but God and Akbar is his caliph." Badauni also claimed that Akbar's universalism, his doctrine of inclusive divine unity (*tawhid-i-ilahi*), was derived from the teachings of Tibetan lamas.

But as we have seen, the praise of the king in such lofty metaphysical and mystical terms is certainly not unprecedented in the Islamic world, as elsewhere. What is perhaps more consequential and interesting is the set of institutional shifts that Akbar oversaw in his efforts to secure increased power, not only by extending the realm into new territory (doubling in size under his rule), but by better controlling the society within the borders of the kingdom.

Early in his career, Akbar saw himself as a devotee of the Sufi saint Sheikh Selim Chishti, naming his first son after him when he correctly predicted the boy's birth, and building a new capital, Fatehpur Sikri, on

FIGURE 17. Akbar, lost in the desert while hunting wild asses. Illustration from the *Akbarnama*, 1586–89, opaque watercolor and gold on paper, by Mahesh and Kesav. Victoria and Albert Museum, South and South East Asian Collection.

the site of the saint's village. Akbar also made a pilgrimage, walking on foot in 1570 to the tomb of Sheikh Selim's famous predecessor Moinuddin Chishti (d. 1230) in Ajmer, Rajasthan, and he interpreted a series of seizures he experienced along the way as divine encounters.

But whatever the personal nature of Akbar's Sufi piety, his gestures of reverence for renowned holy men must also be seen as rather traditional ways of garnering legitimacy and charisma for his rule by means of the saints' blessings. Ironically, the saints' otherworldliness conferred on them a power that exceeded the power of kings; the more they appeared to stand aloof from the world of politics, the more their charismatic power affected the king's capacity to exercise political power. The reclusive Moinuddin was even known by the epithet Sultan-e-Hind ("Emperor of India"). After his pilgrimage to Ajmer, however, Akbar himself took direct control of the shrine's governance. It is also noteworthy that while Akbar was a devoted follower of Sheikh Selim, and after the saint's demise was royal patron of his tomb and shrine in Fatehpur Sikri, he did not leave the shrine in the hands of the saint's sons, the usual practice, but encouraged them instead to enroll as imperial servants.[9] Thus although clearly following well-trodden paths in the Muslim world, Akbar reserved the right to assert his own authority over the successors of charismatic saints.

Akbar's early preference for the religious styles of Sufi saints put him at odds with the piety of the orthodox scholars of *shari'ah*, the *ulama*. It is worth noting that the *ulama* residing in Akbar's kingdom were largely Afghans, an important group who posed a real political threat to his rule. Regional Afghan nobles, dethroned by the Mughals, mounted several rebellions in the early years of Akbar's reign. Moreover, the Afghan *ulama* were wealthy and powerful and given to corrupt practices, especially using their knowledge of the law to dodge taxes. Later on, when Akbar set up his famous Hall of Worship in Fatehpur Sikri, the Ibadat Khana, to encourage religious debate, he found the *ulama* in attendance there to be rigid, contentious, and unimaginative. Though most scholars of Islamic law considered the age of interpretation (*ijtihad*) to be long since over, with fixed schools of law (*maddhabs*) to have already established the scope of *shari'ah,* Akbar began to claim the right to interpret the law anew as the supreme authority (*mujtahid*) on matters of *shari'ah*. Just as liberal Muslim feminists today call for a culturally sensitive reinterpretation of orthodox law, an opening up of the long-closed practice of *ijtihad,*[10] Akbar claimed a similar right, and in 1579 forcefully required the scholars of his realm to recognize him the supreme *mujtahid* of the Islamic world, issuing what S.R. Sharma calls his "Infallibility Decree."[11] In a sense, he wanted to be pope as well as king, bridging the divide of religion and kingship that Barani long ago had discussed as fundamentally opposed.

For a time he much preferred the theological insights of the Jesuit priests he had invited to his court from Portuguese Goa. The Jesuits hoped, of course, to convert the great emperor, and were later disappointed to learn that he simply wanted them included as part of the grand cultural synthesis of his splendid court. He did go so far as to have his son learn Portuguese to converse with the padres, but as with Islam, Akbar held to a religion over and above certain critical particularities, and was unable to accept Christian Trinitarianism, or its requirement of monogamy (his harem was populous).

Akbar was also interested in classical Indian religion and literature. In general, he fostered a spirit of religious and intellectual cosmopolitanism, and patronized major translation projects, such as the Persian translations of the *Mahabharata* and the *Ramayana*. The hallmark of this cosmopolitanism seems to be a spirit of cultural universalism, with Hindu philosophy accepted as more or less the equal of classical Greek thought, neither being disparaged as non-Muslim but both accepted as a natural part of the humanistic heritage of Muslims who represented the culmination of human history and who were thus heirs of all that went before, whether Babylonian, Greek, Indian, or Persian.

The inclusion of Hindus, Christians, Zoroastrians, and others at his religious conferences paralleled his moves to include all his Indian subjects, whatever their religion, in his political project. He removed traditional Muslim privileges at the same time he claimed authority over the *ulama* (1579), canceling the poll tax on protected minorities (*jizya*) and pilgrimage taxes on Hindu devotees. He allowed Muslims to convert to Christianity, an act illegal under Islamic law. He married Rajput princesses (allowing them to remain Hindu) and made important military alliances with Rajput generals as he broadened the number of groups from which he recruited military and bureaucratic talent. Thus no one faction would be big enough to rebel successfully.

Meanwhile, he carried out his own personal religious experiments, unrelated to any of the debates in his Hall of Worship. He celebrated Hindu holidays like Diwali, the festival of lights, experimented with vegetarianism, and adopted the Hindu practice of veneration and protection of the sacred cow. He made use of a non-Muslim solar calendar and celebrated the Iranian New Year (Nawruz). But more interestingly, Akbar began to pray four, not five, times a day, and not toward Mecca, but toward the sun, having the 1,001 Sanskrit names of the sun chanted at his court. This sun worship was the cause of scandal among strict Muslims, but Akbar justified it as consistent with the *Qur'an* (referencing Surah 91, "The Sun"), and Platonic notions of light as the fundamental nature of the divine; Abul Fazl had argued that every flame is derived from Divine Light and "the fire of the sun is the torch of God's Sovereignty."[12]

Certainly the Jesuits were puzzled by Akbar's eccentric piety. Pierre du Jarric, a French Jesuit at his court, wrote:

And yet one does not know for certain what law he follows; for though he is certainly not a Mahometan . . . and he seems to incline more to the superstitions of the Pagans, Gentiles being more welcome at his court than Mahometans, he can not be called an Ethnique; for he adores and recognizes the True God, the maker of heaven and earth; and yet, at the same time, he worships the sun. It is the opinion of many that he aims at making a new religion of which he himself is to be the head, and it is said that he already has numerous followers.[13]

What would be this "new religion" that would transcend not only Christianity and Hinduism, but even Islam? Many have answered: the Din-i Ilahi (the Divine Faith, or Religion of God/Allah), the name given to a special cult of initiates who swore allegiance to Akbar, wearing an amulet with his picture and the inscription "Allahu Akbar," a phrase that could mean either "God is great" or, alternately, "Akbar is God." But many modern interpreters do not accept the designation of the Din-i Ilahi as a new *religion*. Its followers were very few in number, a small corps of elite members of Akbar's court, all Muslims save Birbal, his most trusted Hindu advisor. It was more like a Sufi brotherhood, with Akbar himself serving as the Master, the other members being his disciples. The disciples all pledged to renounce religion (*din*) itself as part of a loyalty oath, but this is consonant with other forms of Sufism in which the disciple so fully accepts the Master's authority that he is willing to transgress dictates normally assumed as part of Islam (the disciple renounces all ego, becoming "a corpse in the hands of its washer"). Other statements emphasize that accepting the loyalty oath of the Din-i Ilahi means the renunciation of "traditional" (*taqlidi*) Islam. Rizvi translates the oath that initiates took: "I, so and so, do voluntarily and with sincere predilection and inclination liberate and dissociate myself from the traditional and imitative Islam which I have seen my fathers practice and heard them speak about, and join the Din-i-Ilahi of Akbar Shah, accepting the four degrees of devotion, which are the sacrifice of property, life, honour and religion."[14]

Other terms used to describe this special devotion to the religious authority of the emperor were: *tawhid-i-ilahi* (divine unity), *ikhlas-i-chaharganah* (the fourfold loyalty), and *muridi* (simply, "discipleship"). All this comes down to the assertion of the king's transcendent authority. Harbans Mukhia quotes Abul Fazl:

Kingship is a gift of God, and until many thousand grand requisites have been gathered together in an individual, the great gift does not emanate from His court. Merely one's lineage, collection of wealth and the assembling of a mob are not enough for this rare dignity. . . . And on coming to the exalted status if he did not establish absolute peace (*sulh kul*) for all time and did not regard all groups of humanity and all religious sects with the single eye of favour and benevolence, and not be the mother to some and the step-mother to others, he will not become worthy of the exalted dignity.[15]

Mukhia argues that Akbar and Abul Fazl favored a method of rule that replaced Islam as the religion of the state with something more universal, beyond all sects, the meta-religious ideology of *sulh kul,* "absolute peace." This was consistent with Abul Fazl's reading of world history, establishing Akbar as a divinely marked ruler with a genealogy, not related to the Islamic community and the Prophet, but to a much bigger story,[16] beginning with Adam, running through the biblical prophets to the Persian kings and the Mongols. To accept one's religion as but one among many, as Abul Fazl and Akbar seem to do, requires its demotion—from being The Truth, the central fact of human experience, to being a limited, humanly created style or denomination along other, similar interpretive communities.[17] Of course, Islam itself was traditionally thought to be *the* universal religion, encompassing all of world history, and not just one community among others, characterized by a particular set of cultural practices. It, too, began with Adam and ran to Abraham and Moses and Jesus. Many venerated the Prophet as a Perfect Man, the manifestation of God's pure light.[18] But faced with the intractable reality that the majority of Indians saw the world in a completely different light, with millions of Hindus and others unlikely to convert, Abul Fazl began to see Islam as a particular rather than a universal religion. What was more universal was a sort of mysterious wisdom shared by the ancient philosophers of India and Greece, and a tradition of kingship shared by Persians and Mongols. And the wedding of all these traditions in Akbar had brought justice and peace to people lucky enough to be ruled by this divinely sanctioned ruler.

Modern admirers of Akbar have thus praised him for his freedom from sectarianism, his tolerance, even his "secularism."[19] But I hope it now seems clear that whatever the sources of Akbar's personal quest for wisdom, we must never forget that all his policies were consistent with his quest for absolute authority and power.

If the Din-i Ilahi was a sort of Sufi cult for elite courtiers, Akbar's ideology of *sulh kul* ("peace for all") represents the sort of meta-religion designed to adjudicate between the various religious communities of his vast and diverse realm. It effectively replaces Islam as the sovereign religion of the realm with something that does not explicitly deny the truths of Islam, but appeals in abstract and universalist language to something that supersedes all religions (including Islam) both in the name of reason and in the name of Akbar's authority as a radiant authority ruling a divinely sanctified state. Rizvi notes that Akbar, like Mahatma Gandhi, challenged himself and others to find a Truth above the teachings of particular religions. The *Akbar Nama* states: "He is a man who makes Justice the guide along the path of inquiry, and takes from each sect that which is consonant with reason."[20]

This approach, often praised as enlightened tolerance, is consistent with a tradition of Indian inclusivism, whereby all religions are seen as legitimate if partial glimpses of the one truth, all paths up the same mountain. A popular folkloric expression of classical Indian inclusivism is the tale of the blind men grabbing hold of an elephant, each claiming to know what they have grasped, but all disagreeing because each has grasped a different part of the whole. What is often overlooked is the fact that the common conclusion of this tale is that a prince, who *can* see the whole, resolves the dispute. The true nature of the elephant—grasped variously and understood differently—cannot be understood fully until one not limited by blindness comes along to transcend their limited perceptions. The idea that all religions are different paths up the same mountain seems plausible until one realizes that s*omeone* must stand above the numerous paths and see that they all lead to the same summit; otherwise, we have no assurance that the different paths do not simply lead to different destinations. In Akbar we seem to have the all-seeing prince, transcending particularity—at least that is what his partisans want to claim.

In its supersessionist role, the inclusivist policy of *sulh kul* does not actually replace traditional religion. Traditional religion, buttressed by ingrained practices, continued to set the mood and rhythms of everyday life for most Hindus and Muslims. Akbar's court only supplemented those practices by adding royal rituals that enhanced his imperial status. But the average person still considered the dietary and impurity codes, the old holidays, and the traditional rites of passage to be markers of identity. *Sulh kul* could stand above these norms, as a meta-religion, a kind of abstract policy, but it could not replace them in their world-building role. Such a policy made the emperor supreme, a man of absolute authority, but even such a potentate could not even hope to dislodge the deeply rooted behaviors of the majority of his traditionally-minded subjects. This is no doubt why, despite his claims, Akbar was careful to respect the pieties of his Hindu subjects—their veneration of the cow, their pilgrimages, their temple worship. The strategy of inclusivism is to claim power *over* those below, but to leave them to their own ideas and way of life as much as possible.

It is understandable that we in the modern world find Akbar so fascinating, but he was not as revolutionary as he at first seems. His son Jahangir largely followed his religious policies, and even Aurangzeb (r. 1658–1707), who professed a much stricter Sunni orthodoxy and is usually seen as Akbar's antithesis, was as careful as any of his predecessors to rule Mughal India in a way that protected his role as a supreme authority in all matters, whether military, political, or religious.

Although Jahangir's son and successor Shah Jahan (r. 1628–58) had followed a more Islamic policy, the prince next in line, Dara Shikoh, seemed poised to return to the inclusivist religious policies of his great grandfather Akbar. Dara, becoming fascinated with Hindu thought and declaring that the *Upanishads* were God's prior revelation, hinted at in the *Qur'an,* had the *Upanishads* and numerous other classical Hindu texts translated into Persian.[21] When his father was imprisoned, and the battle for succession began, he was outmaneuvered by his younger brother Aurangzeb. Unlike Akbar, an able general as well as a speculative thinker, Dara did not have the military skills to inspire a following and win the struggle. Ultimately he was declared a heretic, and after his execution, Aurangzeb assumed total power under a banner of religious orthodoxy.

Many historians today dispute the simple narrative of a struggle between the religious policy of an Akbar or Dara and the later purism of Aurangzeb, but it is undeniable that Aurangzeb was strict in his piety. He memorized the *Qur'an,* sought to more strictly rule by *shari'ah* law, including the reimposition of *jizya* tax on non-Muslims (but only after 1679, twenty years into his reign). He even denounced the more commonly accepted aspects of Islamicate courtly life like wine drinking, music, and dance, and was uninterested in grand architectural projects; and when he died, he was buried in a very simple tomb, far from the capital. Aurangzeb certainly continued to employ Hindu nobles, but did seek to reduce the number of non-Muslim nobles allied to his court, and encouraged high-ranking Hindus to convert to Islam. Of necessity, he could not be absolutely consistent in his pro-Islamic policies, and given the ruthlessness with which he clung to power (for example, imprisoning his own father for eight years),[22] it is not surprising that he was not such a religious zealot that he would follow policies that would obviously weaken his rule, and he continued to rely on powerful Rajput princes (granting those in imperial service exemption from *jizya* taxes), and on occasion—contradicting his image as a temple-destroying icono-clast—even patronized some important Hindu shrines.

During his reign, the boundaries of the Mughal Empire reached their greatest extent, and at his death at the age of ninety, Aurangzeb was still on campaign. He did face at least three sources of non-Muslim resistance: restive Hindu Rajputs and Punjabi Sikh rebels to the west and northwest, and an emergent Maratha power to the southwest. Some of this resistance was no doubt inspired by a rejection of Aurangzeb's religious intolerance.

As we have seen, the growing Sikh community in the Punjab traced its roots to mystical universalists, holy men who tried to transcend Hinduism and Islam alike. They ran afoul of Aurangzeb when they supported his rival brother Dara Shikoh.[23] Several of their leaders, revered by the title *guru,* became martyrs in resisting Aurangzeb's repression of their movement. The result was the reformation of Sikhism, transforming it from a spiritual movement, to a more clearly defined brotherhood of militant believers carrying out guerilla warfare to win independence from Mughal oppression in the Punjab. Sikhs today look back upon this formative period when they adopted the "five *k*'s" (marks of their militant brotherhood all beginning with the letter *k:* uncut hair and beard, comb, dagger, etc.). Their scripture was sealed at this time, when the last of ten gurus, Gobind Singh (d. 1708), declared that after his death, the holy book itself would be the guru—no longer a human leader. It is interesting to note that while Aurangzeb encouraged nobles to convert to Islam, Sikhs were winning followers among the lower classes, a practice scorned by Mughal aristocrats. Made militant by Mughal policy, Punjabi Sikhs grew into a powerful force of resistance, and ultimately succeeded in becoming an important political and military power in the northwest until finally subdued by the British in the Anglo-Sikh wars of the nineteenth century.

Rajasthan's princes continued to be important during Aurangzeb's rule, though their number decreased, and after Aurangzeb became involved in succession issues and threatened to raise an orphaned Rajput prince as a Muslim at his court, a rebellion erupted that lasted for years, resulting, not only in a loss of Mughal prestige and power in the region, but in religious bitterness over the destruction of Hindu temples. Under Aurangzeb, the critical Mughal-Rajput alliance that Akbar had forged was fraying and on the point of collapse.

The third source of resistance was in the Deccan, southern India, where Aurangzeb had long sought expansion. Here rival Muslim sultans, the Adil Shah of Bijapur, the Qutb Shah of Golconda, and the Nizam Shah of Ahmadnagar, had exercised control over regional kingdoms for over a century. One Nizami noble, a Hindu general named Shahji Bhosle, briefly allied with the Mughals during the collapse of the Nizam Shahi during Shah Jahan's time, before migrating further south to become governor of Bangalore. His son, the celebrated Shivaji (1630–80), refused to be content with his father's career path, and unwilling to accept even high office in service to any Muslim sultan, led a sort of independence movement to establish his own Hindu principality in what is today the western Indian state of Maharashtra.[24] After breaking away from the Adil Shah, his father's employer, Shivaji managed to hold off Mughal advance and have himself declared king (Chatrapati Maharaj) in an orthodox Hindu ceremony in 1674, nine years after escaping house arrest at Aurangzeb's court in Agra.

Just as Aurangzeb is often posed against Akbar in a bipolar depiction of the intolerant bigot versus the liberal inclusivist, Indians today remember Shivaji as the Hindu opponent of intolerant Muslim rule, and there is a Persian letter purportedly written by him, urging Aurangzeb to adopt the policies of Akbar and Dara Shikoh.[25] Perhaps both men were in fact trying to break out of old paradigms by foregrounding religion as the basis of their political and military projects, even while constrained by pragmatic requirements to make concessions. So, just as Aurangzeb supported a Muslim agenda but of necessity allied with Hindus, Shivaji employed Muslims and sought Muslim allies while pursuing the goal of an independent Hindu kingdom. It is interesting to note that after Shivaji's death, his grandson was brought to Aurangzeb's court, where he was raised as a Hindu and placed on the throne of the Maratha Kingdom, which, though formally allied to the Mughal throne, ultimately became the most powerful regime in eighteenth century India, propping up a declining Mughal emperor before both succumbed to British rule in the nineteenth century.

Thus, while largely under the political control of Muslim sultans, India in the sixteenth and seventeenth centuries was still fundamentally Hindu in religious culture, and many great Muslim rulers, Akbar most prominently, adopted a rather inclusivist policy to religion rather alien to the Muslim project of promoting Islam as supreme. Meanwhile, a popular Islamic culture unsupported by the royal court and far from the capital, spread among the lower classes in both the Punjab and Bengal, the regions that would form the nations of Pakistan and Bangladesh in the twentieth century. The Mughals, as powerful political and military rulers, did not produce a Muslim population. They did not even really try. Massive conversion to Islam was the work of charismatic Sufis far from the halls of power.[26]

Meanwhile, amid the growth of the broad universalism that characterized much of Mughal rule, the inclusivist Sikhs, who revered a scripture with the anti-institutional messages of the iconoclast Kabir and the Sufi Baba Farid, grew ever more concerned to define the sources of external authority and membership in their group. They evolved from a popular devotional movement into a distinct religion and separate political and social community by the end of the seventeenth century. The Mughals resisted them, not for their heterodoxy, but as political and military rivals in the Punjab.[27]

SAFAVIDS AND OTTOMANS

However wealthy and powerful the Mughals became, they were ever aware of the two great Muslim empires to the west: the Safavid Empire in Persia, and the Ottoman Empire centered in Istanbul and controlling Turkey, much of the Balkans, and the heartlands of Arabia and Egypt. Like Akbar, the emperors of these realms also arrogated to themselves great powers in matters of religion as well as in politics and warfare.

The Safavids made their claims of religious authority based on their adherence to classical Shi'ism. Ismail I (r. 1501–24), inaugurated the Safavid Dynasty as a Sufi *pir* of the Safaviyya order, a descendant of both the Prophet and the last Sasanian monarch. Roger Savory writes:

> Ithna 'Ashari [Twelver] Shi'ism lay at the heart of one of the bases of the power of the Safavid leaders, namely, their claim to be the representatives on earth of the 12th Imam or Mahdi (if not the Imam himself); the cult of Ali had been inextricably bound up with the development in Iran of Sufism, or Islamic esotericism, from at least the thirteenth century, and the position of *murshid-i kamil*, or perfect spiritual director, was the second basis of the power of the Safavid leaders; finally, by asserting that Ali's younger son Husayn, married the daughter of Yazdagird III, the last of the Sasanid kings, Shi'is had linked the family of Ali with the ancient Iranian monarchical tradition, and the divine right of Iranian kings, derived from their possession of the "kingly glory", was the third basis of the power of the Safavid shahs.[28]

Ismail was of mixed ethnicity, spoke Azerbaijani Turkish and Persian, and was the leader of Turkoman warriors (called Qizlbash "red hats") devoted to him as their Sufi *pir*. In ecstatic language he himself proclaimed:

> I am Very God, Very God, Very God!
> Come now, O blind man who has lost the path, behold the Truth!
> I am that *Agens Absolutus* of whom they speak.[29]

Despite his claim of divinity, however, after tragically losing a crucial battle to the Ottomans, he lost his swagger, and took his comfort in wine while his kingdom became less and less theocratic and more traditionally bureaucratic in nature. Nonetheless, an unbending Twelver Shi'ism was to remain the state-supported orthodoxy of Iran for the entire history of the Safavid Empire (1501–1736), and was reborn with Ayatollah Khomeini's revolution in 1979.

Meanwhile, the Ottoman emperors could also lay claim to a certain divine legitimacy, although clinging to a much more orthodox Sunni theology. Their strategy was not so much to elevate their status above Islam as a particular religion, as to embody the traditional claims of Islam itself to be the religion at the center of human history. Suleyman (d. 1566), known as "the Magnificent" in the West and as *Qanuni* or Lawgiver to his subjects, reigned as both a caliph (even claiming descent from Muhammad's Quraysh tribe) and as the successor of his namesake, the biblical Solomon. Ruling from the old capital of the Byzantine Empire, Ottomans saw themselves as the new Romans, and the biblical and Hellenistic legacies as rightly theirs. Bernard Lewis notes that even the nineteenth-century Turkish nationalist Namik Kemal saw the Ottomans in such a universalist way: "In a poem celebrating the 'Ottoman Fatherland', Namik Kemal proudly reminds his readers that it was in their country that Christ was born and ascended to heaven, that the light of God came down to Moses, that Adam found a substitute for Paradise, that Noah's ark came to rest, that 'from the song of David and the moan of Socrates, religion and reason became keepsakes for one another'—that is, the Biblical and Hellenistic heritages merged in Islam."[30] The Ottomans were the great rivals of Christendom; Suleyman was a contemporary of Henry VIII (d. 1547) and Elizabeth I of England (d. 1603); Philip II (d. 1598) of Spain; the Holy Roman Emperor Charles V (d. 1558); and Ivan the Terrible (d. 1584) of Russia, all of whom made the grandest of claims. But the Ottoman Empire was arguably the grandest of them all, spanning the ancient Middle East, including the ancient cities of Medina and Mecca, Jerusalem, Cairo, and Baghdad, as well as the eastern Mediterranean, and much of the lands of the eastern Christian kings in the Balkans (even Vienna was besieged in 1529).[31]

The empire was much enriched by Christian talent, including the famous elite corps of celibate soldiers (Janissaries), as well as notable

FIGURE 18. Hagia Sophia, Istanbul. Arild Vagen, photograph courtesy of Creative Commons.

figures like Suleyman's queen,[32] and his most prominent architect. But unlike the Hindu servants of Akbar, all these converted to Islam as a prerequisite to Ottoman preferment. Thus while both Mughal and Ottoman realms were broadly cosmopolitan and inclusive, the Ottomans still assumed Islam to be the very banner of that cosmopolitanism.[33] Justinian's great Byzantine church Hagia Sophia, today still referred to in Turkish as Ayasofya, was transformed into a mosque after the 1453 Ottoman Conquest. The name, meaning "Holy Wisdom," could be preserved as perfectly consistent with Islamic sensibilities, but gestured toward the Muslims' role as guarantors of an ancient heritage, from Solomon to Justinian.[34] The new Solomon, Suleyman, would codify the law of the land, a thousand years after Justinian did the same from the same capital. In the Ottomans' mind, Islam did not replace Judaism and Christianity by eradication, but fulfilled their historical promise and thus superseded them.

But while the Ottoman emperors pursued a policy of conversion for their elite servants, they, like the Mughals, continued to govern a religiously diverse empire, and they worked to develop a pragmatic system for dealing with their Jewish, Armenian, and Orthodox subjects that is praised as tolerant and far more enlightened than the policies of persecution pursued by their contemporaries in Christian Europe. Often referred to as the "*millet* system," using the Turkish word for "confessional communities," these policies evolved first as a response to the challenges of ruling over the Balkan territories where Christians were the majority population. The Ottomans allowed Orthodox Christian religious officials to serve as the leaders of their communities, and set up a separate Christian court system mirroring *shari'ah*-law judiciary functioning for Muslims. They later tried to create similar arrangements for Armenian Christians, and for Jews, even though these communities did not have a hierarchical clergy well suited for such a system. The important thing about the *millet* system, is that the Ottoman secular and Islamic courts still had final say, and more importantly, the ethnarchs among the Orthodox, Armenian, and Jewish communities were favored and chosen by the Ottomans, and thus came to be loyal servants of the Ottoman state rather than potential rebels stirring up discontent among subjugated minority communities.

Thus the Ottoman emperor followed a religious policy that made all religious leaders, Muslim, Christian, or Jew, servants of the state. Unlike the situation in the classical age, when scholars of Islamic law were often critics of the royal court, Ottoman sultans oversaw the orthodox establishment and appointed the *sheikh al-islam* as the supreme authority in religious matters. The treatment of minorities may have involved a certain level of religious tolerance, but in the interest of *incorporating* all communities as part of the imperial project. A suspect group like the Sufi order that brought the rival Safavids to power in Persia was ruthlessly persecuted, while another Sufi group, the Bektashis, spread a somewhat Christian-Muslim heterodoxy in the Balkans, but were supported as the spiritual advisors of the Janissery recruits.[35] While Akbar might have cultivated a supra-Islamic meta-religious ideology as part of his attempt to rule a religiously diverse society, Ottomans were content to follow the traditional notions of Islam as supreme, the religion that rightly held primacy of place in a society where members of other religious communities were "protected," but only as second-class citizens. In fact, even Islam was subject to the emperor's authority and only those Muslims and those versions of Islam that found his favor would be allowed to flourish in his realm. Thus the great early modern empires of the Ottomans and the Mughals had important similarities. Both were religiously diverse, and in both, absolutist emperors jealously guarded their authority to rule *over*, not just in the name of, religions that claimed access to Truth.

As the Ottomans faced their Shi'i rivals to the east and their Christian rivals to the west, they pragmatically cultivated allies wherever it suited their political and military purposes rather than following a purist policy of attacking religious opponents.[36] Like the Islamic world, Christendom was also not a unified front, and was about to undergo a massive religious and political transformation under the twin forces of the Protestant reformation and nationalism. That forms the background story against which we can evaluate the role of secularism in the modern nation states of the West in the following chapter. Before the separate western European states were to embark on their career of colonialism and worldwide domination, displacing Muslims and destroying the Islamic sense of confident dominion, those Christians, now fractured into warring rivals, first had to sort out sources of meaning and legitimacy in ways that might avoid the utterly destructive religious wars between Catholics and various protestant groups that tore Europe apart in the seventeenth century. The so-called modern world, to which we turn in the following section, was not born with the falling away of religion in the face of a cool and detached scientific mentality, but in a spasm of intense and passionate religious reform and rivalry.

PART THREE

The Modern World

Confronted with the disquieting reality of religious conflict, popular wisdom typically comforts itself with the ironist's refrain: "How sad to see wars in the name of religion, when all religions preach peace." However well intentioned such sentiments may be, they manage to ignore the fact that virtually all religions allow for the righteous use of violence. . . . In similar fashion, academic commentators often regard the religious side of conflicts like those in Sri Lanka or Northern Ireland as relatively unimportant or, alternatively, they deplore it as a debasement of all that is properly religious. Although one can empathize with those who offer such views . . . , their analyses rest on an understanding of what constitutes religion that is simultaneously idealized and impoverished: a "Protestant" view that takes beliefs and moral injunctions . . . to be the essence of the religious.

—Bruce Lincoln[1]

Liberalism presumes to master culture by privatizing and individualizing it, just as it privatizes and individualizes religion. It is a basic premise that neither culture or religion are permitted to govern publicly; both are tolerated on the condition that they are privately and individually enjoyed.

—Wendy Brown[2]

1546   Death of Martin Luther
1555   Peace of Augsburg
1598   Edict of Nantes
1603   Death of Elizabeth I of England

1610   Death of Henri IV of France

1648   End of the Thirty Years War

1704   Death of John Locke

1715   Death of Louis XIV

1776   U.S. Declaration of Independence

1778   Death of Voltaire

1799   End of the French Revolution

1821   Death of Napoleon Bonaparte

1826   Death of Thomas Jefferson and John Adams

1833   Death of Ram Mohan Roy

1861   First Italian parliament proclaims Victor Emmanuel king of a united Italy

1864   End of the Tai Ping Rebellion in China

1865   End of the American Civil War

1870   End of First Vatican Council under Pius IX

1893   World's Parliament of Religions in Chicago

1918   End of World War I

1926   Turkey begins secularization program

1945   End of World War II

1947   Independence of India and Pakistan

1948   United Nations Universal Declaration of Human Rights; founding of the modern state of Israel

1949   Communists founding of the People's Republic of China

1979   Iranian Revolution

1988   Publication of Salman Rushdie's *Satanic Verses*

2001   9/11 attacks

2011   End of the Iraq War

CHAPTER 8

Putting Religion in Its Place, I

Reformers, Kings, and Philosophers
Challenge the Church

The end of a religious society (as has already been said) is the
public worship of God and, by means thereof, the acquisition
of eternal life. All discipline ought, therefore, to tend to that
end, and all ecclesiastical laws to be thereunto confined.
Nothing ought nor can be transacted in this society relating
to the possession of civil and worldly goods. No force is here
to be made use of upon any occasion whatsoever. For force
belongs wholly to the civil magistrate, and the possession of
all outward goods is subject to his jurisdiction.

—John Locke[1]

The existence of Portuguese trading colonies on the coast of Akbar's
India certainly did not signal to him or to any of the great Muslim
nobles in the next two centuries that the Islamic world was about to be
eclipsed by European power,[2] any more than wealthy Venetian merchants in Istanbul threatened the confidence of the great Ottoman Sultan. But in the period from 1500 to 1700, as Muslim emperors ruled
over an Islamic world that was politically divided but culturally linked,
a world still at the peak of its wealth, power, and influence, developments in Europe—religious, political, and technological—prepared the
way for a geopolitical transformation that made the world we live in
today.

One aspect of that changing world, the so-called Age of Discovery,
meant that the ancient trade routes of the Silk Road were supplanted
by shipping lanes dominated by Europeans, bypassing the heart of
the Islamic world. Another great change of this period was the rise of

European nation-states in the context of the complex debates over religious authority during the Reformation and wars of religion. In terms of the central themes of this book, the seventeenth century is when articulated notions of the nation-state began to demand a certain demotion of religion from its supreme status of authority, preparing the way for modern domains of politics, science, and religion. In Europe, the very category of "religion" itself, reified as a general concept within which particular traditions like Catholicism and Lutheranism could fit, became possible, and replaced taken-for-granted notions of The Faith. This process was enormously complex—a complexity often misunderstood when we assume a grand narrative of progress toward modernity, a story that envisions the gradual but inevitable retreat of religion before the forward march of secularism. The irony is that the European transformation, from Latin Christendom to a multireligious, multilinguistic world of national cultures and states was first effected not by secularists but by persons radically committed to a fervently *religious* reform. If the early Renaissance could produce a figure like Boccaccio (d. 1375),[3] who composed the fable of "the three rings," each ring signifying a different but equally legitimate religion (a tale later used by the Enlightenment writer Gotthold Lessing in his classic *Nathan the Wise*),[4] Martin Luther would have had no patience for such relativism. His goal, like John Calvin's, was not to create a pluralistic world with a variety of religions or even a variety of Christian denominations, but to reform the One True Church and bring it back to its original purity, cleansed of Roman corruption. In this, there was a newly vigorous attempt to sanctify all of life rather than be content with a realm of monastic sanctity set apart from a realm of worldly concerns. In other words, the purism of the Puritans meant a rejection of the medieval idea that some souls will pursue the religious life—mostly monks and nuns, the religious virtuosi praying for us all—while others remained "in the world," not particularly pious or devout, but outwardly conforming to the demands of the church and relying on Her many graces.[5] Of course the political fractures that occurred with the Protestant challenges were the unintended consequence of this initially theological and moral critique. Simply put, the Reformation was not a movement to win the freedom to worship freely and separately from the Catholic Church, but to thoroughly reform the One True Church of Christ. It assumed nothing like the modern notion of tolerance and pluralism.

But even Luther came to believe in the principle that each principality had to separately affirm but one religion so as to preserve peace, the idea

FIGURE 19. Portrait of Martin Luther, by Lucas Cranach, 1529.
Image courtesy of Creative Commons.

of *cuius regio eius religio* ("whose realm, his religion" or "religion belongs to the ruler") that was affirmed among the princes of the Holy Roman Empire at the Peace of Augsburg in 1555. According to this treaty, each of the German princes could choose either Lutheranism or Catholicism, and that would be the recognized church of his realm. No accommodations were made for other groups, Calvinists, Anabaptists, and the like. Here we see a sort of pragmatic acceptance of the idea that even in the battles that pitted The Truth against an Evil Heresy, a truce had to be called to prevent bloodshed and unceasing warfare. It was not

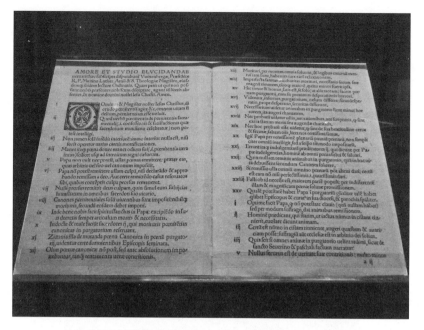

FIGURE 20. Martin Luther's ninety-five theses. Wittenberg, 1522. Image courtesy of Creative Commons.

to achieve, however, an end to religious strife, and it would require another period of massive suffering, the Thirty Years' War (or the "wars of religion"), before a new European attempt was made in 1648 to lessen the violence provoked by religious differences across the continent.

In the age of absolutism, however, both England and France saw the rise of monarchies that elevated the power of the crown over the power of the church, even while developing ways of mitigating domestic religious differences, nationalism thus beginning to trump religion (at least institutional religion). England's Henry VIII famously declared himself supreme head of the church in England, ruthlessly beheading Catholics Thomas More and Bishop Fisher for not supporting his claims, while nonetheless opposing the more truly Protestant ideologies that might threaten the church's role as an effective instrument of power. His successor Elizabeth I (d. 1603) also supported a basically Anglo-Catholic position, "Catholicism without the pope," but was notably more lenient toward her Catholic subjects during her long reign.[6] If they did not plot against her, she had no interest in learning the content of their personal faith and theological views. Similarly, Henri IV of France, who converted twice to Catholicism, issued the Edict of Nantes (1598) to protect the rights of his Calvinist subjects.

Henri IV provides a very interesting case. Baptized a Catholic but raised a Protestant by his zealous mother in the Protestant region of southwestern France (Navarre, Béarn), he was briefly forced to conform as a young man of eighteen and kept in confinement in Paris for several years, before escaping and reverting to his mother's Protestant faith. When he became the primary heir to the French throne, his Protestantism became an even more pressing problem. The French monarch was the "Most Christian King," a divine-right monarch whose quasi divinity was enhanced by a series of Catholic anointings at his coronation (*sacre*). The whole ideology of divine-right kingship was bound up with Catholicism, and the idea of a non-Catholic king seemed oxymoronic to many. Some Catholic nobles formed the Holy League to oppose Henri's accession, and called for his conversion, or for another person to accept the throne, provoking civil war. Of course, the Holy League position was somewhat self-contradictory. If one believed that a certain individual had the duty to reign and rule by right of a divine authority discerned by a sacred law of succession (the so-called Salic Law), then how could that law be put aside on religious grounds? Their position was also tainted by their alliance with Spain, whose king clearly wanted to expand his influence in France and with the papacy (Henri called them "Spanish Frenchmen"). The pope too clearly had a political agenda, thereby reducing his spiritual stature among the French. Other French Catholic nobles ("royalists") supported Henri, but still hoped he would convert. They resisted any attempt to pry apart their joint support of their Catholic Church and their prince of royal blood. And again, we must avoid the modern temptation to interpret these events in a way that would separate religion and politics. No sixteenth-century French nobleman, Catholic or Protestant, could imagine a politics divorced from religion. A king was by his very nature a religious figure, an instrument of God.

Thus sixteenth-century France was divided by three groups of armed nobles: (1) the ultra-Catholic Holy League, for whom the king's Catholicism was of utmost importance. They were willing to overlook the Salic Law of succession, and thus threaten the doctrine of divine right of kings, the assumption that there was one "prince of the blood," in order to have a Catholic monarch; (2) the Huguenot Calvinists, taking the opposite position, that the king's blood made him the monarch, and since the Roman Church was in their view idolatrous, corrupt, and false, it could hardly claim the Most Christian King's commitment; and (3) the Catholic royalists, attempting in a conservative way to maintain the claims of both blood and religion. In short, the Holy Leaguers emphasized religion, the Huguenots blood, the royalists both. The Leaguers could appear insufficiently French, the Huguenots insufficiently Christian, but the royalist Catholics hoped to maintain an allegiance to both sources of legitimacy.

After years of civil war and equivocation, Henri finally agreed to "take instruction" from prominent Catholic theologians and clerics, and he converted to Catholicism in 1593, an act intended to quell civil war and resolve the constitutional crisis of the French monarchy, an institution wed to Catholicism for the previous thousand years. Some, of course, doubted his sincerity, and many people today assume that he rather cynically converted just to win the throne. As Ronald Love points out,[7] however, the claim that the king acted without sincerity is belied by the fact that he temporized so long, clearly reluctant to endanger his soul's salvation and turn against the oaths he had made to his intensely pious mother. Moreover, the question of sincerity is itself a rather Protestant worry, since a more traditional Catholic view, going back to Augustine, would be that the very act of conversion, sincere or not, was a concrete step on the path, and would be followed by acts meant to induce a greater, if gradual, transformation of the convert's inner faith. But the rigorous Holy League Catholics certainly adopted their Protestant enemies' emphasis on sincerity to continue to challenge Henri's legitimacy.

The cynical interpretation of Henri's conversion usually begins with the statement attributed to him, "Paris is worth a mass," but, in fact, he never actually said that. What he did say to his disappointed Protestant allies as he converted is more interesting: "I am entering the house not to live in it, but to cleanse it."[8] Henri seemed to resolve his personal crisis of conscience (and France's crisis of authority), *not* by assuming a separation of church and state, according to which, Protestants and Catholics could peacefully coexist as subjects of the same king, but by reuniting the claims of his God and his kingdom. One could read the sixteenth-century events as a struggle *between* politics and religion, and many today do so. But of course kingship *itself* was sacred; Henri was a divinely blessed figure chosen by God. Neither he, nor most Frenchmen at that time, could imagine a patriotic devotion to a secular state, and no doubt both Protestants and Catholics assumed that sooner or later, all of France would return to a single church. That True Church might turn out to be more Protestant in nature (the Huguenots' passionate hope) or Catholic (the natural triumph over heresy, according to Catholics), but neither group could really imagine a world in which crown and state and church were not singular, mutually reinforcing institutions based on the One Truth.

Henri did seem to move toward a position that assumed a singular Christianity that preceded both a corrupt Catholicism and politically rebellious Calvinism. He declared: "Those who unswervingly follow their conscience are of my religion, as I am of all those who are brave and virtuous."[9] While his mother could not tolerate Catholic observance in their Béarnaise principality (just as Calvin's Geneva was rigidly intolerant of Catholicism or any other "heresy"),[10] Henri repealed his mother's anti-Catholic statutes there in 1576, just as he later issued the Edict of Nantes, promising toleration of Huguenots even as he assumed the crown as a Catholic. "Religion" thought Henri, "is placed in the hearts of men by the force of doctrine and persuasion, and is confirmed by examples in life and *not* by the sword."[11] This principle of toleration, argued at the time by the famous essayist Montaigne, was a pragmatic policy of avoiding civil war, not a relativist position that no one religion had a final claim on truth.

At this stage, Elizabeth I and Henri IV took a position similar to their Muslim contemporaries. Islamdom had long been fractured and multiple kings took on an increasing glow of divinity, their crowns elevating them above the authoritative claims of divines (the *ulama*). As we have seen, the great Muslim emperors of the sixteenth and seventeenth centuries, whether in India, Persia, or Turkey, often claimed a divinely ordained position that gave them an authority superior to that of saints and religious scholars. Granting that the holy men of their realms might not always confirm that authority, it was still a charisma sufficient to give them real power. Just so, Elizabeth and Henri IV tried to rule like Akbar or Suleyman the Magnificent, as divine-right monarchs of kingdoms with subjects adhering to rival faiths.

A generation ago, when a notable historian of the Reformation, Roland Bainton, argued that "nationalism . . . eclipsed religion for those who came to feel that the unity and security of the nation were of more importance than the victory of a single religion,"[12] he thus argued from a Eurocentric position, assuming the centrality of European history to global history as the natural conclusion of the rise of modern secular nationalism. But these European monarchs, like Akbar, were struggling to expand their royal power by claiming authority over religion while nonetheless trying to maintain the sort of legitimacy that religion alone could confer. Bainton's language, still free of the critique of postmodernism, captures the mentality of those who see the transcendence of religion by secular nationalism in fairly unproblematic terms:

> After the collapse of the universal Church and universal empire, where could a solid basis for internationalism be discovered? The canon law would not do because it was rejected by Protestants. The Roman law would not do because it was not conceived in terms of international relations. The Bible would not do because both vague and controverted. The answer was discovered by Hugo Grotius in the theory of natural law, but a new kind of natural law it was, no longer identified with the law of God . . . but secularized and thereby rendered immune to religious division; grounded in experience and nature like Locke's theory of knowledge, valid even if there were no God, accessible to the understanding of the natural man.[13]

Of course, all our previous references to kings seeking unity over division by appealing to a nonsectarian *logos* or *dharma* or *sulh kul* (Augustus Caesar, Ashoka, Akbar) suggest a commonly available premodern structure for dealing with religion and politics in a pluralistic setting. We have already and often seen appeals to a universal law, expressed in the language of cosmopolitan reasonableness, declared from on high, above and thus immune from the claims of religious partisans. So perhaps the insights of Grotius were not so novel, but an obvious move to escape the clash of knights and bishops on the chessboard of religion and power.

Hugo Grotius (d. 1645) is less well known than John Locke, whose social-contract theories reflect his influence and were to shape the thought of America's founding fathers. But in Grotius, we see the intellectual steps that take us beyond a world in which kings challenged ecclesiological institutions, now problematically plural, in the name of their own sacral monarchic power, to something more properly secular. In two works, *The Freedom of the Seas* (*Mare liberum,* 1609), and *The Rights of War and Peace* (*De jure belli ac pacis libri tres,* 1625), Grotius laid the foundations for what we today consider international law. To have something properly international, it had to transcend a fractured Christianity (Grotius was himself a radical Protestant), and be based in something that at least appeared to be the truths to which all reasonable men could assent. Although exiled from Holland for much of his life on account of his religious beliefs, Grotius developed a natural-law argument that favored the sort of free, international trade that the Dutch republic needed to compete with Spain and England in the colonial era.

He based his belief in free trade on an understanding of natural law still firmly rooted, as Ivan Strenski has clearly shown, in theology.[14] Strenski quotes from *The Freedom of the Seas:*

> God Himself says this speaking through the voice of nature; and inasmuch as it is not His will to have Nature supply every place with all the necessaries of life, He ordains that some nations excel in one art and others in another. Why is this His will, except it be that He wished human friendships to be engendered by mutual needs and resources, lest individuals deeming themselves entirely sufficient should for that reason be rendered unsociable? So by the decree of divine justice it was brought about that one people should supply the needs of another, in order, as Pliny the Roman writer said, that in this way, whatever has been produced anywhere should seem to have been destined for all.

Hence, Grotius concludes, "every nation is free to travel to every other nation and to trade with it . . . on the following most specific and unimpeachable axiom of the Law of Nations."[15] This invocation of Nature, reminiscent of the ancient Indian idea of *dharma,* is here employed in a postimperial way. Whereas the ancient ideal of one king, one God, one law, imagined the possibility of world dominion, the dawning of seventeenth-century Europe imagines a plural world of many nations, no longer subject to one king or even one religion, but still clinging to a rather univocal notion of Nature, speaking for an utterly transcendent (if not yet quite absent) God, a nascent economic, if not political globalism that protected free trade, and ultimately spurred colonialism, a novel form of the imperial project, but one still requiring meta-religious justifications.

Grotius and Locke were both trained in philosophy and theology but worked out their social and political theories within what Charles Taylor calls "the immanent frame."[16] The question for us is whether the creation of taken-for-granted categories of nature, human rights, and the like are really all that different from religious dogmas based on revelation, or all that different from the universalist meta-religious notions of *logos, dharma, and sulh kul.* This seventeenth-century transition must be comprehended as the preparation for the emergence of Enlightenment politics in the following century. What was the nature of absolutist politics in England and France as well as the intellectual shifts that Grotius and Locke made possible? Nationalism and secularism arose together, however much their initial impulses were ideologically at odds.

In France, the national unification made possible under Henri IV continued under the leadership of Cardinal Richelieu, who served as prime minister from 1624 until his death in 1642. While France was internally unified and largely free of civil war, Europe continued to be torn apart by the Thirty Years' War (1618–48), and although a man of the church, Richelieu had no qualms about supporting Protestant powers like Sweden when it was in France's interest to do so. Within French borders he was wholly committed to the defense and the revitalization of the church. But in foreign affairs he was not reluctant to oppose the Catholic Hapsburgs or even the pope himself. So once again, it is tempting for the modern scholar to see Richelieu as an unprincipled Machiavellian, whose support of the notion of *raison d'état* meant a grasp of power for its own sake, and that image was furthered by his fictional portrayal as an antagonist in Dumas' *The Three Musketeers*. But his legacy remains as the chief architect of strong nationalism, a centralized state triumphing over regional feudal power and foreign threats. His support of the monarch and the French state against all opponents was still an endorsement of a Catholic Christian monarch and kingdom, however ruthless and morally questionable the means he adopted in that support. Richelieu's approach assumed that without an absolutist monarchy and centralized state, the Christian realm of France would be torn apart by religious conflict and overrun by rapacious Hapsburg invaders. The end of a peaceful, prosperous, *Christian* nation justified almost any means to that end.

The goal of absolutism, the establishment of a monarch so powerful so as to guard against anarchy and unrest, triumphing over the chaos of religious conflict and the ambitions of feudal lords, was already imagined during the reign of *le bon roi* Henri IV, remembered by secularist French patriots today as the gallant king with the common touch, who sought to guarantee the humblest Frenchman the minimal prosperity of a chicken in the pot every Sunday. Already the word *patrie,* "fatherland," was in use, two centuries before "patriots" and "citizens" of the French republic replaced "subjects" of the French monarch. But this strong monarchy, this center, was threatened in the years after Henri's murder at the hands of a Catholic fanatic in 1610.[17] Pierre de la Mare, voicing the longings of those who remained devoted to the royal myth, wrote his *Discours sur la justice et science royalle* in 1618, in which he portrayed the king as the perfect man, resplendent as the sun in heaven. The solar imagery and the belief in the king's religious and royal superiority call to mind the similar language of Akbar's courtier, and more distantly, the image of Constantine and even Alexander the Great. Such an ideology, revived by Richelieu, came to full realization in the reign of the absolutist monarch par excellence, the Sun King Louis XIV.

Under Louis XIV, we have the ascendancy of royal splendor and the emphasis on power, wealth, and order, but now at the expense of the common touch, the welfare of the peasant, and of religious toleration. "Let them eat cake" replaces the chicken in every pot, and Louis XIV seems to signal the return to both the power of the monarchy and the greatness of the French kingdom, while at the same time a tenacious clinging to Catholic traditionalism. The initial steps toward religious toleration under Henri IV now seem to halt and reverse, a hundred years before the French Revolution.

Between the age of Henri IV and the age of Voltaire (d. 1778), lies the age of Louis XIV (d. 1715) and John Locke (d. 1704). Louis represents the high point of absolutism, and his cousin monarchs in England, Charles II and James II, shared his view of divine-right kingship, even while being challenged by a parliament seeking to limit their royal power. Locke on the other hand represents the rationalism that would both challenge the divine right of kings and begin the discourse of human rights and religious tolerance that would be a hallmark of the eighteenth century, shifting sovereignty from the crown to the people. Since many Enlightenment notions of religion and politics have become so taken for granted in our own day, it is instructive to go back to their origins, when it was a bloody struggle to see them come into being and to influence the polity of England, France, and the newborn United States of America. If America's founding fathers took "these truths to be self-evident" (to quote the Declaration of Independence), they did so as partisans of Locke's philosophy. Surely when Locke was making such declarations, they were hardly so self-evident.

The long, splendid reign of Louis XIV (1638–1715) seemed to resolve the French crisis of governance in favor of a return to the rule of a legitimate, absolute monarch fully supportive of the French Catholic Church. Under Louis XIV, France was an expansive, paramount power in Europe, victorious in war abroad, and possessed of a strong, central-ized government that curbed the powers of nobles. Louis believed that unity of religion was necessary for the unity of the state, and revoked the Edict of Nantes in 1685, making Protestant worship illegal, destroy-ing all Protestant churches, and closing Protestant schools. (In France today, Protestant churches are even still often called "*temples*," implic-itly suggesting that there is but one Church.) It is interesting that Louis' revocation granted Protestants the freedom to *believe* their aberrant doctrines, just not engage in any public practice of their religion: "Liberty is granted to the said persons of the Pretended Reformed

Religion Protestantism . . . on condition of not engaging in the exercise of the said religion, or of meeting under pretext of prayers or religious services." Such a requirement of public conformity, contrary to the emphasis on personal sincerity voiced by Henri IV, provides an important counterpoint to the notions of Locke and his Enlightenment heirs, who were so concerned with freedom of conscience and the rights of the individual. It recalls the medieval tradition we noted above, going back to Augustine, that practice precedes personal transformation—that, for example, if one performs *acts* of penance, the inner *feeling* of penitence will follow. By extension, it assumes as a corollary that the establishment of institutions shapes individuals, not the other way around. However one evaluates this argument, the net result of Louis' revocation of Nantes was the emigration of over two hundred thousand Huguenots to the Netherlands and elsewhere.

In contrast to the absolutist splendor of Louis XIV's France, England after Elizabeth experienced several new spasms of conflict over religion and political legitimacy, and it was the difficulties of this period that created many of the ideas that shaped modern notions of the proper places of religion and politics in a modern society. During the seventeenth century in England, civil war and revolution, and the deposing of two kings on largely religious grounds, accompanied by the growing power of the parliament, brought all these questions to a head.

While Elizabeth had sought to establish a strong monarchy wed to a Church of England still fundamentally Catholic, with the sense of authority and sacramental grandeur this implied, more truly Protestant impulses remained among some Anglican clergy and among members of a variety of dissenting Protestant sects. The dissenting sects, Calvinist Presbyterians and Puritans, and, somewhat later, Quakers and Baptists, threatened the social and cultural unity thought necessary for successful monarchical rule. And indeed, Oliver Cromwell, the Puritan commoner and member of parliament, led a revolution that established England briefly as a republican commonwealth. He reigned as "Lord Protector" from 1653 to 1658, but his rule was preceded and followed by kings who resisted parliament's reach, claimed to reign by divine right, and were either Catholic or High Church Anglicans, and thus opposed to Puritanism and its suppression of sacramental religion. Charles I (r. 1625–49) was an Anglican, but married to the French Catholic daughter of Henri IV. Headstrong and resistant to parliamentary influence, he was deposed by the Puritan revolution and executed, becoming, for a small group of conservative Anglicans, a martyr. In fact, he remains today the only Anglican canonized a saint, and thus represents the conservative Anglo-Catholic wing of the Church of England. There are stories of various omens that accompanied his death, suggesting the persistence of beliefs in the special sanctity of kings—kings chosen by God. Stories were spread of Charles's loyal, grieving subjects, dipping their handkerchiefs in his blood after the beheading, and keeping these cloths as holy relics.

After Cromwell, the High Church Anglicans ultimately regained control of the parliament and sought the suppression of Puritans with the restoration of the monarchy and the accession of Charles II (r. 1660–85). Charles II was also married to a Catholic, and as the cousin of Louis XIV, was thought to be a Catholic sympathizer. But he was a popular king, whose hedonism (he fathered at least twelve illegitimate children and allowed a rebirth of popular theater) seemed a welcome relief after the austerity of Puritan rule. He issued a Declaration of Indulgence in 1672, providing religious freedom for both Catholics and dissenters. The declaration was rejected, however, by the pro-Anglican forces in parliament in 1679, and as Charles II's wife was unable to give birth to an heir, fear mounted that Charles II's brother James, a Catholic, would inherit the throne and begin to return England to Catholic rule. Led in part by the Earl of Shaftesbury, the patron of John Locke, the parliament began to author bills of exclusion to prevent James from attaining the throne. Although James did succeed in obtaining the crown, his reign was a brief three years (1685–88), and he was deposed in the Glorious Revolution, ending any chance that England would return to Catholic rule, and moreover, ending the possibility of truly absolutist rule. James II's sister Mary, and her consort William of Orange, came to the throne as constitutional monarchs, agreeing to parliamentary limits on their power and a bill of rights protecting the freedom of their subjects. The issues that bedeviled the French with the accession of Henri IV now reemerged in England. Henri IV's ultra-Catholic Holy League opponents and James II's Anglican opponents really had the same problem. Either one believes in a divine-right monarchy—God chooses the king—or not. If one believes that God necessarily chooses the right person, then one can't accept that choice while claiming that the person has renounced his right to rule by adopting the wrong religion. How would God get that choice wrong? Or if one says religion is the decisive matter, why have a royal monarch at all? (Indeed, Cromwell was offered the crown.) Why wouldn't any religious exemplar serve just as well? Is there something in the royal *blood*? And if one is committed to the notion of royal blood, one continues to face the prospect that the very idea of royalty is protected by noble marriages contracted with the Catholic royal families of Europe (as was the case with Charles I, Charles II, and James II). This was the context in which Locke wrote his philosophical reflections on religion and politics. Although he presented himself as an Anglican and supporter of a constitutional monarchy, he was sympathetic to dissenters. His views on religion and politics evolved over a twenty-year period, but he ultimately supported an expansive view of toleration, based upon a well-earned skepticism about the state's claim to legitimate authority in matters of religious doctrine:

> Our modern English history affords us fresh examples in the reigns of Henry VIII, Edward VI, Mary, and Elizabeth, how easily and smoothly the clergy changed their decrees, their articles of faith, their form of worship, everything according to the inclination of those kings and queens. Yet were those kings and queens of such different minds in point of religion, and enjoined thereupon such different things, that no man in his wits (I had almost said none but an atheist) will presume to say that any sincere and upright worshipper of God could, with a safe conscience, obey their several decrees.[18]

Born to Puritan parents, Locke worked as the Earl of Shaftesbury's personal physician, and his advisor on many political matters. The staggering breadth of his thought and his great importance to the history of philosophical thought are beyond the scope of this book, but it is important to see that his very fundamental questions about epistemology, how it is that we can be sure of the knowledge we claim to have, are central to his analysis of the relationship of religion to politics, and his position on the rights of individuals to be free of religious persecution at the hands of state authorities.

Like his patron the Earl of Shaftesbury, Locke went into exile in the Netherlands in 1683 when it became clear that their efforts to block the Catholic James II's succession had failed. He witnessed there the flood of Huguenot immigrants from France, and composed his famous *Letter concerning Toleration* while abroad.[19] Locke asserts in that critical text that since no one can be sure of the rectitude of his theological position, and since even if one's position is the right one, he must hold it in all sincerity or else be a liar and hypocrite, then no one has the right to challenge the beliefs of any other unless they contravene laws that enforce the common peace and weal of the society.

In this, Locke upholds the sanctity of individual conscience, and authorizes the civil authority ("the magistrate") to govern matters of civic welfare ("life, liberty, health, and indolency of body; and the possession of outward things, such as money, lands, houses, furniture, and the like"),[20] but to avoid intrusion into matters concerning the salvation of souls, since one could never be coerced into adoption of the truth. If one is coerced, one is only capable of making an insincere declaration. In other words, Locke has taken here a very long stride toward what we would call the separation of church and state. He does so, not as a secularist, but as a man convinced of the "simple truths" of Christianity, such as the virtues of charity, forgiveness, and peace, truths that he cannot square with any impulse to coerce belief through persecution, torture, or the threat of execution. Moreover, he demotes the significance of those theological debates over matters not explicitly mentioned in scripture, such as a debate over transubstantiation. The heart of Christianity, for Locke, is its capacity for moral reform; everything else is a matter of personal speculation and opinion and should not set one Christian against another.

In opposing those who would use government as a coercive instrument to induce a particular faith, Locke sets himself against the tradition of Augustine, who was invoked by his opponents. As we have seen, the Augustinian position assumes that government can support institutions and practices that will discipline wills and induce dispositions.[21] Locke, on the other hand, envisions individuals in a very modern way, as persons of conscience individually coming to affirm a truth, and then voluntarily joining like-minded persons in forming a particular church ("a church, then, I take to be a voluntary society of men, joining themselves together of their own accord in order to the public worshipping of God in such manner as they judge acceptable to Him, and effectual to the salvation of their souls").[22]

According to Locke, then, human beings can come together voluntarily under different social contracts to form both governments ("a society of men constituted only for the procuring, preserving, and advancing their own civil interests") and churches.[23] Gone is the idea that king and church come first, the individual after, that the Holy Mother Church commands obedience and conformity. Both kingdom and church are thereby desacralized and imagined as contractual. Members of the several churches should have free rein to worship and believe as they choose insofar as they do not endanger the civil society. Returning to England with the Glorious Revolution and crowning of the Protestants William and Mary, Locke was in favor of complete religious toleration, except for Catholics, whose allegiance to a foreign ruler, the pope, made them in effect, traitors. Here Locke felt that one can extend toleration only to those religions that themselves recognize the principle of tolerance: "That Church can have no right to be tolerated by the magistrate which is constituted upon such a bottom that those who enter into it do thereby ipso facto deliver themselves to the protection and service of another prince."[24]

So the seventeenth-century transition, post-Reformation and pre-Enlightenment, seems to have two contradictory tendencies in the arguments of constitutional and absolutist monarchists, but both represent the common framework of the problems caused by religious civil war. In this context, reflecting on the context that ultimately gives rise to "the secular age," Charles Taylor writes of the neo-Stoic natural-law theory developed amid "bitter and violent inter-confessional strife," as well as asserting that "the most prominent answer in seventeenth century Europe to the disorder of religious war was the absolute state."[25] Both responses then, though pulling in different directions, are attempts to go beyond institutional religion, to find a basis for common political life in something besides the taken-for-granted authority of the church. Since divine-right kings assumed a sacralized authority, they retained the church, but now as their creature. The natural-law theorists seemed to anticipate the Enlightenment in limiting, if not completely casting aside, the authority of both church and crown. But, of course, in the name of freedom and reason, they still had to imagine a way to govern, with institutions that claimed a taken-for-granted authority, and thus something very like the religious authority they rejected.

To gain an understanding of the distinctive ways that modern, especially western European and North American people approach the relationship of religion and politics, we must first appreciate the profound changes that occurred during the eighteenth century, when the Enlightenment and the growth of democracy and nationalism fundamentally altered the place and scope of religion in western society. One simple way of formulating the issue would be to say that whatever tensions existed between religion and politics during earlier times, and whatever dynamic sparring existed between popes and kings, *ulama* and caliphs, the ancient, medieval and early modern world was one where institutions of power found their legitimacy guaranteed by claims of divine authority. The Enlightenment formulations shifted sovereignty from divine-right kings to the people, and grounded legitimate authority on claims of reason and natural rights. Perhaps these new self-evident truths were only superficially novel, mere God-replacements, articles of faith masquerading as the products of rationality. But at the time, the revolutionaries saw themselves as offering the final liberation from oppression at the hands of kings, nobles, and priests, breaking what Peter Gay called the "sacred circle" of churchmen legitimizing the rule of kings, who in turn, protect the church.

Prior to the eighteenth century, many ingredients of the Enlightenment were already present in western Europe. There were scientists accumulating knowledge of the world based on empirical data rather than making assertions based on authoritative sacred sources. The church was fractured, never to be unified again, and thus growing doubts about the role of any church in providing a firm foundation for political legitimacy. But it was in the eighteenth century, particularly in France, when intellectuals fully embraced the role of skeptic, and claimed the freedom to question all authorities and dogmas.

The quintessential Enlightenment figure was Voltaire (d. 1778), the French writer who lived an adventurous life in Paris, the Netherlands, London, Lorraine, Potsdam, and Geneva. Though buried today in Paris in the Panthéon (once a church and now a secular temple to the nation's great men and women), Voltaire spent much of his life on the run from the many authorities he criticized in his witty and irreverent writing. He was a student of Newton's physics, a friend of Benjamin Franklin, and ready to give authority to scientific truth rather than to any church. He was also a fan of John Locke's ideas of religious toleration, writing his own *Treatise on Toleration* (1763), and an epic poem glorifying Henri IV. But unlike Locke, who was arguing primarily for toleration among a variety of Protestant churches, excluding Catholics and Muslims for their unpatriotic support for foreign monarchs (the pope and the sultan),[26] Voltaire was not only disdainful in his rejection of the authority of France's national Church, he was an early practitioner of biblical criticism and dismissive of many aspects of Christianity, and far more ready to extend religious tolerance to everyone:

> It does not require great art, or magnificently trained eloquence, to prove that Christians should tolerate each other. I, however, am going further: I say that we should regard all men as our brothers. What? The Turk my brother? The Chinaman my brother? The Jew? The Siam? Yes, without doubt; are we not all children of the same father and creatures of the same God?
>
> But these people despise us; they treat us as idolaters! Very well! I will tell them that they are grievously wrong. It seems to me that I would at least astonish the proud, dogmatic Islam imam or Buddhist priest, if I spoke to them as follows:
>
> "This little globe, which is but a point, rolls through space, as do many other globes; we are lost in the immensity of the universe. Man, only five feet

high, is assuredly only a small thing in creation. One of these imperceptible beings says to another one of his neighbors, in Arabia or South Africa: 'Listen to me, because God of all these worlds has enlightened me: there are nine hundred million little ants like us on the earth, but my ant-hole is the only one dear to God; all the other are cast off by Him for eternity; mine alone will be happy, and all the others will be eternally damned.'"[27]

To some extent, Voltaire's expansive, nonparochial spirit, claiming spiritual kinship not just with Christians of different sects but with persons of different religions altogether, was a result of a growing knowledge of the rest of the world. The quest for knowledge drove the French *philosophes* to try and summarize all human learning into a massive, twenty-eight-volume *Encyclopédie.* Not only did this work express the great optimism of the age, the grand hope that knowledge could be amassed that would rid the world of superstition and ignorance, but many of the articles took for granted a very radical view of religion. Its editor, Diderot, shared this attitude with Voltaire and many other cosmopolitans in the eighteenth century, not just the *philosophes,* but American revolutionaries, and even baroque musicians and the later German romantics. Montesquieu (d. 1755), often quoted by America's founding fathers in support of government with balanced powers, wrote a novel, *Lettres persanes,* in which two Persians visit Paris and make various satirical critiques of French society. Voltaire also had great admiration for Confucius's ethical humanism and China in general, ironically cultivating a positive view of China based upon accounts sent home by Jesuit missionaries. A few years after Voltaire's death, Europeans were reading translations of Sanskrit classics, and Goethe became a devoted admirer of the great Sanskrit playwright Kalidasa before the turn of the century. The religiously quite conservative John Adams, second president of the United States, was nonetheless an admirer of Hindu and Buddhist philosophy. Even Mozart, who as a devoted Catholic despised Voltaire, wrote an orientalist opera set in an Ottoman harem (*Die Entführung aus dem Serail,* "Abduction from the Seraglio") in which the plot turns on the gracious and generous act of a Turkish *pasha*. Perhaps what was once utterly "other" was now becoming simply "different," and it is not a far jump to imagine that the different may, in some cases, even be better.

Voltaire, like many thinkers of that day, was hopeful about the possibility of more enlightened rule, and watched the evolution of constitutional monarchy in Britain with interest, but he was never a convinced democrat; he was too much of an intellectual snob to trust "the people."

Like many intellectuals of that century, he became interested in Freemasonry, a club indicted by the Catholic Church as deist, but in general thought to be a fraternal organization with esoteric rituals and a broadly inclusive philosophy and set of ethical principals. Just before he died, Voltaire went to a Masonic lodge in Paris with Benjamin Franklin and was inducted as a member.

In tracing the story of religion and power from Henri IV to Voltaire and Henry VIII to John Locke, we see a world emerging that included people who could imagine only one legitimate religion as the source of truth and thus political authority giving way to people who could imagine a realm in which authority was exercised in the name of something that transcended multiple religions. For a long time there were still large numbers of people in the first camp. But what is so consequential about these developments is the fact that once Christendom was fractured, no one could *take for granted* the simple unity of religious and political authority. As we have seen, this is not a completely novel situation or a revolutionary European idea, but it does produce an understanding of religion that produces a rather different relationship between religion and power across the entire globe. Revolution, the Enlightenment, and imperial colonialism are the strange bedfellows of that new world.

CHAPTER 9

Putting Religion in Its Place, II

Revolution and Religious Freedom

When in the Course of human events, it becomes necessary
for one people to dissolve the political bands which have
connected them with another, and to assume among the
powers of the earth, the separate and equal station to which
the Laws of Nature and of Nature's God entitle them, a
decent respect to the opinions of mankind requires that they
should declare the causes which impel them to the separation.

—Declaration of Independence, 1776

Man will never be free until the *last* king is strangled with the
entrails of the *last priest.*

—Denis Diderot[1]

Paris would have become the capital of Christendom, and I
should have governed the religious as well as the political
world.

—Napoleon Bonaparte[2]

The Enlightenment impulses to secularize, rationalize, and reform—
thus breaking with the *ancien régime*'s instinct to revere without question the doctrines of the church and sacrality of royal power—first bore
fruit in North America, with its less aristocratic social system, to be followed perhaps more radically, if fitfully, in France. American and French
revolutionaries were intellectual cousins. Both Benjamin Franklin and
Thomas Jefferson were quite at home in France, Franklin a darling
of Paris salons from 1776 to 1785, as ambassador, and Jefferson his

successor there from 1785 to 1789. Both were enthusiastic rationalists and empiricists, committed to exploration and invention, and neither beholden to any religious orthodoxy. But the shape of the revolution in America differed from the French Revolution, not least in the way the Americans approached the issue of how religion related to politics. The Revolutionary War may have begun with the battle cry, "No taxation without representation!" but in breaking with their monarch, the colonists were raising profound questions about legitimacy, questions rooted in a rebellion against an authority that claimed a certain divine sanction. While King George III (r. 1760–1820) was a Protestant king of a Protestant kingdom, the American colonists saw many aspects of British rule as rooted in an ideology they rejected as "Romish."[3] Inherent in John Locke's belief in the sanctity of the individual person's liberty of conscience is the acceptance of religious pluralism, and the American experiment in democracy, over time, became an experiment in religious freedom.

Of course the Puritans who first sought freedom of religion in America were hardly believers in pluralism and tolerance. These seventeenth-century settlers sought to build a godly city in Massachusetts and were strict in their attempts to maintain their particular brand of Calvinist orthodoxy. As we shall see, even well into the nineteenth century, as Americans debated the precise meaning of "separation of church and state," New Englanders long continued to assess taxes for the support of their churches and clergy. The history of the ideas Americans associate with the notion of freedom of religion is a contentious one, in some respects not resolved even today.

The democratic impulses of revolutionary America were seen as inconsistent with Catholicism, and from the 1760s, Catholic bashing was the norm, with holidays set aside just for denouncing the pope. In this, popular sentiment was with the early Locke, who had difficulty imagining a freedom of religion to those who did not, in his view, believe themselves in liberty of conscience, and who gave allegiance to a "foreign monarch." Catholics had been persecuted in England, and some of them came to America to found the colony of Maryland, but by the late eighteenth century, Protestants made up over 95 percent of the population (as opposed to about 50 percent today), and in the thirteen original colonies, only three allowed Catholics to vote, and many forbade Catholics from holding public office. Even Maryland became a place where "popery" was legally persecuted. As Americans contemplated the addition of the Bill of Rights to the constitution of their young nation, including the First Amendment, which would secure freedom of religion, they operated in what Noah Feldman refers to as a "sea of Protestant assumptions." He notes that the "framers assumed a whole set of principles that grew out of Protestant Christianity as interpreted by English liberals such as John Locke."[4] Put simply, the generation of the Founding Fathers was one in which the vast majority of people assumed that America would be a Protestant Christian nation. In that context, religious tolerance meant the belief that a variety of Protestant denominations would find a home in this society. Early on, even Quakers and Baptists had a difficult time winning acceptance, more so than rather freethinking and deism-influenced intellectuals. Very few eighteenth-century Americans were ready to embrace a tolerance that might extend to Catholics and Jews.

Among those few were Benjamin Franklin (d. 1790) and Thomas Jefferson (d. 1825), who personally held religious views consistent with French Enlightenment ideals. Both rejected the miraculous as inconsistent with the scientific and rationalist worldview. Franklin edited the Nicene Creed to remove references to Christ's virgin birth and resurrection. Similarly, Jefferson created two expurgated "Bibles," one entitled *The Morals of Jesus,* the other *The Philosophy of Jesus,* both being "cut and paste" texts of Jesus's teachings, with all references to his divinity, or to the miraculous, excised. For Franklin and Jefferson, religion was about virtue, and individual persons had the right to evaluate this religious doctrine or that religious practice in terms of what they meant for society's benefit. Both admired Jesus the moralist, but neither claimed him as a divine savior.

Though the Unitarian movement was flourishing by the late eighteenth century, most Americans adhered to a Bible-based Christianity and it is noteworthy that Jefferson was vigorously attacked for his unorthodox religious views during his campaign for the presidency in 1800. And in one way, even the most broad-minded and Enlightenment-influenced American leaders of this period rejected one aspect of philosophical deism. The true deist makes room for an orderly universe, free of miracles and subject to unchanging natural laws, by assigning God the role of a Creator who then withdraws from His Creation. But neither Franklin nor Jefferson would go that far. Both believed that supplication of God could be efficacious, and that God was actively intervening in human events; the very victory of the American Revolution was taken as a sign of God's grace. And more than either of them, George Washington publicly called upon and thanked God for his military success.

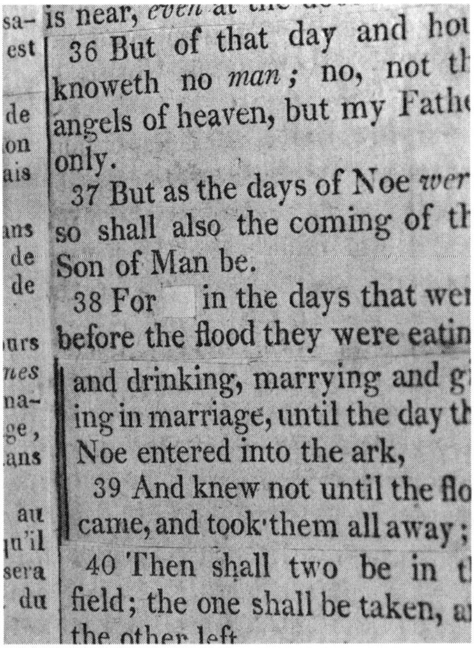

sa-
est
de
on
ais
ans
de
de
urs
nes
na-
ge,
ans
au
ju'il
sera
du

is near, *even at the door*

36 But of that day and hou
knoweth no *man ;* no, not th
angels of heaven, but my Fathe
only.

37 But as the days of Noe *wer*
so shall also the coming of th
Son of Man be.

38 For   in the days that wei
before the flood they were eatin
and drinking, marrying and gi
ing in marriage, until the day th
Noe entered into the ark,

39 And knew not until the flo
came, and took them all away ;

40 Then shall two be in th
field; the one shall be taken, an
the other left

FIGURE 21. Jefferson's Bible.
Smithsonian Museum of
American History. Photograph
courtesy of Creative Commons.

Father of the nation, victorious general and first president, George Washington is today memorialized in the U.S. capitol building in a painting surprisingly entitled *The Apotheosis of Washington,* by Constantino Brumidi. Not unlike Voltaire's burial in the Panthéon, this painting thus divinized Washington in 1865 in a rather pagan manner (he is surrounded by Roman deities). His own religious views are inherently interesting, and were consequential for the history of religion and politics in the United States. A wealthy Virginia planter, Washington was a respectable if not particularly pious Anglican. He seemed to believe fervently that God had blessed America and that His divine protection should be sought. He believed that chaplains should be hired with public funds for both the military and the Congress, and he declared national holidays of prayer and thanksgiving. On the other hand, he was a Freemason and seemed to embrace rather universalist ideals in favor of a strictly Christian theology; and he avoided taking communion when he attended church. Perhaps most importantly, he was outspoken in his criticism of those who abused Catholics (among other things he sought alliances with French Canadians and recruited Hessian Catholic defectors in fighting the British), and as president made a trip to a

FIGURE 22. *The Apotheosis of Washington*, by Constantino Brumidi, 1865. Visible through the oculus of the dome in the rotunda of the United States Capitol Building. Courtesy of Creative Commons.

Rhode Island synagogue to publicly express his solidarity with Jews he considered full-fledged American citizens.[5] As general, and later as President, he had no qualms in publicly invoking God, but tellingly, his pronouncements were non-sectarian and inclusive. Scholars today speak of an "American civil religion" of shared public values and presidents end most of their speeches with "God bless America."[6] Religion is thus very much present in the public square, but it is a civil religion—one where Jesus Christ is not mentioned. Such traditions seem to go all the way back to the first inauguration of the first president of the United States.

The second president, John Adams, was something of an "accommodationist." Coming from Massachusetts, he continued to support the right of individual states to make provisions for the support of clergy and churches. In this he opposed the views of Jefferson and Madison, who argued for a strict separation of church and state. But even Adams was opposed to establishing a particular church, and his personal views, as a Unitarian, were broadly inclusive. He once wrote, "Ask me not . . . whether I am Catholic or Protestant, Calvinist or Arminian. As far as they are Christians, I wish to be a fellow-disciple with them all."[7] Even more striking is his distaste for Bible societies promoting missionary work abroad: "I wish Societies were formed in India, China and Turkey to send us gratis translations of their Sacred Books."[8]

But in spite of such liberal sentiments, Adams's commitment to the idea of government support for churches cost him votes among dissenters like Baptists and Methodists, and they voted for Jefferson in the election of 1800. Though Jefferson was sharply criticized as an infidel deist, his belief in the strict separation of church and state turned out to be a popular position among many zealous Christians. For these groups, evangelical piety meant a special emphasis on the individual's sincere faith, and they equated any government involvement with a Catholic value of institution building. Late in life, Jefferson still wrote to Adams that he felt the New England practice of using taxes to support churches and clergy was "a protestant popedom."[9]

So, ironically, it was Jefferson's secularism that won the backing of evangelicals. And he certainly agreed with their emphasis on the individual as the site of true religion, having once proclaimed, "I am of a sect by myself as far as I know."[10] In fact, the early history of the principle of the separation of church and state is a history of the cooperation of intensely religious Methodists and Baptists with Enlightenment-inspired deists. The principle was first articulated during the fight to disestablish the Anglican-Episcopalian church in the state of Virginia. Jefferson, who had already written the Declaration of Independence, with its language of "Nature's God," worked with James Madison to produce the Virginia Statute on Religious Freedom, finally ratified in 1786. Jefferson considered it as one of the three great achievements of his life, a fact etched on his tombstone. There were those Virginians, most importantly, the patriot Patrick Henry ("Give me liberty or give me death!"),[11] who might have favored dis-establishment, but nonetheless wanted the state to affirm Christianity in general. It was not to be, however, as Jefferson writes in his autobiography: "The insertion [of the name of Jesus Christ into the state constitution] was rejected by the great majority, in proof that they meant to comprehend within the mantle of its protection the Jew and the Gentile, the Christian and the Mahometan, the Hindoo and infidel of every denomination."[12] These expressions of broad tolerance were not always popular; consider his declaration: "The legitimate powers of government extend to such acts only as are injurious to others. But it does me no injury for my neighbor to say that there are twenty gods, or no god. It neither picks my pocket nor breaks my leg."[13] Such statements were used against him in the election of 1800. We might note that he remained a member of the

Episcopalian Church his entire life, and avoided publishing his demythologized "Bibles." It seems clear, however, that he always embraced a very rationalist view of the world and religion's place in it. After he wrote the Declaration of Independence, he spent four years in France in the period concluding with the outbreak of the French Revolution. In France, the revolutionaries saw the Catholic Church as a reactionary support of the monarchy and all that impeded liberty. Jefferson was largely sympathetic to their views and returned to the States in 1789 committed to the idea that the government should be protected from the meddling influence of religion. It is this attitude that prevails among modern secular liberals and makes Jefferson their hero.

But while Jefferson was in France, his ally James Madison was steering the Virginia Statute toward ratification in 1786. Whereas Jefferson may have viewed the separation of church and state as a matter of protecting the state from the church, Madison tended toward the opposite view, with churches being protected from state intervention. In his youth, Madison had witnessed established Anglicans harshly persecuting Baptist preachers in Virginia, and he won Baptist support for the Virginia Statute. His opponent, Patrick Henry, sought to assess taxes that could be directed to a variety of churches, thus avoiding the establishment of any one, but Madison rejected such a compromise, and he was supported by religious men leery of any government involvement with religion.

Madison's later career as a major framer of the Constitution (he is dubbed "Father of the Constitution") preceded his role as secretary of state (1801–9) and election to the presidency in 1809, following Jefferson. In these formative years he took the lead in firmly establishing the separation of church and state, resulting in the first amendment to the Constitution, first of the ten amendments known as the Bill of Rights that were ratified in 1791. The language of that amendment ("Congress shall make no law respecting an establishment of religion, or prohibiting the free exercise thereof") reflected the earlier Virginia statute and has come to be interpreted in terms of its two clauses, the "establishment clause," and the "free exercise" clause.[14] At the time of its ratification, there were many who supported it as a statement disallowing the government from establishing a national church, and allowing for liberty of conscience in the sense that Locke intended. Such a reading meant that although Congress and the national government could not establish a single church, states could continue to assess taxes for the support of churches and clergy, as happened in New England until

1833. The modern reading of the First Amendment depends on an acceptance of a greater and more uniform authority for the federal government than was accepted at the end of the eighteenth century.

In discussions of church and state today we often hear the phrase "wall of separation," Jefferson's language, meant to express an unequivocal separation of church and state. He actually used that phrase not in an official document but in a letter to a community of Baptists in Danbury, Connecticut. They had written to Jefferson early in his first term as president, complaining of their status in Connecticut, a state where Congregationalists were established and tax-supported, and where only Congregationalist ministers were authorized to perform marriages. They appealed to Jefferson's Lockean views: "Our Sentiments are uniformly on the side of Religious Liberty—That Religion is at all times and places a Matter between God and Individuals—That no man ought to suffer in Name, person or effects on account of his religious Opinions—That the legitimate Power of civil Government extends no further than to punish the man *who works ill to his neighbor.*"[15] In response, Jefferson composed a letter in which he articulated his support for their rights, and most importantly, his view that any government involvement with, or interference in, the religious lives of citizens was unwise and harmful to both. He states that it is on this basis that he avoids calling for national days of prayer, fasting, and thanksgiving as his predecessors had done. He quoted the establishment clause of the Constitution, noting that this built a "wall of separation" between church and state. His position seems abundantly clear. And yet we must not overlook the fact that he took no concrete steps to ameliorate the Baptists' situation, for at that time, he could not justify asserting federal authority to coerce a particular state.[16]

However much America was assumed to be a Protestant Christian country, and however much the question of church and state was unresolved in the late eighteenth and early nineteenth centuries, the nation did *not* always present itself to the outside world as a "Christian nation." Consistent with Washington's domestic use of the nonsectarian language of civil religion to his own people, the first presidents engaged in diplomatic relations with a Muslim power by making it clear that the United States was not operating as a Christian nation and held no particular hostility toward Muslims. With their independence from Britain, Americans lost the protection of the British navy, and several of their ships were commandeered and held for ransom by the Barbary pirates, North African raiders loosely affiliated with the Ottoman Empire. Years of diplomacy and naval war ensued, but the earliest treaty declared: "As the Government of the United States of America is not, in any sense, founded on the Christian religion—as it has in itself no character of enmity against the laws, religion, or tranquility, of Mussulmen—and as the said States never entered into any war or act of hostility against any Mahometan nation, it is declared by the parties that no pretext arising from religious opinions shall ever produce an interruption of the harmony existing between the two countries."[17] Jefferson inherited the problem of dealing with the Barbary pirates when he became president, and he met their call for increased tribute with military force. But it is interesting to note that Jefferson's interest in Islam preceded these events by three decades. He had purchased an English translation of the *Qur'an* as a law student in the 1760s. He even began a program to teach himself Arabic, and throughout his career as diplomat and president, he sought to read what he could about Islam.[18] Jefferson did not seem to harbor the usual anti-Islamic prejudices, but neither did he hold romantic orientalist views. After his administration hosted a diplomatic visit from Tripoli in 1805, and prostitutes were requested by the Tunisian ambassador, Jefferson could hardly have continued to hold naïve ideas about the consistency with which followers of Islam followed the dictates of the religion.[19]

As Americans argued over the precise meaning of the separation of church and state, and still argue about it, it is important to attend to some of the sites of tension. As we have seen, many Americans were worried that without strong religious institutions, the nation would lack proper moral support for society. In this, they were in agreement with many Frenchmen who had second thoughts about the course of the French Revolution. If a society were to reject a particular religious institution, where would it turn to find a foundation for a moral way of life? If it rejected the Catholic Church, could it turn to Christianity more broadly conceived, as Locke seemed to think? If so, who would speak authoritatively on behalf of this generic Christianity? More radically, if Christianity were rejected, could it turn to a sort of generic religion, deriving a rational morality from Nature's God, as Jefferson seemed to think? Would democratic institutions provide moral leaders, secular saints who could speak with authority on the moral life, rationally derived and defended?

In America, such worries were largely assuaged, as separation of church and state proved to result in stronger religious institutions, not weaker. Church memberships (in all denominations) increased from

17 percent of the population in 1776 to 34 percent by 1850.[20] Voluntary association, as opposed to state intervention and coercion, turned out to be good for religion. The government's neutrality to religious institutions allowed those institutions freedom to innovate and flourish, and the national culture could draw upon a common civil religion that remained strategically vague, but assumed a broad consensus based on Christian moral values and democratic political values.

Adam Smith, the great laissez-faire economist, had a similar belief in the value of religious freedom, a commitment to a pluralism that would produce good fruits in the free marketplace of ideas. He did worry, however, that fanatical religions appealing to the ignorant could disrupt social harmony, and he prescribed quality education as a necessary balance to uninformed religious enthusiasms. Education could provide the inculcation of rationality that would protect society from the dangers of religious extremism. Thus rather implicitly, the role of religion as the source of authority and truth, and the role of religious institutions as the schools for moral edification and formation, are to be now assumed by secular institutions. It will be a long time before America has a fully developed system of public schools, but it is noteworthy that schools become the site of future anxiety and debate about the relationship of religion and politics, a topic we pick up below.

In France, without the possibility of encouraging a true religious pluralism, the revolutionary moment was not one of religious "freedom *to*" (practice and follow the religion of one's choice), but rather "freedom *from*" (the demands of the Catholic Church). And unlike the United States, what emerged was not the separation of church and state so much as a radical experiment in replacing the church with the state. The very social world that one inhabited, so saturated with Catholicism, was to be remade. One clear example of this was the French revolutionaries' experiment in creating a new calendar. The French revolutionary calendar was used by the French government from 1783 to 1805. Consistent with the adoption of the metric system in general, the new calendar had ten-day weeks with the names of the days being simply *primidi* ("first day"), *duodi* ("second day"),[21] and so on. Meant to be a more rational system for marking time, the more important reason for the adoption of the new calendar was to make the average Frenchman's experience of the passage of time unrelated to the traditional culture of popular Catholicism. Gone would be the experience of Friday abstinence and Sunday rest, gone Christmas and Easter. Gone would be all those reminders of the sacred foundations of everyday experience. But this remarkable effort at secularization did not simply remove symbolic meaning from the passage of time, making that experience neutral and disenchanted. The revolutionaries, by way of compensation, sought to establish a whole new festival life, with holidays to recognize virtue, talent, labor, and so on, coming at the end of the year, as well as seasonal festivals for things like youth, agriculture, and marriage. Mona Ozouf has referred to this as a part of the project to "transfer sacrality" from the church to the state.[22] We read of one priest objecting to the fact that a statue of liberty was left in his church after a republican ceremony was conducted there, and wanting it removed, much to the chagrin of republican authorities.[23] At the height of the revolutionary period, the goddess Reason was worshiped in the Notre Dame Cathedral, as tens of thousands of priests were either exiled, stripped of their office, or killed.

Such a radical and all-consuming revolutionary effort has to be seen as the attempt to eradicate the one religion that served as a final court of legitimacy in France, shaken but reestablished at the time of Henri IV. The revolutionaries sought to re-create for every Frenchman a new sense of the world, not just a newly acute sense of the moral, but a new world of sacred time and space. This was not the separation of church and state, not just the shrinking of the role of the church, or religion, but their wholesale replacement by the state. Henceforth, the state was to have no rivals, its power manifest not only in a coercive way, but deeply inherent in the very culture. And so even these revolutionary prophets often consciously embraced the language of religion to describe the ideas and institutions inaugurating the new dispensation of equality, fraternity, and liberty. David A. Bell has explored in an insightful way the way "the cult of the nation in France" grew out of the models of religious reform, even while resisting simplistic comparisons of religion and nationalism.[24]

If millions of French subjects, peasants and nobility alike, were to become citizens, if sovereignty was to reside in them and not in a single monarch, they would require education. And education-as-indoctrination and as the site of character-building would draw upon the example of religious reformers. Citizens should share a common French language, dropping their old dialects, and share a common creed, one not founded on a celestial destination but on a terrestrial fatherland. Bell highlights the call of the revolutionary Jean-Paul Rabaut de Saint-Étienne to create a revolutionary program of education to shape the entire population into a single people of shared culture and ideals. Rabaut's speech, later published as "Projet d'éducation nationale" in 1792, envisioned "a long list

FIGURE 23. *Culte de l'Être suprême* (Cult of the Supreme Being), by Pierre-Antoine Demachy, 1794. Carnavalet Museum. Courtesy of Creative Commons.

FIGURE 24. *La Liberté guidant le peuple* (Liberty Leading the People), by Eugène Delacroix, 1830. The Louvre. Courtesy of Creative Commons.

of obligatory civic functions, including physical exercises, parades, festivals, 'morality lessons,' the reading and memorization of key political texts, and the singing of patriotic songs."[25] Such a comprehensive program, sounding very Maoist to modern ears, went well beyond anything imagined for the medieval Catholic peasant. It was presaged, however, by the Jesuit Catholic reformers of the previous century. Whereas in medieval times, monastic institutions had embraced such utopian notions, monks never dreamed of thoroughly reforming "the world" but only created isolated schools of otherworldly men and women. Rabaut envisioned villagers gathering in national temples to sing patriotic hymns to the nation and learn from catechisms on how to be good citizens. Here he saw the goal as the remaking of this world, but the methods were drawn directly from religious reformers, who had taken the Protestant challenge to reform the religious lives of lay people.[26]

Bell notes that the nationalist quest for a common French language was colored by the background of the Catholic Reformation. It was reform-minded priests that used local patois for literary purposes, and many of their successors were quick to translate revolutionary documents into local languages in the 1790s. For a brief period (1790–92), leaders of the revolution embraced a multilinguistic program of translating all the decrees of the revolutionary assembly into the several languages of France. Soon they abandoned this course in favor of supporting a program of educating each and every French citizen in standard French.[27]

The Enlightenment project of education, like the colonial project, confidently assumes a universalism. Rather than going out into the world (whether that world be the rural provinces of France or to distant colonies in Africa, Asia, and America) to save souls, educational reformers and colonizers hoped to create rational men, sharing their vision for a civilized society. The rich diversity of cultures we purport to value today were seen by Enlightenment thinkers as vestiges of backwardness, to be supplanted by the singular culture of universal Reason. Although it is fashionable nowadays to criticize such views as hopelessly chauvinistic,[28] vestiges of such logic continue to pervade the discourses that shape the policies toward religion embraced by the modern secular regimes of Europe and America.

Early on, Enlightenment reformers and revolutionaries had difficulty squaring their utopian universalism with the diversity of human beings with whom they had to work. Replacing the single monarch with an assembly of Rational Men representing an equal citizenry would mean that that citizenry would include women and Jews. And in the colonies, would African slaves be liberated to participate in the universal project of civilization?

One enlightened priest, the *abbé* Henri Gregoire (d. 1831), remained Catholic, but followed these strands of universalism to their logical conclusion. Joining the revolution, Grégoire even accepted the idea that bishops be elected under the revolutionary Civil Constitution of the Clergy. Under this provision, even protestants and Jews could vote for the bishop of their region, and Grégoire was duly elected bishop of Blois, and became the first priest to swear allegiance to this constitution in 1790). Unlike many revolutionary priests who used local dialects to inspire the peasants, Grégoire fought for the primacy of the French language, a position consistent with the nationalist impulse to unity and monoculturalism. Even today, French is constitutionally the sole official language of the nation, and despite recent efforts to revive minority languages and dialects, the long history of repression has radically reduced the use of these tongues. Grégoire was also an abolitionist and friend of the Jews, taking the position that both groups were degraded by their position in society, and both were capable of advancement to a point when they would be full participants in society. But in his search for unity, Grégoire called for the renunciation of particulars. In the case of gender, where difference could not be overcome by education, conversion, and cultural adaptation, Grégoire had difficulty, and could never accept full political equality for women.

A friend of several prominent Jewish intellectuals and leaders, Grégoire harbored few of the prejudices of his contemporaries that Jews were an irredeemably alien racial group. He did dismiss their Talmudic religious practices as superstitious nonsense, and looked to the day when they would abandon their role as usurers. He thus reinforced many negative stereotypes about Jews, but unlike many French Enlightenment figures, truly believed in a singular human nature. All differences in human beings could be attributed to environmental causes. In time, with the development of proper social institutions, all the people of France would become one.

Arthur Hertzberg, who singles out Voltaire for criticism, sees Grégoire as an exception to the general pattern of Enlightenment thinkers to view Jews as forever inferior, alien, inassimilable. But even those tolerant of Jews and optimistic about their future as French citizens accepted "not the concretely existing one, but ... some new Jew that they would remake, or who would remake himself."[29] Voltaire had, however, no faith in Grégoire's project to rehabilitate the Jews, and his position remained a profoundly influential one, a toxic seed germinating to later form a virulent twentieth-century anti-Semitism.

One problem the Enlightenment project faced was its assumption of roles once taken by the church. If it were to relegate religion to a private sphere where its fanatic intolerance would no longer incite violence against sectarians and freethinkers, the modern nation-state would have to claim its own authority in the name of reason. But this authority, vested in the People, assumed that those republicans, those democrats, those egalitarians, could agree upon a common secular framework. That broad secular space could not admit those for whom religion took up too much space, if any at all. And Jews clinging to orthodox practices, unwilling to dine with others, seemed a group positively at odds with the secular Enlightenment dream. The revolutionary dream was a nation of equals, but equals unified in culture and carrying little luggage.

In his wish to dethrone Christianity, Voltaire looked to classical times, to see how Greeks and Romans governed a society housing many religions. Tellingly, he sided with the tolerant Romans, who were annoyed by Jewish and Christian claims of superiority. Jefferson would agree with him, and even Grégoire, who befriended many Jews and sought their welfare, assumed that in time, they would undergo reform, reject their backward ways, and become members of a common society founded on reason. The Enlightenment dream of creating a society based on a singular universal rationality confronted an intractable pluralism, and continued to suffer blind spots. In declaring the universal truths of *liberté, égalité,* and *fraternité,* the French revolutionaries continued to struggle with the idea that their new egalitarian society might necessarily be open to women, Jews, and black Africans (slave and free), just as Jefferson penned the noble words of the Declaration of Independence ("We hold these truths to be self-evident, that all Men are created equal") while he was a slave owner, and took his slave Sally Hemmings as a concubine, *in France,* and fathered six children with her. Grégoire, supporting the struggle of Haitians to win their freedom, even wrote to Jefferson to encourage him to the abolitionists' view, but though Jefferson wrote a respectful reply, he never freed his mistress, even in his will, though he did free their children, some of whom were later able to "pass" as white, thus obtaining equality and freedom by surrendering difference.

Thus, at the turn of the nineteenth century, both France and the United States had carried out revolutions to establish governments founded on principles of freedom and equality, rejecting old sources of legitimacy and authority in favor of rational and empirical principles. But in both places, real equality and universalism were unrealized. The scandal of slavery remained as a rebuke to the very principles that Americans invoked, and would tear the nation apart a half-century later. If all men were created equal, slavery could only be justified by arguing that Africans were not "civilized," and perhaps not fully human. The reluctance to extend suffrage to women was based on a similar biological determinism, associating women with the body while associating men with the mind.

TEMPERING THE RADICAL REVOLUTION: NAPOLEON BONAPARTE

In France, worries about the instability of their utopian society led to a revival of both monarchic and Catholic impulses. Even Robespierre, a leading figure during the Terror, opposed many of the policies of the de-Christianization of France and tried to establish a deist "cult of the Supreme Being" as a national religion supporting the cultivation of virtue in its citizens. When Napoleon came to power as a military hero in 1799, he publically supported many of the aims of the revolution, but opposed the radical attempt to uproot Catholicism from French culture. He negotiated the Concordat of 1801 with Pope Pius VII, an agreement that restored the civil status of the Catholic Church as the majority religion (if not the sole official religion) of the French nation, and granting Rome the right to depose bishops. Within a few years, the revolutionary calendar was dropped in favor of the old Gregorian one. In a sense, and in what seemed to be a popular move, Napoleon restored Catholicism to its central role in French culture.

He did retain many powers, however, that made the state dominant in its relation to the church. The government still nominated bishops, and paid the salaries of priests, who in turn, took oaths of allegiance to the nation. He appended the "Organic Articles" to the Concordat that further stipulated the state's oversight role in religious matters, for Protestants and Catholics (an addition not to the pope's liking). But perhaps the pope was sufficiently mollified, as a few years later, he crowned Napoleon emperor in a ceremony that seemed to restore the *ancien régime* of church and monarchy, a tradition going back to Charlemagne's crowning a thousand years before.

Such amity was, however, short-lived, as Napoleon later invaded Italy and exiled the pope, who in turn, excommunicated him. Napoleon, who once described himself as a deist with a fondness for Catholicism, pursued policies that advanced a revolutionary agenda of human equality and freedom of religion, while accommodating the church as a force for social order. And in pursuing both of these, he was primarily concerned with advancing his own power. The ultimate pragmatist, he wanted to avoid conflict, and issued orders that saw to it that Protestants and Catholics confined their worship to their respective church buildings in those towns where public processions might cause offense. He, like Grégoire, believed in the "regeneration" of the Jews, and he emancipated them from the ghetto in every land he conquered. In conquering Egypt, he took pains to listen carefully to Muslim clerics there, and even toyed with the idea of converting to Islam and emulating Alexander the Great in conquering the known world.

> O people of Egypt, they will tell you that I have come to destroy your religion. Do not believe it. Answer them that I have come to restore your rights, to punish the usurpers, and that I respect God, his prophet and the Qoran even more than the Mamluks.
>
> Tell them that all men are equal before God, and that only wisdom, talent, and virtue make differences among them. . . .
>
> O you judges, sheikhs, Imams and shorbadjis, tell the people that we, too, are real Muslims. Are we not the one who destroyed the Pope, who said that war must be made on the Muslims? Have we not always been the friends of the Grand Signior (may God accomplish his designs) and the enemies of his enemies? On the other hand, have not the Mamluks not always rebelled against the authority of the Grand Signior, that authority that they still do not recognize?[30]

But despite such public pronouncements, it is clear that Napoleon was always a pragmatist in matters of religion. He followed policies that advanced his power and prestige. He once declared: "It is by making myself Catholic that I brought peace to Brittany and Vendée [regions where royalist Catholics opposed the Revolution]. It is by making myself Italian that I won minds in Italy. It is by making myself Moslem that I established myself in Egypt. If I governed a nation of Jews, I should reestablish the Temple of Solomon."[31] Exiled to St. Helena at the end of his life, Napoleon had time to reflect on his exploits as conqueror and leader: what if he had returned victorious from Russia? Perhaps then relations with the pope might have been better. Napoleon makes a fascinating declaration on this:

> What then would have been the result, had I returned victorious and triumphant? I had consequently obtained the separation, which was so desirable, of the spiritual from the temporal, which is so injurious to his Holiness, and the commixture of which produces disorder in society in the name and hands of him, who ought himself to be the centre of harmony; and from that time,

I intended to exalt the Pope beyond measure, to surround him with grandeur and honours. I should have succeeded in suppressing all his anxiety for the loss of his temporal power; I should have made an idol of him; he would have remained near my person. Paris would have become the capital of Christendom, and I should have governed the religious as well as the political world. . . . I should have had my religious as well as my legislative sessions; my councils would have constituted the representation of Christianity, and the Popes would have only been the presidents. I should have called together and dissolved those assemblies, approved and published their discussions as Constantine and Charlemagne had done.[32]

Well read in history, Napoleon might fantasize thus, that like Constantine and Charlemagne, he would reign as a great emperor over a united Christendom with the Vatican in Paris. As with Akbar and the Ottoman sultans, the power of religion would be harnessed to the mystique of kingship. Religious authority would not be destroyed, as the revolutionaries had hoped, but absorbed by the political. The unity of church and state, as realized under Constantine, emperor and bishop, could have once again been achieved.

But Napoleon's dream of united imperial and sacred power was not to be. Despite his importance in spreading revolutionary ideals throughout much of Europe, his military and political dreams were reversed, and in France itself, the nineteenth century remained a tumultuous period after Napoleon, with monarchy replaced by republican rule followed by another monarchy followed by another republic, the Third Republic (1870–1940). Throughout this period, there were repeated battles between church and state, but the state retained its power over religion, as it does today. After the many battles between Catholic royalists and republicans, new laws in 1905 abrogated Napoleon's Concordat of 1801, definitively separating church and state.

Central to the effort to minimize Catholic influence in French culture, the Republicans struggled to establish state schools and forbid priests, brothers, and nuns from teaching. David Bell sees the establishment of secular education as central to the Third Republic project. He points specifically to the École normale superieure, calling it a "high temple" charged with inculcating patriotism in its students, many of whom go on to become important politicians. This was education in the eighteenth-century sense, intended to produce a certain cultural uniformity, dare we say orthodoxy:

The French republican nationalism born in the eighteenth century remained powerful and active through the middle of the twentieth, shaping the policies of the French state both at home and abroad and providing to its élites, educated in large portion at the Ecole Normal Superieure, a unique sense of mission. In this somber building on the rue d'Ulm in Paris, within site of the Panthéon, so reminiscent of a monastery in its architecture . . . the Republic trained its own secular Jesuits to go forth and forge not the church, but the nation.[33]

The church in nineteenth-century Europe would make one last stand against the forces of nationalism and secularization. The papal states, the pope's central Italian principality of three million people, fell to the armies of Italian nationalists in 1870, and the Vatican state, still a recognized "nation" in the center of Rome, shrank to its present size: two-tenths of a square mile. Pope Pius IX (r. 1846–78), having lost all his temporal power, responded by a vigorous new assertion of his spiritual power. The once progressive pope became an arch-conservative, issuing his famous *Syllabus of Errors,* a document that fundamentally rejected every aspect of Enlightenment thinking. Among its most striking statements, we find these examples of "false thinking":

> Human reason, without any reference whatsoever to God, is the sole arbiter of truth and falsehood, and of good and evil. [Number 3.]

> All the truths of religion proceed from the innate strength of human reason; hence reason is the ultimate standard by which man can and ought to arrive at the knowledge of all truths of every kind. [Number 4.]

> In the present day it is no longer expedient that the Catholic religion should be held as the only religion of the State, to the exclusion of all other forms of worship. [Number 77.]

> Protestantism is nothing more than another form of the same true Christian religion, in which form it is given to please God equally as in the Catholic Church. [Number 18.]

> The Church ought to be separated from the State, and the State from the Church. [Number 55.]

> Every man is free to embrace and profess that religion which, guided by the light of reason, he shall consider true. [Number 15.]

> It has been wisely decided by law, in some Catholic countries, that persons coming to reside therein shall enjoy the public exercise of their own peculiar worship. [Number 78.]

> The Roman Pontiff can, and ought to, reconcile himself, and come to terms with, progress, liberalism and modern civilization. [Number 80.]

FIGURE 25. Pope Pius IX blessing troops before the Capture of Rome, 1870. Photograph courtesy of Creative Commons.

This declaration, following his declaration of the immaculate conception of Mary (1854), set the stage for his calling of the First Vatican Council in 1869, as Italian nationalist soldiers fired cannonballs against the Vatican walls. With many liberal bishops, especially from Germany, staying away, the pope called for a declaration of papal infallibility. Despite some controversy, the council confirmed that doctrine, declaring that the pope was infallible when making a statement on faith and morals from the chair of Peter (*ex cathedra*). In modern times, only once was this power exercised, when Pius XII articulated the doctrine that the Virgin Mary was assumed bodily into heaven (the Assumption). Thus in all these ways, the role of the pope and the veneration of Mary, so alien to Protestants, let alone Enlightenment liberals, the Catholic Church sought to regain ground lost to the secular world. It is worth noting that this antimodernist Catholicism was ascendant at precisely the moment when over thirty million European Catholics—Irish, Germans, Poles, Italians—immigrated to that most Protestant nation, the United States.

CONCLUSION

Thus by the end of the nineteenth century, many parts of the western world saw secular institutions gain authority at the expense of religious

FIGURE 26. Pope Pius IX, 1870. Photograph courtesy of Creative Commons.

ones, even if large numbers of people still thought of themselves as religious. This meant the progressive shrinkage of the religious domain, and a clearer articulation of religion as something separate. This new definition of religion, largely based on a modern Protestant model that emphasized individualism and sincerity of belief, and implied pluralism, became dominant at exactly the same time as European colonialism made the religious worlds of non-Christians something to be studied and comprehended within this new paradigm. As Europeans encountered Hindus, Buddhists, Confucians, and others in their colonies, they conceived of those peoples as belonging to clubs similar to Protestant churches, and they gave those clubs names: Hindu*ism,* Buddh*ism,* Confucian*ism,* where no such names had hitherto existed. Those telling – *ism*s attest to the European project of seeing the religious life in the colonies as understandable in post-Enlightenment Protestant terms: belief, voluntary membership, and so on, even while those very Hindus, Buddhists, and Confucians did not think of their religion that way, since they lived in cultures where religion permeated life and had not undergone the shrinkage necessary for secular domains to be dominant. They were thus expected to undergo a crash course in that project. In the twentieth century, the secular age encompasses the whole world, not without fits and starts, and most everyone is expected to have an identity, both religious and national. Even so, the confident secularists who run that world assume that civilized and reasonable people can come to agreements even while they hold these different national and religious memberships. They can come to those agreements because they all can agree on a common framework of universal human rights, a moral regime that restricts the role of religion to the private sphere and keeps it in proper perspective. The United Nations and the first-world powers defend that regime; it is the meta-religion of the world order and supersedes all particular religions by the very fact that it seems so obvious. To that world, our world, we now turn.

CHAPTER 10

The Contemporary Era

The Worldwide Regime of Meta-Religion

Everyone has the right to freedom of thought, conscience and
religion; this right includes freedom to change his religion or
belief, and freedom, either alone or in community with others
and in public or private, to manifest his religion or belief in
teaching, practice, worship and observance.

—Universal Declaration of Human Rights, Article 18

In the nineteenth century, Europeans and Americans embraced religious
and philosophical views that emphasized the freedom of the individual
and with that, a consequent pluralism. They tried to uphold these ideals
even while clinging to practices like colonialism and slavery that stood
in direct contradiction to their egalitarian values. In much of the contemporary world, especially in the West, we are still plagued by similar
tensions. The developed world is one where old Enlightenment notions
of the freedom and dignity of individuals are upheld with a sort of religious assurance, and even promoted with missionary zeal, while being
tested by new notions of the legitimacy of diverse cultures to promote
their own values—values which may not accord with Euro-American
values promoted as universal. Before we turn back to a final examination of the would-be universalism that serves as a meta-religion for the
dominant, worldwide, neocolonial regime of the capitalist West, we
must first consider the encounter with countries like India and China,
which sought to forge, not only political independence from western
powers in the twentieth century, but intellectual and spiritual independence as well.

INDIA: RELIGIOUS CONFLICT AND SECULARISM, 1820 TO THE PRESENT

As noted in the previous chapter, Thomas Jefferson twice constructed versions of the New Testament gospels by literally excising those passages that presented Jesus as a divine figure capable of performing miracles. He wanted a Jesus who was a profound moralist but not an incarnate deity. The second of these projects he completed after his presidency, in 1820, late in his life. In the very same year, another child of the Enlightenment completed a similar portrait of Jesus as a moral teacher. He was at the other end of the world that Britain had colonized. His name was Rammohun Roy (d. 1833), a Bengali businessman and intellectual. And as Lynn Zastoupil has argued, the fact that Thomas Jefferson and Rammohun Roy created such similar works was not pure coincidence.[1] Both were committed monotheists, influenced by a worldwide Unitarian movement, both profoundly cosmopolitan rationalists, and both were part of an increasingly interconnected world. In nineteenth-century New England, seekers like Ralph Waldo Emerson and Henry David Thoreau would read Indian scriptures made public by people like Rammohun Roy and his successors. Thoreau would even "fain practice the yoga."[2] By the end of the century, the famous yogi Vivekananda would arrive in Chicago to captivate audiences at the Parliament of the World's Religions in 1893. He was able to do so in part because he had received a thoroughly English education.

Rammohun led a fascinating, intellectually adventurous life. A well-to-do Hindu brahmin, he studied Sanskrit in his youth, but tellingly, Arabic and Persian as well, and he first operated in an intellectual world where Islamic influences were still dominant. As a teenager, he composed Persian texts in which he explored the nature of the world's many religions in a comparative manner. Here it seems likely he was influenced by a Persian text, the *Dabistan-e Mazahib* (School of Religions),[3] written soon after Akbar's death but still well known in Rammohun's intellectual circles. In his own early work, Rammohun refers approvingly to Akbar's Din-i Ilahi (the Divine Faith, or Religion of God/Allah) as one of the world's religions that he evaluates. Thus before he learned English and entered the European intellectual world with such vigor, he was already heir to an Indian Islamicate tradition of universalism and Greek rationalism.[4]

In the decades before the British formally incorporated much of India as part of Queen Victoria's empire, Rammohun Roy worked with East

India Company managers, learned flawless English, and began a career as a social and religious reformer. In the latter capacity, he cultivated friendships with a number of missionaries in India, Unitarians as well as Christians upholding more orthodox creeds. He became a critic of aspects of Hinduism, especially traditions of "idolatry" and polytheism, thus encouraging these missionaries in the hope that he would soon convert to their faiths. He never did convert, but did win many fans among social reformers in India and Britain, taking up causes like the abolition of *sati* and child marriage. When he came to Britain at the end of his life, he was a celebrity and public intellectual, and may have even entertained the ambition of running for parliament.[5]

Unlike the French and the Portuguese, the British never pursued a policy of Christianization as part of their imperial project.[6] In fact, missionaries were often discouraged by those British officials more concerned with governing and transacting business in a profitable manner. Missionaries were always capable of getting in the way. In the famous words of Macaulay: "We must at present do our best to form a class who may be interpreters between us and the millions whom we govern; a class of persons, Indian in blood and colour, but English in taste, in opinions, in morals, and in intellect."[7] Taste and morals, but not religion. In many ways, Rammohun Roy was already an incarnation of Macauley's ideal.

Or so it seemed to those British liberals who tried to cast the imperial project as an exercise in bringing the benefits of civilization to a backward world. In fact, Rammohun was quite aware of the real purpose of the British in India—the extraction of wealth—and he was not reticent in pointing out to the British their tendency to withhold from colonized subjects the very rights that they proclaimed as universal to British subjects at home—things like freedom of the press. He thus embodied the contradictions inherent in the colonial subject and enterprise. In the imbalance of power, he sought some of the goods to be obtained from his colonial masters, including intellectual and spiritual goods, but in adopting these, and in debating and his English tutors in their own language, did he not submit to their paradigms of knowledge and power even while trying to resist them? Such dilemmas were to characterize the colonial world in the nineteenth and early twentieth century, and are surely still present today in neocolonial cultures across the world.

Successors to Rammohun Roy, especially in the vibrant British colonial domain of Bengal, sought both to reform Hinduism and Hindu practices, producing a sort of neo-Hinduism that resembled a tolerant

FIGURE 27. Swami Vivekananda, 1893. Thomas Harrison, photograph, courtesy of Creative Commons.

Unitarianism in ideology and a privatized Protestantism in practice. They did so, all the while, in order to revive what they saw as a decadent and weak culture incapable of competing with an increasingly powerful and intrusive British presence. The Bengali spiritual leader Vivekananda (d. 1902) captivated both Indian and western audiences with a message that today seems to be quintessentially Indian in its inclusivism, tolerance, and universal appeal. He became the face of Indian spirituality and "yoga" with his charismatic speech at the World Parliament of Religions in Chicago in 1893,[8] but however much he was largely followed by people interested in a very individualistic and apolitical religion of personal development, he nonetheless harbored great dreams of Indian empowerment and independence. As such, he was a bridge to the extraordinary figure of Mahatma Gandhi.

Central to the construction of a modern Indian identity, especially among the majority Hindu population, was the notion of religious tolerance, and no one was more important in articulating this ideal than Vivekananda. Drawing on classical Vedantin ideas, he spread the gospel of inclusivism, that all religions were different paths up the same mountain. Ironically, since Vivekananda saw Hinduism as the tradition that best embodied such inclusivism, he thus also asserted its superiority. So Vivekananda could appeal to outsiders by claiming them as spiritual brothers and sisters, and insiders by the proud assertion of Hinduism as the clearest exponent of tolerance and inclusivity. He also adopted the orientalist trope that while the West excelled in worldly matters, India was great in the spiritual realm: "This is the great ideal before us, and everyone must be ready for it—the conquest of the whole world by India—nothing less than that. . . . Let foreigners come and flood the land with their armies, never mind. Up, India, and conquer the world with your spirituality! Aye, as has been declared on this soil first, love must conquer hatred, hatred cannot conquer itself. Materialism and all its miseries can never be conquered by materialism. . . . Spirituality must conquer the West."[9]

Oddly enough, Vivekananda's religious inclusivism became the intellectual basis of modern India's version of secularism. Whereas people the world over revere Mahatma Gandhi as a modern saint, in India, Gandhi's political movement to win independence was premised on the idea of a multireligious society, and that multireligious society depends on meta-religious assumptions that Indians refer to as "secularism." This distinctively Indian version of secularism has its Hindu roots (just as western secularism has Christian ones), but has nonetheless been opposed by those who have felt the Indian nation-state should be founded on explicitly Hindu cultural ideals.

Thus from the colonial period to the present, Indians have clashed over the question of national identity. Could India be a secular state with an inclusive common culture that had room for Muslims as well as for Hindus (and numerous other minorities as well)? Or did the Muslim minority represent an alien and inassimilable group? Was India *Hindustan,* an essentially Hindu culture and nation? Followers of Gandhi felt that India was one nation, with a capacious and welcoming culture that could embrace and accommodate members of all religious communities.

FIGURE 28. Mahatma Gandhi, late 1930s. Photograph courtesy of Creative Commons.

Their view, upheld by the Gandhian Congress Party, has largely won the day, but Hindu nationalists have continually tested them, and secularists more generally.[10]

In Gandhi's day, the British justified their continued rule over South Asia on the grounds that their powerful presence prevented conflict between the Hindu and Muslim populations. Many have indicted the British for a "divide and rule" policy that exacerbated tensions between the two communities. Meanwhile, Gandhi fought hard to win independence for an India that would not exclude Muslims, but he was unable to win over Muhammad Ali Jinnah (d. 1948), leader of the Muslim League, who agreed with the British that partition of India was necessary in order that Muslims not live as an oppressed minority in a nation dominated by Hindus.

Some have characterized this disagreement as one between the "one-nation theorists" and "two-nation theorists." One-nation theorists look back to the age of Akbar and argue that under Muslim rule India evolved a common culture of tolerance and syncretism. Against that view, two-nation theorists argue that Hindus and Muslims are two distinct groups and that without a British presence, would revert to violent conflict. As it turned out, independence did indeed come to a divided India, which suffered a bloody partition in 1947 with the creation of two independent nations: a *secular* India (that still had a Muslim population of 12–15 percent), and an Islamic Pakistan, made up of regions in the east (Bengal) and west where Muslims were in a majority. In 1971, East Pakistan broke away in a war of independence, becoming the nation of Bangladesh, thus giving the lie to the claim that religious identity trumps other factors. The Bengali-speaking east, separated from the west by nine hundred miles, formed a new nation in which the national anthem was written by the Bengali Nobel laureate Rabindranath Tagore, a Hindu who lived his whole life in India. Those who died in this military conflict are referred to as the "language martyrs," a fact which suggests that theirs is a nation of Bengali speakers more than it is a nation of Muslims.

Thus modern South Asia includes three countries, India, Pakistan, and Bangladesh, which were all formerly part of colonial India, and each with a Muslim population of over 150 million. India has fought several wars against Pakistan since independence, and for many Indians, Pakistan represents an Islamic enemy, and thus Indian Muslims are often seen therefore as unpatriotic and disloyal to the Indian—read Hindu—cause. Nonetheless, following Gandhi's lead, the postindependence Congress Party has continued to forge a secular alliance that includes the support of Muslim voters.

Gandhi himself, even while winning a following largely through a spiritual charisma one would characterize as Hindu in nature, cultivated a personal piety that included acts like devotional readings of the *Qur'an*. He was also much moved by Christian scriptures and hymns. In his own mind, his religion was a personal quest open to the truth of all religions, the embodiment of tolerance and inclusivity. The fact that the very ground of his inclusivism was, as it were, a Hindu ground, was not something he was largely conscious of, and the legacy of Gandhian thinking in modern India is a secularism that is Hindu in its spirit.

Hindu nationalist opponents of Gandhi and his way of thinking, from those who plotted his assassination to current members of organizations and parties devoted to asserting Hindu supremacy, have opposed accommodation and placation of Muslims and other minorities. For them, Gandhi's Congress Party has promoted a "pseudosecularism," in that it recognizes a particular religion's rights in law rather than treating all citizens as equal. One example of this debate over secularism occurred in the 1980s over the question of a separate "personal law" for the Muslim community. This case involved the divorcée Shah Bano Begum, who asked the court to grant her a financial settlement in line with the common civil code rather than the smaller amount she received according to the personal law of the Muslim community to which she belonged.[11] It thus raised fundamental questions: Do not all Indian citizens deserve a common civil code? Or would the enforcement of such a code mean the destruction of any legal protection for distinctive cultural practices of minority communities? In other words, does the law recognize individuals or communities? If the first, all persons stand equally before a single law without regard to their community or religion. If the second, the right of a religious community to maintain a distinctive way of life can be accommodated and protected. The first position is one kind of secularism, in that it claims that one's religion is irrelevant. It avoids facing the fact that the common, secular civil code may assume values of the majority community and thus quietly but powerfully maintain Hindu dominance. The second position upholds a secularism which accepts that a truly tolerant society must recognize and protect religious communities, otherwise individual members of minority communities will always be subject to the hegemony of majority opinion.

With the rise of the Bharatiya Janata Party (BJP) in the 1990s, Hindu nationalists posed a real challenge to the long dominant Congress Party. They appealed to Hindus who felt Congress placated the Muslim minority and that the Hindu majority population should assert its primacy. They did so under an ideology called *Hindutva*, "Hindu-ness," claiming rather disingenuously that this term did not assert a "Hindus first" policy of *religious* nationalism, but rather the rightful place of a certain Hindu "culture." Surprisingly, the supreme court of India authorized their right to campaign under the *Hindutva* banner even though explicit appeals to religion are disallowed under current campaign laws. By emotional appeals to Hindu pride, the BJP managed to manufacture violent symbolic conflicts that provoked political crisis and ultimately won for them parliamentary supremacy in 1998, where they remained in power until 2004, and again in the 2014 election.

The BJP's most significant campaign appealing to Hindu pride was the effort to destroy a mosque in the northern Indian town of Ayodhya. That mosque, the Babri Masjid, was alleged to have been built above a destroyed Hindu temple marking the birthplace of the Hindu avatar Ram.[12] Even though such stories of the mosque being built atop a Hindu temple to Ram seem not to predate the British period, and even though Ram is a legendary figure said in the scriptures to have lived eons ago, the emotional campaign had salience, and resulted in the mob destruction of the mosque in 1992, with the clear collusion of the police. The riots associated with the campaign both in 1992 and again in 2002, when Muslims were blamed for burning a train with Hindu pilgrims returning from Ayodhya,[13] have claimed the lives of thousands and again raise the question of the power and meaning of secularism in a country where religious identity is so marked, and where government institutions (state governors, local police forces) can be controlled by a Hindu majority prejudiced against Muslims as a group.

The goal of Gandhian politics was to create an Indian national identity that, though infused with spiritual values, transcended identification with particular communities. The primary identification of many people in India, however, is with a religious or caste identity, and thus their patriotic identification with the nation is rather weak. Some take pride in the rich diversity of a country with thousands of castes and hundreds of languages and dialects, where Jews, Christians, and Zoroastrians have lived alongside Hindus, Jains, Buddhists, Muslims, and Sikhs for centuries. But managing that diversity while trying to create the conditions for equality has been a staggering challenge. The meta-religion of tolerant Gandhian inclusivism has been relatively weak, but the nation has nonetheless maintained a stable democracy and in recent decades, a fast-growing economy.

CHINA: MANAGING RELIGION AND IDEOLOGY, 1839–PRESENT

With a far more robust tradition of central government than India, China has had a kind of secular meta-religion at the heart of its imperial ideology since at least the Qin Dynasty, but the turmoil of the nineteenth century resulted in major disruptions. Since then, China has struggled to find a replacement for the classical structure of centralized imperial authority buttressed by a Confucian ideology of self-sacrificing, gentlemanly virtue. In this section, we will consider three telling moments in the history of modern China and its search for meaning, legitimacy, and power: the Taiping Rebellion (1850–64); the rise of Maoism as a meta-religion for the state (1949–76); and finally, the state suppression of Falun Gong (1995–2004).

Unlike India, most of China avoided direct British colonization, but western political and economic domination still meant that the period 1839–1949 was surely a low point in the history of Chinese civilization. The century of weakness and poverty began with the disastrous Opium Wars. Worried about an imbalance of trade, and following the sort of logic implied in Grotius's defense of free trade, the British intervened militarily to assert their right to import opium into China to a population increasingly addicted to and debilitated by the drug. After a devastating and humiliating military defeat in that conflict, once-proud China entered a century of economic, political, and social crisis. The result was the destruction of the Confucian ideology at the heart of Chinese religious and political life for the past two thousand years.

One response to this malaise was the Tai Ping Rebellion (1850–64). In many ways, it was the sort of utopian and millenarian movement that characterized previous challenges to the imperial state, but oddly enough, it was a movement led by a man, Hong Xiuquan (d. 1864), who thought of himself as a Christian. Hong's family had hoped that he would pass the civil service examination and win a coveted position as an official in the government. But after long study and repeated failures, he suffered something of a nervous breakdown, accompanied by visions that he later interpreted as revelations from God that he was Jesus's younger brother, on earth to destroy demon worship and idolatry. His exposure to Christianity had been slight, and his unorthodox teaching appalled the Protestant missionaries with whom he had contact. Despite his vigorous denunciation of idolatry, Hong nonetheless believed that Guan Yin, the Buddhist goddess of mercy, dwelled in heaven with Jesus as his divine sister.[14] Moreover his movement, the Tai Ping (Great Peace), bore a name reminiscent of ancient Daoist millenarian groups, and had many of the marks of older Buddhist and Daoist sectarian rebels.

Surprisingly, Hong was able to win a large following, first among members of his own minority community, the Hakkas, but later among a large number of other disaffected peasants, who followed him in a quest to remake China into an egalitarian society. At the peak of his power, Hong was the leader of a successful rebel army, and governed a large portion of southern China. The central government ultimately subdued his forces, but only with great effort. The human cost of this rebellion, from war, disease, and famine, is estimated to be over twenty million deaths.[15] One might be tempted to write off Hong's visions as those of a madman, but the strength of his movement, the very fact that such a large part of China fell under his power, suggests that we must appreciate the fact that the Taiping God worshipers were, like so many peasant movements in the past, driven both by a sincere religious fervor, and by the passionate desire to create a truly egalitarian society.

Where Hong's revolution failed, his admirer Mao Zedong succeeded a century later. Mao (d. 1976) became a committed Marxist when China was at its lowest point, and he battled for decades to finally emerge as the Great Leader of a single-party socialist state. As a Marxist, Mao saw religion as superstition, to be replaced by scientific principles. Like the leaders of the French Revolution, Maoists replaced traditional religion with a Marxist ideology and practice that took on many aspects of religion, and, in many respects, began to resemble the meta-religious ideology of the old Confucian state they had so vigorously destroyed.

Mao himself became the object of a personality cult, and a small book of his quotations known as *The Little Red Book* served as a scripture for party members. The tone of many of these sayings is religious in nature, exalting noble self-sacrifice for the glory of China and the liberation of the workers. For example: "Wherever there is struggle there is sacrifice, and death is a common occurrence. But we have the interests of the people and the sufferings of the great majority at heart, and when we die for the people it is a worthy death."[16]

Ambitious central planning did not produce the economic and agricultural miracles expected, but no one could challenge Mao's authoritarian rule. Only later did the outside world learn of the massive starvation of perhaps twenty million people that resulted from the failed experiments. With the Cultural Revolution (1966–76), Mao initiated even more radical efforts to totally disrupt resistant forms of social hierarchy, turning over much authority to teen-aged bands of Red Guards. It was an effort to make revolution permanent, an ongoing process of renewal that disallowed any group from claiming elite status. Intellectuals were banished to the fields to learn from peasants, and doctors were banished from hospitals that were turned over to untrained students.[17]

In the years since Mao's death, China's leaders have maintained an official allegiance to Maoism, but have introduced a wide range of policies to liberalize the economy and link it to market forces. While embracing capitalism in deed if not in theory, they have held tight to the reins of power. Most prominently Deng Xiaoping authored the major shifts in

FIGURE 29. *Mao, the Great Helmsman,* by Zhang Zhenshi, 1950. Courtesy of Creative Commons.

economic policy while at the same time cracking down mercilessly on protesting students in the Tiananmen Square democratic uprising of 1978.

As China grew prosperous and people lost faith in Maoist egalitarian ideals, many Chinese suffered personal crises of faith and meaning, but consistent with the long history of state suppression of "cults," contemporary Chinese leaders have continued to view alternative religious systems as suspicious and dangerous. Christian churches are supposed to be registered with the government; Muslims in western China and Buddhists in Tibet are persecuted as troublesome schismatic groups; and "sects" of all kinds are monitored, controlled, and suppressed.

Scholars have noted the tendency of the Chinese state, throughout its long history, to treat all sectarian religions as political rivals, whether or not their adherents do indeed have political inclinations.[18] In time, however, even apolitical groups, under the pressures of official disapproval, become political. Thus the state's policy of suspicion and repression becomes self-fulfilling. Such is the pattern that seems borne out, once again, in the story of the rise of Falun Gong.

Falun Gong (Dharma Wheel Practice) is one name for a sectarian movement founded in 1992. In a very short period it became enormously popular, by 1999 growing to a following of tens of millions of Chinese.[19] Despite the Buddhist name and teachings drawn from both Buddhism and Daoism, Falun Gong's charismatic founder, Li Hongzhi, claimed that his movement was not a religious one, but rather a "practice" or system of personal cultivation, a primary aim of which was good health. It was one of many such movements originating in the mid-twentieth century, and described in Chinese as *qigong* (the cultivation of *qi,* or *chi,* the "vital force"). Li's reluctance to claim the title of religion is telling. Given government suspicion of all "cults," it was doubtless safer to market the movement as one of cultivation and health. In this, we see a similarity to the way yoga is marketed in the West, first as a healthful practice, then perhaps as a kind of no-name "spirituality," but almost never as a religion, or branch of Hinduism. In the Chinese setting, Falun Gong first gained popularity as a "practice" that promised bodily healing, but it also answered the needs of many Chinese for a sense of spiritual growth. At first, the government embraced Falun Gong and other *qigong* movements as based on science, albeit traditional Chinese science. Like acupuncture, here was something scientific and thus respectable, and free from the taint of superstition so repugnant to forward-looking Marxists. On the other hand, it was authentically Chinese, and thus also not imported slavishly from the West.

But with such a Buddhist name, and with such explosive popularity, it was doubtless too much to hope that the government might continue to grant its approval. In the end, the government condemned it as an evil and heretical cult. When the government first became threatened by its popularity, and cracked down, Falun Gong followers, ten thousand strong, demonstrated in Beijing on April 25, 1999. Massive repression resulted, with the government incarcerating thousands of Falun Gong followers, torturing many.

Thus we see that the Chinese state, like the ancient Chinese imperial regime, sees itself as the guardian of unity. It can tolerate a degree of religious diversity, but is quick to respond to any challenge to its final authority, and given its modern efficiency, it can repress any religious movement with brutal results. So while every modern state has an inter-

FIGURE 30. Falun Gong demonstration. E. Christman, photograph courtesy of Creative Commons.

est in managing religion and restricting it to those forms that do not threaten it directly, Chinese leaders do not hesitate to use massive force to crush any movement that even suggests that there may be sources of truth and meaning not emanating from the central government.

WESTERN EUROPEAN SECULARISM AND THE CHALLENGE OF ISLAM: CHRISTENDOM REPLACED

Europeans were drawn into the two great world wars when nationalism was at its peak, and colonialism was in its last chapter. For Germans, the radical nationalism of the Nazi period was the attempt to forge a common national identity by scapegoating the Jewish minority, and the horrific result of such an ideology meant that nationalism based on race lost any claim to legitimacy. That fact, in addition to the staggering losses of the great wars, led European leaders to establish a common market in 1957 (later called the European Union) to find economic and political incentives to unity and peace. Ironically, despite the poverty of the idea of racial identity, the now racialized Jews were offered a new Jewish homeland, the modern state of Israel, carved out of old Ottoman lands in Palestine.[20] Jews, who had lived for centuries in Europe as a religious minority, were now offered, based on their ethnicity rather than their religion, a place to build a Zionist nation. For Palestinians and the other Arabs and Muslims of the Middle East, this represented simply another face of European colonialism, with consequent political results still with us today.

At the end of World War II, Britain and France had survived the German challenge to their sovereignty at great cost and began the process of relinquishing their hold on their colonies. In 1947, India and Pakistan gained their independence. In 1949, China won its war of independence and established a Maoist state. French colonies, especially in North Africa, gained independence in an agonizing manner over the two decades following the end of World War II.

If the nation-state took over many functions once considered the domain of the church, the formation of a multinational body like the European Union created something of a replacement for medieval Christendom, forming a cultural and political realm in which certain values are assumed and institutionalized. Wendy Brown writes: "In the mid-nineteenth through the mid-twentieth centuries, the West imagined itself as standing for civilization against primitivism, and in the cold war years for freedom against tyranny; now these two recent histories are merged in the warring figures of the free, the tolerant, and civilized on one side, and the fundamentalist, the intolerant, and the barbaric on the other."[21] The European Union is one multinational attempt to embody such a postreligious ideology. Early attempts to include religious statements in the EU charter were easily turned aside, but broad support for basic human rights is at the heart of the EU project. So, for example, no nation may enter the EU if it does not abolish capital punishment; as part of its candidacy to join the union, Turkey abolished the death penalty in 2004.

Given the heritage of the seventeenth-century wars of religion, Europeans by the twentieth century had come to assume that the nation-state was the final arbiter, and that religion was largely restricted to the private sphere. But this quiet assumption requires people to ignore the fact that imbedded in the secular regime of the nation state are meta-religious values. Moreover, in Europe, more so than in the United States, the state may attempt to control and manage religion, but still cooperate with those religious institutions which support its social programs, especially in the domain of education. And since education is the realm in which liberal societies invest so much energy in producing proper citizens, it is in that realm that the greatest anxieties about the future of the nation and society are likely to manifest.

In the modern capitalist West, the diminution of religion, its demotion before a regime of Enlightenment universalism, is now so fully naturalized that the meta-religion replacing Christendom is almost invisible. There are places, however, where it is defended in ways that make it more obvious. Two that I will consider are (1) arguments about the nature of secular/state education (soft power); and (2) the war on terror (the response to relatively weak, nonstate actors who use terror to challenge the massively powerful, militarized state on the basis of nonsecularist religious ideologies). Those terrorists are then declared barbarians and attacked not so much because their religion is odious, but because they have challenged the right of the state to exercise unquestioned authority in the name of a naturalized meta-religious ideology. The idea of acting on the basis of absolute *religious* commitments and using violence to pursue a religious agenda, historically something perfectly legitimate, is now framed as barbaric and perverse, while the *state's* use of violence in pursuit of political goals is assumed to be reasonable.

When western Europe was torn apart by religious violence in the seventeenth century, the last vestiges of a singular Latin Christendom were destroyed and nation-states asserted their ultimate authority—an authority that extended to the religious as well as the political realm. The Enlightenment solution of the eighteenth century was the elevation of a secular rationality and the consequent demotion of religion and the growth of the idea of tolerance. With the nation-state claiming the authority to manage the multiple religions of the realm, patriotic national identity could not rest easily upon religious foundations. As we have seen, this was especially true in France, home to the Enlightenment, where notions of a secularism rooted in a universal rationality ultimately triumphed and became the hallmark of the French Republic.

During the twentieth century, a number of political and institutional changes made possible the development of institutions, especially educational institutions, that would support a French republican state and a French identity. By progressively removing the church from public life in general, and the schools in particular, the state was able to establish what has become known as *laïcité*, a secularism that emphasizes the necessity of establishing "neutral" public spaces, where religion cannot enter. The French approach to nation building involved the replacement of religion as the system of meaning in the public sphere, making all persons equal members of society, regardless of their religion. Of course the price of that equality was the erasure of religion as a public force. To be a citizen was to embrace a French identity as one's primary identity, and to limit one's religious identity—Catholic, Protestant, Jewish—to the private domain.

With this heritage, the French today are less inclined to support the ideas of multiculturalism. As several writers have noted, there is no place in France for "hyphenated identities," no equivalent of the American terms Irish-American, Italian-American, African-American. Even regional identities in France have been discouraged and massive educational efforts have been taken to assure the use of standard French nationwide in opposition to those who would promote regional languages and dialects.[22] It is this commitment to a singular French identity and cultural unity that explains "why the French don't like headscarves," as John Bowen argues in his book about controversies surrounding the banning of Islamic dress in public schools and offices in contemporary France.[23]

For anyone convinced of the necessity of accommodating multiple cultures, the 2004 French ban of all "conspicuous signs" of religious identity from places like public schools seems boorish, but it is consistent with French republican ideals, and for a fairly large majority of Frenchmen, schools have the role of producing a united society in the face of two challenges: regional and religious difference.[24] After a century of struggle against the Catholic Church to achieve this end, the contemporary worry that a population of mostly North African immigrants would develop a separate, ghettoized subculture became especially worrisome. While the French law forbids the wearing of *any* conspicuous sign of religious identity, the Sikh turban, for example,[25] the popular discourse concentrated on the headscarf worn by Muslim women. The headscarf became a dense symbol of resistance to certain French values assumed to be sacred.

Most prominently, the French saw the headscarf as an affront to the ideal of sexual equality. Joan Scott argues: "Sexual equality (like *laïcité*) has become a primordial value. Those who don't share this value (Muslims in this case) are not only different but inferior—less evolved, if capable at all of evolution. The ultimate proof of the inassimilability of Islam thus comes down, or adds up, to sexual incompatibility. This incompatibility was so profound that it compromised the future of the nation. . . . The French gender system was represented then not only as superior but 'natural.'"[26] Thus, according to this view, the intolerance for this particular cultural expression is not a critique of Islamic religion per se, but the critique of something that transgresses the universal value of equality and human rights. Both the state and society are now, after much travail, founded on universal principles that transcend the views embedded in culturally specific, particular religions. To reintroduce those sorts of claims to an enlightened society would be a tragic regression. There are, of course, French opponents of such thinking, but this summarizes a republican ideology that has widespread allegiance on the left and the right.

What must be stressed here is that principles thought to be universal are not considered as products of a particular history and culture. They are treated as transcendent and over and above "culture." Thus what minority groups, especially European Muslims, uphold as their distinctive way of life is treated as a "culture," while the hegemonic values of the majority are products of rationality and not marked as coming from one culture among many. They descend from on high, a gift to humanity.

We should note that French *policy,* as opposed to its secular ideology, often involves government engagement with religious communities. The former interior minister and later president Nicolas Sarkozy (2007–12) argued that mosques should be funded by the state rather than through foreign investment. He was instrumental in working with Muslim organizations to develop representative bodies like the Conseil français du culte musulman (French Council of the Muslim Faith, CCFM), with which the government could consult. Such a move was motivated by the desire to encourage leadership among "moderate" Muslims. Sarkozy even wrote a book on religion, *La république, les religions, l'espérance,*[27] in which he admitted the centrality of Catholicism to French culture and even suggested that secularism left the culture without a firm moral anchor. Sarkozy's willingness to engage Muslim groups, to recognize them politically as groups, goes against the traditional French secularism, and suggests some of the tensions present in *laïcité.*

Western European nations have seen a large influx of Muslim immigrants in recent decades. In the early stages of this process, they were often treated as racial minorities, but since the Iranian Revolution (1979) and the Salman Rushdie affair (1989), and especially since 9/11 (2001), they have come to be considered, and have come to consider themselves, first and foremost, as Muslims. In other words, ethnic or racial identity has given way to religious identity, and a religious identity of the most self-conscious and ideological sort. Nonetheless, the story of European Islam since the 1970s is not a simple narrative. Muslims coming to Europe have come with different cultural and religious styles, and the host countries have developed different policies in accommodating these populations. Finally, the children and grandchildren of original immigrants develop new understandings of Islam and their place in European society.

Although there are fascinating tales to tell of Muslim immigrants in some of the smaller countries of western Europe (e.g., Denmark, Sweden, the Netherlands), I will turn here to two larger nations—Britain and Germany—with significant Muslim populations. As we have seen, France, with its revolutionary and republican heritage and Europe's largest Muslim minority of close to six million, most from North Africa, has sought to assimilate Muslims as equal citizens while minimizing the degree to which the Islamic community is recognized as a site of communal identity. Britain, with a Muslim immigrant population of close to three million, a majority of whom have come from South Asia, has sought to accommodate Muslims within a multiculturalist framework. Germany, which has a population of more than four million Muslims who originally came as "guest workers" (*Gastarbeiter*), mostly from Turkey, has struggled to evolve policies to deal with the fact that these visitors are now unlikely to return "home."

In contrast to the French situation, Britain has never maintained a completely secular school system. Students are able to attend tuition-free schools that are funded by the state and follow national curricula, but which are supported by religious communities and maintain the ethos of those communities. The vast majority of these institutions are affiliated to the Church of England and the Roman Catholic Church, but there are also Methodist, Jewish, Sikh, and Muslim schools. When people imagine that schools are perhaps the most important institutions for shaping children's worldviews, we see that Britain has embraced the notion that those children can be both good British citizens and faithful followers of diverse faiths.

In Bradford, where 16 percent of the population is Muslim, mostly of South Asian descent, and Muslims are often elected to parliament, an elite Muslim high school for girls (ages eleven to eighteen) receives full state funding. That school, Feversham College, boldly states on its website:

FEVERSHAM COLLEGE IS A COLLEGE WITH AN ISLAMIC ETHOS

The foundation of the college is based on the Quran and Sunnah (tradition) of the Prophet Muhammad (peace be upon him). Therefore, Islamic Ethos is at the heart of everything we do. As a college with an Islamic Ethos we seek to help our students develop the core universal principles of equality, fairness, justice, tolerance and respect for others. We nurture our students so they can become confident individuals, responsible citizens and successful learners.

Throughout the year we celebrate the events of Eid ul Fitr and Eid ul Adhaa. The month of Ramadan brings about a special and unique spirit throughout the school. We have many activities during this blessed month such as whole school reminders about Ramadhan, Iftar bags and Ramadhan activities. Our students also have the opportunity to reflect upon the blessings that have been bestowed on them and also to empathise with those people less fortunate. During the month of Ramadan fundraising takes place for a variety of charities in order to support families across the world.[28]

Consistent with that ethos is the school's uniform, the *jilbab,* or conservative outfit involving complete coverage of the body except for the face and hands. Here the sort of tensions produced by the French resistance to schoolgirls wearing any clothing blatantly religious in nature seems to be happily tolerated under a system that allows for different religious groups to maintain enclaves where their values are protected. And yet, despite this commitment to multiculturalism, we find signs of tension, where "British values and culture" are promulgated to the minority Muslim community out of the fear that society cannot tolerate too great a degree of diversity and still cohere. Bradford was also the site of Muslim protest of the publication of Salman Rushdie's novel *The Satanic Verses,* a book many Muslims considered blasphemous, so much so that the Iranian leader Ayatollah Khomeini pronounced a *fatwa* calling for the author's death.[29] The Muslims of Bradford gathered for a ritual burning of the book, provoking in return a liberal backlash among those who see freedom of speech as something sacred. Then the deputy home minister, John Patten, wrote an open letter to the Muslim community entitled "On Being British."[30] As Talal Asad has ably analyzed it, we have here a sort of neocolonial document lecturing the minority community (as if they were not citizens) on essential British values, including a fluent command of English, and a "clear understanding of British democratic processes, of its laws, the system of Government and the history that lies behind them."[31] In other words, Patten is calling for Muslims to commit to a British way of life in which Islam can have a role, but one circumscribed by a common culture. Following Raymond Williams, Asad writes of the meaning of that word *culture:* "Where once culture meant the training that provided mind and soul with their intellectual and moral accomplishments, it now also means an entire way of life—the common way of life of a whole people."[32] So, "culture" now stands in for the role once played by a dominant Christianity, and now is deployed as a means of control and power, a totalizing project not all that different than the French version of universalism. Accepting British "culture" means accepting the idea that religion is a private matter.

Enrolling large numbers of Muslims students, not all schools in Britain have been able to establish a school uniform policy without controversy.

The complexity of the very idea of "British values" can be seen in a long legal case and controversy concerning the right of a Muslim girl to wear the conservative Muslim attire (a *jilbab*) to a school which had 80 percent Muslim students and had previously agreed upon a uniform consistent with the cultural values of most of those students, but one less restrictive than the *jilbab*. In this case, the girl, Shabina Begum, after attending the school for several years and wearing the uniform, decided at the age of sixteen to adopt the more conservative dress. The school, located in a suburb of London, had a uniform policy that was developed by the school administration, a group that included Muslims, and local mosques and Islamic organizations. The students, mostly of South Asian descent, were expected to wear the *shalwar kameez,* commonly seen in Bangladesh, India, and Pakistan. Shabina Begum felt that the school uniform was not consistent with more conservative Muslim traditions and she adopted clothing more common to the Arab Middle East.

The school's resistance seemed to be motivated by a number of concerns. First, they did not want students competing, as it were, in an effort to exhibit ever more strict standards of Islamic behavior. Secondly, they did not want radical Islamists influencing their policies; it became known that the girl involved, an orphan, was under the influence of her brother, a member of a radical group, Hizb ut-Tahrir. Finally, school officials felt that the whole point of a school uniform is that everyone dresses similarly, and that girls should not feel pressure to conform to the ideals of external groups.

In 2002, initial court rulings backed the school. It was noted that students could choose to attend other schools where the *jilbab* was permitted, so this was not a human rights issue of freedom of religious expression. Moreover the school was already accommodating the religious sentiments of the majority of its students and their parents. Several years later, however, Shabina Begum, employing the Prime Minister Tony Blair's wife, Cherie Booth, as her lawyer, won on appeal. Finally, when the case finally reached the House of Lords in 2006, the original ruling was upheld in favor of the school.[33]

This tortuous path illustrates the British ambivalence about the limits of multiculturalism. Unlike the French, there are numerous attempts to accommodate the minority Muslim community, but such accommodation is still primarily a community matter, rather than an individual matter of self-expression. Given that a community had come together and reached a commonsense agreement on a uniform, no individual would have the right to disrupt that consensus.

Despite his wife's advocacy in the Shabina Begum case, Prime Minister Blair stated in 2006 that the most restrictive Islamic dress, the *burqa*, which entirely covers the woman's body, including the face, had no place in modern European society. Sarkozy agreed with him, and in 2009 the French made such attire illegal on French streets, a crime subject to nominal fines for the wearer, but much harsher fines for men demanding this dress of their wives. Thus for both leaders, there were definite commonsense limits to religious freedom. Integration and assimilation were values that allowed for religious diversity, but not when it led to social separation.

Whereas Britain, and especially France, have struggled with the idea of assimilation, and basically concluded that to be a citizen, one should adopt certain shared cultural values, the Germans have long felt that being German was something in the blood. Their many Turkish *Gastarbeiter* were never expected to assimilate, settle down, or become German. Ultimately, they would return home. But of course that did not happen and today perhaps a million German citizens are of Turkish descent, and a German-Turkish woman was recently elected to parliament. Nonetheless, Angela Merkel, the German chancellor, was quoted in 2010 as saying that multiculturalism was an utter failure.[34]

It is ironic that Turks in Germany are trying to establish a legitimate Islamic identity, whereas Turkey has undergone almost a century of strict French-style secularization, though Prime Minister Recep Tayyip Erdoğan has embodied a more open acceptance of religion in the public square. Thus during the period of Turkish immigration, when Germans treated the Turks as temporary guests, the Turkish government ministered to its people abroad through an organization called DITIB (Diyanet Isleri Turk-Islam Birligi, or Turkish-Islamic Association for Religious Affairs). DITIB built mosques and supplied imams who were trained and salaried by the Turkish government. Since DITIB was secularist and "moderate" in its orientation, those German-Turks of a more conservative bent established rival organizations, most notably associations related to the militant Milli Görüs movement, an Islamist party exiled from Turkey.[35]

With the ancient heritage of the Augsburg treaty of the sixteenth century (where the principle of *cuius regio, eius religio* was first proclaimed), Germans have continued to see the state government as legitimately involved with religious organizations. After World War II, the West German constitution (*Grundgesetz*, "Basic Law") recognized as public corporations (*Körperschaft des öffentlichen Rechts*) certain prominent religious communities, and about 9 percent of federal tax monies were earmarked for the budgets of these corporations. Article 140 of the Basic Law states: "Other religious communities shall be granted like rights upon application where their constitution and the number of their members offer an assurance of permanency."[36] What is noteworthy here is that the government supports through tax money only a few well-established religious institutions, basically the Roman Catholics, Lutherans, and Jews. So far, no Muslim organization has convinced the courts or the government that it is truly representative of the Muslim minority, and thus none have received government recognition (and funding) as a public corporation.

We see, then, in Germany a willingness to blur the boundary of church and state because of the sense that religious institutions serve the public good. There is a certain diversity and tolerance, but at the institutional level as opposed to the individual level. Only those groups that are organized as large representative associations can avail themselves of government support and cooperation.

Political parties in Germany on the right profess a commitment to a *Leitkultur* ("leading culture") that should guide government policy and social norms. Thus, as in Britain and France, we find in Germany some support for something that would replace religion as a common bond among the populace. Muslims are often suspected of being incapable of embracing this culture, and thus it is perhaps not surprising that their religion is not a club member among those religions comfortably superseded by the state. It seems that Muslims have not succeeded in convincing their fellow Germans—Lutherans, Catholics, Jews, nonbelievers—that they are willing to submit their religion to the higher authority of Enlightenment ideals.[37]

When opinion polls in Britain show that younger British Muslims report in high numbers that apostasy from Islam deserves the death penalty, they provoke the same worry among secular people.[38] In varying ways, Europeans have accommodated a growing Muslim population with varying degrees of success. All across western Europe there are attempts to comprehend and contain Islam within the framework of secular democracy, a framework that for over a century has presumed that religion should be a private and personal affair while the politics of public life is governed by the meta-religious discourses of Enlightenment rationality. That rationality has come to be so taken for granted that it often remains unnamed. To oppose it is to oppose, not another system of belief, but a basic reasonableness available to all humans, at least all modern humans. The fear of many Europeans is that those Muslims who seek to bring religion back to the public square represent a population who desire to turn back the clock and thus reject the peace and prosperity that comes with a truly modern outlook.

AMERICAN POWER AND ITS META-RELIGION

While the most difficult issues of community and multiculturalism for Europeans today involve the accommodation of immigrant Muslim populations, Muslims make up a much smaller percentage of the American population, and thus the multicultural question for them continues to be how to come to terms with the legacy of slavery that produced a minority population of African-Americans, scarred by history and marked by race. A nation founded on Enlightenment ideals of equality has struggled to come to terms with a history that denied the full humanity of people treated as unequal. It is striking, however, that the civil rights movement, turned on the ability of a black preacher to describe the issues of racial inequality and injustice, not just in the language of the French egalitarianism that inspired the Founding Fathers, but more powerfully in biblical themes. Dr. Martin Luther King Jr.'s famous "I Have a Dream" speech, delivered at the Lincoln Memorial in 1963, reminded Americans of the unfulfilled promise of Emancipation, but called on a great tradition of messianic hope, a message drawn from Isaiah (40:4–5): "I have a dream that one day every valley shall be exalted, and every hill and mountain shall be made low, the rough places will be made plain, and the crooked places will be made straight; 'and the glory of the Lord shall be revealed and all flesh shall see it together.'" At a time when America saw itself as the preserver of freedom from the threat of worldwide communism, it also faced this shameful contradiction to its founding ideals. It is ironic that King, today revered as a sort of Gandhi-like secular saint, was at the time investigated by the FBI as a possible communist. In time, however, his murder, like that of President John Kennedy and his brother Robert F. Kennedy, and more distantly, like that of Abraham Lincoln, made him a martyr for racial equality and ideals that most Americans would claim to uphold. He is recognized with a national holiday and revered in schools as a patriotic ideal.

As seen in the recent history of India and France, the goal of equality can be imagined in two different ways. Either all persons are assimilated as equals into a singular culture, or the different communities, the different ethnic subcultures, can be celebrated in a multicultural agenda. In the case of the latter model, equal treatment does not entail the homogenization of cultures. In India, that may mean a protection for Islamic family law and affirmative action for members of oppressed castes and communities, with opponents of such measures calling for a secularism that recognizes and sets apart no religious communities and calls for a meritocracy without affirmative action of any sort. In France, official policy discourages the cultivation of distinctive subcultures and encourages assimilation.

Similar debates about affirmative action take place in the United States, but debates about the accommodation of religion takes a different form. The cleavage in contemporary American culture and politics is not between Christians and non-Christians or Catholics and Protestants, as it is between what Bruce Lincoln has called "maximalists" and "minimalists," those who wish to see religion manifest in society and politics, and those who prefer the more secularist option of restricting the role of religion in public life.[39] This can create some interesting inconsistencies. In recent decades, following a French laicist model, the courts have kept public prayer out of public schools, and attempts even to have "moments of silence" when students could choose to pray (or not) have lost legal fights. On the other hand, following a multiculturalist model, Muslim students are often accommodated in American public schools at the time of prayer. They are allowed time and space to perform ablutions and a room to which they can retire for prayer at the designated time.[40] A distinction is thus made between school support and sponsorship of religion (forbidden by the "establishment clause" of the First Amendment), and school accommodation of the cultural requirements of the religion (allowed under the "free expression" clause).

But as we saw in the British case, accommodation of religion requires something of an essentialist model of religion. If the school is to accommodate Muslim practice, say daily prayer or *halal* diet, it depends upon what is deemed standard Muslim practice. If suddenly members of a hundred new sects emerged, all claiming distinctive practices required by their religions, how could the school respond? Here the impulse in American culture to recognize that individualism founders, and face limits to the free expression guaranteed in the First Amendment to the Constitution. As the British school sought to accommodate Muslim students, but had to set limits on that accommodation, likewise in this instance. The school, as a state institution, gets involved in the managing and defining of the nature of religion in general and religions in particular. So, for example, if some Muslims claim that foot washing is required in the process of ablution before prayer, and others claim it is unnecessary, how far should the school go in providing facilities for students to wash their feet before prayer?

These sorts of issues get to the heart of a problem highlighted by Winnifred Sullivan in her book *The Impossibility of Religious Freedom.*[41] As a scholar of American religion and law, she shows convincingly that in order for the state to protect religious freedom of expression, it must first define what genuine religion is. Otherwise, to offer a hypothetical situation germane to the case of prayer in schools, any group of students could form a new religion that requires all members to go shirtless or shoeless (both of which are well-attested ritual requirements in a variety of settings), or claim most any other practice as a religious requirement. In most such cases, the state has an interest in restricting the degree to which it must go in accommodating religious expression, and does so by only recognizing well-known and well-established religious institutions. Thus, absolute religious freedom is an impossibility. The German case of only recognizing a very few large groups is just an extreme case of this principle.

Islamophobia has come to the United States not as the result of a growing immigrant community but largely because of two notorious incidents, incidents that were prompted by America's role as a global superpower: the taking of American hostages in Iran in 1979 and the attacks of September 11, 2001 (9/11). American leaders, especially since 9/11, have had to distinguish what they would characterize as "true Islam" from some false terrorist version. In so doing, they generally assume a definition of religion that accords with Protestant definitions and places religion in a private and nonpolitical realm. Thus they can continue to portray American military strikes against Islamist groups in the quasi-religious language of patriotism while avoiding what might seem the language of Christian crusades against a Muslim enemy. Their opponents do not always grasp this fine distinction.

As Bruce Lincoln has analyzed in his book *Holy Terrors,* President George W. Bush had to respond rhetorically to the 9/11 attack with a sort of double message. First, he had to affirm that the United States was not at war with Islam. Appealing to all good people everywhere, including the majority of (reasonable) Muslims, Bush asserted a shared commitment to peace and prosperity: "we are friends of almost a billion worldwide who practice the Islamic faith," but enemies of the "barbaric criminals who profane a great religion by committing murder in its name."[42] Thus, in pursuing the war on terrorism, Bush had to make an authoritative distinction between good Islam and perverted Islam, and his ability to articulate and define which versions of the religion are acceptable and which not, rested upon unstated gestures of reasonableness. Lincoln further points out that even as Bush's approach protected American claims of being based on secular rationality, he used subtle references to biblical themes that would win the support of more explicitly Christian maximalists. While presidents may conclude speeches with a perfunctory "God bless America," a phrase sufficiently vague and pluralist to win the approval of many and offend only a tiny minority of "hardcore secularists," Bush's new line "May God continue to bless America" (a phrase President Obama also has used) further affirmed to more religious people the belief that America enjoys divine favor and is guided by God's plan for the world.[43] More importantly, Bush used unmarked biblical language that would appeal to evangelical Christians but go unnoticed by others.[44]

With the support of more secular and pluralist voters, President Obama has not used coded biblical language to appeal to evangelical Christians. Since he bears a middle name of Hussein, and spent part of his childhood in Indonesia, some suspect President Obama has been harboring a secret Muslim identity. Thus he must take some pains to assert that he is a Christian. For the most part, however, despite gestures to Martin Luther King Jr. and the Christian language of civil rights and care for the poor, he approaches his role as a world leader in the cosmopolitan language of pluralism, tolerance, and peace.

Obama reached out to the Muslim world in his 2009 speech at Cairo University.[45] There he sought to use his complicated background to his advantage, and employed the idea of the common bonds of the three Abrahamic religions to claim common values and goals of Americans and Muslims around the world, even while admitting current tensions. Like his predecessor, he had to engage in a process of defining which Muslims were friends by declaring who the real Muslims, or good Muslims, might be, as opposed to the false Muslims, or bad Muslims.

> America is not—and never will be—at war with Islam. We will, however, relentlessly confront violent extremists who pose a grave threat to our security. Because we reject the same thing that people of all faiths reject: the killing of innocent men, women and children. . . .
>
> The Holy Koran teaches that whoever kills an innocent, it is as if he has killed all mankind; and whoever saves a person, it is as if he has saved all mankind. The enduring faith of over a billion people is so much bigger than the narrow hatred of a few. Islam is not part of the problem in combatting violent extremism—it is an important part of promoting peace.[46]

There are several things we must note in Obama's rhetoric here. First, he denies an opposition between America and Islam. America's fight is with violent extremism. Muslims, true Muslims, like true Christians, are people of peace. What is not said in such a formulation is that Americans, as preservers of the peace against violent threats, may legitimately use military power (legitimate violence), while Muslims should not. So, for example, Obama declares: "Palestinians must abandon violence. Resistance through violence and killing is wrong and does not succeed." And yet no such stricture is urged either for Israel or the United States.

Obama's approach to the Muslim world is then essentially the same as Bush's. On behalf of his country, he declares Americans to be friends of all those Muslims, optimistically declared the majority, who will renounce violence. He further declares that they must recognize Israel, and adopt an agenda of equal rights for women and policies of religious tolerance. Muslims who adopt those positions, consistent with cosmopolitan ideologies of the United Nations and the worldwide regime of human rights, can be members of an international club which operates under the protection of a great power that jealously guards its military superiority and position of economic and political dominance.

The point is not to criticize either President Bush or President Obama for their rhetorical language, but to understand it. Such language is part of the necessary exercise of power. To exercise power one must speak authoritatively in the language of truth, and any claim to speak the truth in a world of religious pluralism, one must claim a truth that transcends the multiple religions. One must present it as obvious, natural, and reasonable. Such language must go beyond the relativism of multiculturalism. It is "above" the many religions, or their "common ground." It is a meta-religion, and its effective deployment requires that it remain unmarked, unnamed, and unnoticed as such.

Conclusion

Here's something else that's weird but true: in the day-to-day
trenches of adult life, there is actually no such thing as
atheism. There is no such thing as not worshipping. Every-
body worships. The only choice we get is what to worship.
And the compelling reason for maybe choosing some sort of
god or spiritual-type thing to worship—be it JC or Allah, be
it YHWH or the Wiccan Mother Goddess, or the Four Noble
Truths, or some inviolable set of ethical principles—is that
pretty much anything else you worship will eat you alive.

—David Foster Wallace
 Commencement Address
 Kenyon College, 2005

I hope that in this survey of religion and power from the age of Alexander the Great to our own day that I have shown a few critical things
about this relationship:

*Any commonsense understanding of religion should assume that claims
about the Truth will have political consequences.*

Mahatma Gandhi had a supreme confidence that his political activ-
ism was based on a truth not derived simply from Hinduism, but a truth
that transcended all religions, a truth reflected in teachings found all
over the world. It gave him the authority to challenge Hindus, Muslims,
and Christians, to critique the ideas of the British rulers and the South
Africans and Indians they colonized and ruled. His very legitimacy
came, then, from his assertion of a *religious* authority, and thus challenged those whose authority seemed less rooted in righteousness and
truth. Yet he would not be constrained by the boundaries of any one
religion and thus could appeal to people of any and every religion. His
God was simply the Truth; who could disagree with that?

In asserting his allegiance to something so nonspecific and universal as the Truth, Gandhi followed a long tradition of political figures who appealed to vague but compelling and inclusive values. Ashoka appealed to *dharma*, not in sectarian Buddhist terms, but in the broadest sense of righteousness, only to provoke a five-century backlash from those brahmin intellectuals who sought a far more particularist understanding of the term. Meanwhile, Greco-Romans ruled in the name of a universal reason they called the *logos*, only to see that *logos* claimed as consubstantial with Christ. The Chinese developed a Confucian ruling ideology that assumed that the *Dao*, the Way, was best discerned and followed by conservative scholar-officials who adhered to traditional rituals and behaviors of deference. Daoists, and later Buddhists, rejected such traditionalism in the name of truths they believed to transcend culture, even the culture of the sages of the Golden Age, but the Confucian scholars withstood these challenges and ruled China until the early twentieth century.

In the end, I think we can say that Gandhi prevailed, even though he was assassinated by those who rejected his vision of religious pluralism. In his own time, Ashoka too was successful, but Hindu particularism ultimately triumphed over Buddhist universalism in India. Christians came to rule in the Roman Empire, not without absorbing much of paganism, and Confucians overcame Buddhist and Daoist challenges to maintain power for centuries, again not without absorbing many of the ideas of their opponents. But whether India would be more Buddhist or Hindu, whether Rome more pagan or Christian, whether China more Confucian or Buddhist, were all matters of great struggle—intellectual, spiritual, political, military. These struggles were real fights, and most often resulted in bloody conflict. If we attend to the teachings of Jesus, Confucius, and the Buddha, but ignore conflict, we are constructing portraits of religion that are perhaps beautiful and inspiring, but surely false and misleading.

The modern, western understanding of religion, derived from thinkers like John Locke, is inappropriately applied and assumed in many times and places where religion is not a private matter of individual conscience and choice.

We tend to think that people with insights about the truth of things should be free to share their views with others who in turn will be free to consider and perhaps adopt them. Those adhering to the new ideas could then form a club that should be tolerated. We might call those ideas and that new club a religion. We tend then to be completely unsympathetic to those who oppose them, those who feel that the new religion is a threat and deserving of censure and even violent repression. In fact, we tend to leave the fact of such opposition uninvestigated and, without much thought, we confidently ascribe it to narrow-mindedness, intolerance, or bigotry.

But the fact that people in power saw Jesus and Muhammad and Gandhi as threats demands reflection, especially since violent reaction to prophetic figures is such a recurrent theme in the history of religion. We cannot simply wring our hands and lament the fact that most people in most times and places felt that religious ideas were potent enough to pose dangers and to disrupt the peace. A quick survey of the material covered in this book shows how powerful new religions can be. Followers of Jesus expected his return in glory to oversee an apocalyptic overthrow of the corrupt world order and the establishment of the Kingdom of God. Romans saw such an idea as revolutionary and its proponents as immoderate and antisocial. If they were not terrorists, Jesus and his ilk were, in their eyes, close enough such to deserve repression. Ultimately though, that superstitious and rebellious cult won the allegiance of Emperor Constantine and partly destroyed and partly absorbed the religious culture of the vast and powerful Roman Empire. Perhaps conservative Roman aristocrats and officials were not so crazy to fear the charismatic preacher Jesus, who gathered restive crowds in their colonies of Galilee and Judea.

On the basis of his profound religious experiences, Muhammad claimed the authority to reveal God's Word and to form a community of monotheistic believers. The powerful Quraysh tribesmen who controlled the lucrative Meccan trade system were right to see Muhammad's teaching as more than a matter of private religious reflections. Although he was run out of town with only a tiny band of followers, Muhammad returned to Mecca in 630 A.D. at the head of an army of ten thousand men to sweep away both the pluralistic religious system of the Ka'ba and the economic system that it undergirded. This was the beginning of a movement that would dominate the world for the next thousand years.

The British who jailed Mahatma Gandhi and the Hindu nationalists who murdered him knew that he was a powerful man in large part because of his religious ideas and charisma. Gandhi himself wrote, "I can say without the slightest hesitation, and yet in all humility, that those who say that religion has nothing to do with politics do not know what religion means."[1]

Speak truth to power, and you will generally provoke a powerful response.

The political management of multiple religions requires that those religions are not just tolerated, but managed according to criteria set by a meta-religious discourse. Those who would claim the authority to manage multiple religions must do so from a higher vantage point. Their effectiveness depends upon their ability to assert values that can be taken-for-granted as reasonable, natural, and obvious.

As we have seen, the pluralism of ancient India, Rome, and China involved the development of ideologies that made a place for numerous religions and diverse religious expression. Nonetheless such ideologies still maintained boundaries. Ashoka might declare a universal *dharma* and patronize religions of all sorts while at the same time criticizing and limiting animal sacrifice and challenging the authority of brahmins. Romans could happily accept foreign deities from Egypt and Syria into their pantheon, but had difficulty with Christians whose God was too jealous to allow proper patriotic reverence for Caesar, the one act that declared allegiance to a unified empire. The Chinese similarly allowed a range of folk-religious practices and in some cases were open to, even supportive of, Daoist and Buddhist ideas and piety. However, when any group seemed to challenge the idea that the emperor was at the apex of a system of meaning, it was persecuted fully. From the Han Dynasty to the present, the Center would claim the role of final arbiter of truth and meaning, and those alienated from that system, as members of alternative societies, secret sects, or cults, found themselves subject to the full power of the state.

The Abbasid Empire ruled from Baghdad in the name of a singular Islam, but could tolerate important minority communities of Christians, Zoroastrians, and Jews as long as those groups posed no threat to their authority and power. The Ottomans basically extended that project in early modern times by granting some authority to Christian and Jewish leaders to govern their communities' internal affairs. The Ottomans thus ruled a religiously plural empire, but in the name of Islam. Their contemporaries in India, at least during the rule of Akbar, went one step further in recognizing Hindus and other communities as on a par with their own Muslim community, while Akbar himself ruled in the name of something that transcended even Islam, the ideology of *sulh kul* (absolute peace) or perhaps the Divine Faith (Din-i Ilahi). Such transcendent, universalist inclusivism reaches back to the approach of Ashoka, and forward to the secularists of our own day, European and Indian.

However enlightened and attractive Akbar's policies seem to us today, we must recognize that they were in service of absolute royal power. His contemporaries in Europe certainly would have recognized the king's desire to claim authority over religion. In face of the fracture of western Christendom in the age of the Reformation, rulers in Europe began the process of arrogating absolute authority to the nation-state over and above the claims of the Catholic Church, of any church. In the end, the very idea of religious tolerance, as articulated by Locke, worked to enable the state to take over functions previously claimed by religion. Over a two-century period in England, France, and America, religion was thus "demoted," even as religious freedom was affirmed and enshrined in law.

The more a meta-religious ideology can be taken for granted, the less it need be articulated and named. The claims of its opponents are best countered by marginalizing those opponents, declaring them to be barbarians and terrorists, persons undisciplined by acceptable norms of civilization and rationality. The language of tolerance is deployed not simply to bestow the blessings of freedom of religion to diverse communities and individuals. It also serves to authorize and yet hide the meta-religious language that distinguishes the persons and religions that deserve approval, support, and toleration, from those that are out of bounds. It distinguishes good religion from bad religion, true religion from false.

The demotion of religious institutions and the diminution of their authority, whether by enlightenment-influenced political figures, or by ambitious kings like Akbar and Henry VIII, did not result in the articulation and construction of new patriotic superreligions, though the French and Maoist revolutionaries seemed to try. The demotion of religious authority (and the consequent tolerance of multiple religions) generally results from the propagation of something reasonable and taken for granted, but something that needn't be named as a new player in the game of debate and discussion. Thus meta-religious discourse of the reasonable and scientific, of universal human rights, must appear embedded in the nature of things and not be seen as arising from a specific teacher from a particular time and place and culture. It must be ahistorical and acultural, transcending all. Modern secular claims of universality and rationality have their ancient antecedents in the similarly vague terms of *dharma, logos, Dao, tawhid, suhl kul.*

Even within the capacious universal inclusivism of those who would rule religiously plural realms there are important limits. Gandhi centered his quest for Truth on the practice of *ahimsa,* nonviolence, and hence however tolerant and affirming he might be of different religions, all would be judged in light of this central value. Thus, once again, he followed in the footsteps of Ashoka, who valued a variety of traditions, especially ascetic ones, but had no time for animal sacrifice or rituals he deemed magical and superstitious. Gandhi read his own favorite scripture, the *Bhagavadgita,* as referring to battle only in the most metaphoric sense. Enlightened European and American secularism espouses a tolerance of all religions, but only in the sense that there are versions of those religions whose ideas and practices are acceptable to general standards of egalitarianism. So, for example, polygamy is outlawed even when there are religions (Islam, Mormonism) that might recommend it, but this legal restriction is ostensibly upheld *not* because that is the view of most Christians, the majority community, but because it is seen as in accordance with values all modern civilized people should recognize.

And finally, though I have concentrated on the relation of religion to power in the context of politics, and especially imperial politics, I must add that many people without much political power still use meta-religious language to secure their worlds, and everyone must engage in discursive practices to exercise power and secure his or her place. Many modern people would never dream of asserting the binding truth of their particular religion. If I am a Christian, I may not assert my right to demand of you, a Muslim, that you adopt my creed. Nor should Buddhists or Hindus make such demands of others. Such would be the reasonable stance of the tolerant, modern, democratic person. But this modern humility hides the fact that there are nonetheless universal criteria that I apply in judging the religious ideas and practices of others. I apply those criteria by shifting the register of my language from a religious language, which in a pluralist world can no longer easily claim ultimacy, to the language of science and rationality. In secular western democracies today, all religions are subject to such rationalist critique. "True religion" must uphold certain reasonable and universal values: egalitarianism, peace, freedom, and the like. Not only do outsiders judge religious institutions according to those principles, insiders do as well. Thus many American Catholics disagree with their own church's teaching on sexual ethics and gender equity. Those Catholics have decided that certain values, derived from Enlightenment principles, are more authoritative than "out of date" religious principles. A meta-religious ideology has supplanted their church as the final authority, even when they could not name that ideology; it just seems reasonable and fair and obvious.

Similarly Buddhists in America who follow Tibetan teachings do not seem to claim an absolute authority for those teachings, but nonetheless might pursue a program, abstracted from Buddhist teaching, of "compassion based" secular ethics, recommended for all.[2] Children cannot be taught in public schools that the Dalai Lama is the reincarnation of the Buddhist deity Avalokiteshvara, but who would object to their learning principles of compassion? Thus by shifting from an explicitly religious language to one of science and reason, one may argue not only from a neutral and unthreatening position, but gain real power to influence the world.

Consider these claims: *Secular Ethics is based on neuroscience, as yoga is on physiology. Falun Gong is not a religion, but a program of cultivation. Meditation is a useful technique. Spirituality transcends particular religions. The Judeo-Christian tradition undergirds our legal system.* All such claims seek to move from the particular to the general and thus gain discursive advantage. If "religion" nowadays refers to something particular, the product of a specific culture and thus necessarily limited in its claims, one can regain the authority to speak from a position of universality and ultimacy only by using a new language, operating above the several religions. That language (with the institutions it often produces) is one example of what I have called a meta-religion; and its function, like the function of religion in many traditional societies, is the function of claiming authority and exercising power. So if we puzzle over the ability of ancient people to assert the truth of their faiths with an assurance we cannot imagine, we must remind ourselves that those truths had power insofar as they were taken for granted as obvious. In a secular age, our religious truths are never so obvious, but perhaps, when we recognize the power of our largely unrecognized meta-religions, we can see that those faithful ancestors were, after all, not so very different.

Notes

PREFACE

1. I am not the only one. See the following collection of review-essays: Mark MacWilliams et al., "Religion/s between the Covers: Dilemmas of the World Religions Textbook," *Religious Studies Review* 31 (2005): 1–36. I have in mind here textbooks like Huston Smith's classic *Religions of Man,* later retitled *The World's Religions* (New York: HarperOne, 2009), which has sold two million copies since 1958; as well as popular books like Karen Armstrong's best seller, *A History of God: The 4000-Year Quest of Judaism, Christianity and Islam* (New York: Random House, 1993). Textbooks like Michael Molloy's *Experiencing the World's Religions* (New York: McGraw-Hill, 2010) and Mary Pat Fisher's *Living Religions* (Upper Saddle River, NJ: Prentice Hall, 2008), also assume that the goal of understanding is primarily empathetic. Like Huston Smith, they seek to understand the tradition from the believer's perspective. Such accounts leave out facts that might lead to disparagement.

2. For example, one can find accounts of abstruse Buddhist philosophies of consciousness alongside Australian aboriginal rituals of rainmaking, as in David S. Noss and John B. Noss, *A History of the World's Religions* (New York: Macmillan, 1990), 202–3, 24.

3. It is not clear how one defines Hinduism and thus considers it a single religion, and Judaism has far fewer followers than the others in this group.

4. See Jack Goody, *The Eurasian Miracle* (Cambridge: Polity Press, 2010), who faults historians for promulgating a narrative that sees something unique in Europe that leads to advanced urban culture. The phrase "the rise of the West" alludes to W.H. McNeill's book *The Rise of the West* (Chicago: University of Chicago Press, 1963), a stunning world history that is free of most parochialism, but does indeed "end up with us."

INTRODUCTION

1. Peter Berger, *The Sacred Canopy* (Garden City, NY: Doubleday, 1967), 3.

2. To use the phrase of James C. Scott. Cf. his book *Weapons of the Weak* (New Haven, CT: Yale University Press, 1985).

3. Thus it is quite natural for modern persons, who think of themselves as personally religious, to be appalled by "theocracy."

4. Thus it is important to attend not only to issues of explicitly *political* power exercised by members of the governing elite, but the power of social discourses and institutions that actually precede and set limits for political action. I often emphasize the importance of "taken-for-granted" truths: truths so obvious to members of their societies that no one can imagine a sane, civilized person as rejecting them. Thus notions of rebirth and caste in classical India, the value of harmony in ancient China, or egalitarianism in contemporary France are not doctrines to be defended and protected by government actions, but inescapable, largely unchallenged realities in these cultures.

5. See for example the classic work of Carlo Ginzburg *The Cheese and the Worms* (Baltimore: Johns Hopkins University Press, 1980). Ginzburg describes the heretical views of a sixteenth-century Italian miller.

6. See William A. Christian, *Person and God in a Spanish Valley* (Princeton, NJ: Princeton University Press, 1988); and E. Valentine Daniel, *Fluid Signs: Being a Person the Tamil Way* (Berkeley: University of California Press, 1984).

7. See David Brooks, *Bobos in Paradise* (New York: Simon and Schuster, 2000).

8. After the Enlightenment, sacral kingship in the West largely gave way to democratic forms of government in a process that ended up with the sacralization of democracy itself.

9. This is why evangelicals seek to rewrite the history of the American Revolution in a way that obscures the secular, deist, and French Enlightenment roots of the founding fathers' ideology.

10. *Inclusivism,* especially applied to Indian religion, was first coined by the German scholar Paul Hacker. Cf. *Inklusivismus: Eine indische Denkform,* ed. Gerhard Oberhammer (Vienna: DeNobili Library, 1983). In English, one may turn to Wilhelm Halbfass's book *Philology and Confrontation* (Albany: State University of New York Press, 1995), to read translations of Hacker along with Halbfass's commentary.

11. Thus Americans may be tolerant of Muslims and Mormons, but intolerant of polygamy, which offends an almost instinctive notion of individual dignity.

12. One can read the Universal Declaration of Human Rights on the United Nations' website: www.un.org/en/documents/udhr (accessed July 3, 2014).

13. Stephen L. Carter, *The Culture of Disbelief: How American Law and Politics Trivialize Religious Devotion* (New York: Basic Books, 1993), 23–43.

14. Cf. President Obama's speech at Cairo University, June 4, 2009, at the White House website: www.whitehouse.gov/the_press_office/Remarks-by-the-President-at-Cairo-University-6-04-09 (accessed July 22, 2014). Also cf Rory Stewart, *The Places in Between* (Orlando: Harcourt, 2006), 234–38, , where he

shows how the well-meaning but misguided British prime minister Tony Blair carried about an English version of the Qur'an, drawing teachings from it as though it could be used as an easily accessible summary of creeds, as a sort of alternative Bible, with no awareness of the complex Islamic notions of its talismanic and sacred properties, much less its doctrinal complexity. Blair now heads his own faith foundation: see www.tonyblairfaithfoundation.org. It is worth noting that, like Blair, former President Jimmy Carter also heads up a foundation devoted to what we would call enlightened meta-religious policies (www.cartercenter.org).

CHAPTER I. ALEXANDER AND ASHOKA

1. *Oikoumene*, meaning "the inhabited world," or "the known [civilized] world," is the Greek root for our word *ecumenical*. Some historians anglicize the word as *ecumene*. Cf. Erik Voegelin, *Order and History*, vol. 4, *The Ecumenic Age* (Baton Rouge: Louisiana State University Press, 1974).

2. It is noteworthy that biblical scholars date the spread of Iranian or Zoroastrian religious ideas to Judaism from this period, when Jews, like later Christians and Muslims, began to believe in angels, life after death, and a cosmic struggle at the end of history.

3. *The Edicts of Asoka*, ed. N.A. Nikam and Richard McKeon (Chicago: University of Chicago Press, 1959), 27–30: *Rock Edict* 13. See Amulyachandra Sen, *Asoka's Edicts* (Calcutta: Institute of Indology, 1959), 101, where Sen notes that the phrase *one faith or another* translates the word *pasade*, which later connotes heresy.

4. Ashoka may have heard of Alexander the Great from his grandmother: Romila Thapar, *Asoka and the Decline of the Mauryas*, 2nd ed. (Oxford: Oxford University Press, 1997), 20.

5. See ibid., passim.

6. Stanley Tambiah, *World Conqueror, World Renouncer* (Cambridge: Cambridge University Press, 1976), 54–72.

7. See Alf Hiltebeitel, *Dharma: Its Early History in Law, Religion, and Narrative* (Honolulu: University of Hawai'i Press, 2010), 12–18. Garth Fowden has compared Ashoka to Constantine, who also played the role of king but thought of himself as a kind of bishop. Cf. Fowden, *Empire to Commonwealth* (Princeton, NJ: Princeton University Press, 1993), 82–85.

8. *The Edicts of Asoka*, trans. N.A. Nikam and Richard McKeon (Chicago: University of Chicago Press, 1959), 36.

9. *Edicts of Asoka*, 51–52: *Rock Edict* 12.

10. W.W.Tarn, *Alexander the Great and the Unity of Mankind* (London: Milford, 1933).

11. Peter Green, *Alexander of Macedon, 356–323 B.C.: A Historical Biography* (Berkeley: University of California Press, 1991).

12. Jonathan Z. Smith, "Differential Equations: On Constructing the 'Other,'" in *Relating Religion: Essays in the Study of Religion* (Chicago: University of Chicago Press, 2004).

CHAPTER 2. IMPERIAL RELIGION

1. Michael Loewe, "The First Emperor and the Qin Empire," in *The First Emperor: China's Terracotta Army,* ed. Jane Portal (Cambridge, MA: Harvard University Press, 2007), 78.

2. Maximus of Madaura, writing in a letter to Augustine. *The Works of Saint Augustine,* vol. 2, pt. 1, *Letters 1–99,* trans. Roland Teske (Hyde Park, NY: New City Press, 1999), 46. This was written long after the period under review here, but captures the enduring spirit of Roman inclusivism.

3. An extremely popular museum exhibit of the terracotta warriors has recently toured Europe and the United States. Cf. *The First Emperor: China's Terracotta Army,* ed. Jane Portal (Cambridge, MA: Harvard University Press, 2007).

4. The Qin (pronounced *chin*) Dynasty lasted from 221 to 207 B.C. and is probably the basis for the English word *China* and the Sanskrit word *Cina.*

5. Said by the regime to be using the past, i.e., accounts of ancient history, to criticize the present. Such traditionalist Confucians became the support of the Han Dynasty a century later.

6. The Han Dynasty is divided into two periods, the "Former Han" or "Western Han" and the "Later Han" or "Eastern Han," divided by the brief Xin Dynasty (9–23 A.D.). For simplicity's sake I will treat the period from 202 B.C. to 220 A.D. as one era. One should note that the effort to portray China as ethnically united obscures the history of many different and contentious ethnic groups that have been absorbed into modern China. Cf. Terry Kleeman, *Great Perfection* (Honolulu: University of Hawai'i Press, 1998), 3 n.

7. *Sources of Chinese Tradition,* ed. William Theodore de Bary and Irene Bloom (New York: Columbia University Press, 1999), 1: 46–47.

8. Ibid., p. 59. Also cf. Edward Slingerland's translation, *Confucius' Analects* (Indianapolis: Hackett Publishing, 2003), 175. He numbers this verse as 15.5 and provides a useful commentary.

9. *Chuang Tzu: Basic Writings,* trans. Burton Watson (New York: Columbia University Press, 1964), 94–95.

10. Walter Scheidel has done much collaborative work on the comparative history of imperial Rome and Han China. In the introduction to his edited volume *Rome and China: Comparative Perspectives on Ancient World Empires* (New York: Oxford University Press, 2009), he notes numerous points of comparison, most importantly for our purposes here: "ideological unification through monumental construction, religious rituals, and elite education"; "ideologies of normative empire sustained by transcendent powers"; but also, "later on, religious change leading to the formation of autonomous church systems and philosophical and religious shifts in emphasis from community values to ethical conduct and individual salvation" (4). Thus, critically, both the Roman and the Han Empires depended on a sort of metareligious system that supported the empire and community values, and both faced, in Christianity and Buddhism, the rise of an alternative system of values that appealed to individuals. Consequentially Christianity survived to become the basis of empire, but in China, as we will discuss in the following chapter, the old imperial system revived to crush the Buddhist challenge to its final authority.

11. The four books of the Maccabees are included in the Roman Catholic canon, but excluded from the Protestant version of the Bible.

12. The author of this text uses the Greek word for piety (*eusebeia*) that Ashoka used to translate *dharma* a century before.

13. Cf. Ronald Williamson, *Jews in the Hellenistic World* (New York: Cambridge University Press, 1989), 128–30, quoting Philo on elements of creation: "So also the universe which consisted of ideas could have no other location than the divine reason, which had made them"; or: "[The] world discerned by the intellect is nothing other than the Word of God."

14. Ibid., 25.

15. Philo is quoting Agrippa's letter in his *Embassy to Gaius*, 278–80.

16. Williamson, *Jews in the Hellenistic World*, 16.

17. Jon Dominic Crossan, *Jesus: A Revolutionary Biography* (San Francisco: Harper, 1994); Richard A. Horsley, *Jesus and Empire: The Kingdom of God and the New World Disorder* (Minneapolis: Fortress, 2003).

18. Horsley, *Jesus and Empire*, 23–24.

19. Ibid., 27–31.

20. *Latrones* is the Latin equivalent of the Greek word *lestai*, used in the New Testament with a similar connotation of terrorists or bandits. Jesus was crucified with two *lestai* (Mark 15:27; Matt. 27:44).

21. Cf. Daniel Boyarin, "The IOUDAIOI in John and the Prehistory of Judaism," in *Pauline Conversations in Context; Essays in Honor of Calvin J. Roetzel*, ed. Janice Capel Anderson, Philip Sellew, and Claudia Setzer, special issue of *Journal for the Study of the New Testament*, supplement series 221 (2002): 216–39. Boyarin argues that "the Jews" (*Ioudaioi*) of John's gospel are not an all-inclusive group of Jews, but a very specific group of Judeans associated with the temple in Jerusalem. Note that when Pilate asks whether he should crucify their king (Jesus), the chief priests answer, "we have no king but Caesar" (John 19:15).

22. George W. MacRae's translation in *The Nag Hammadi Library in English*, trans. James M. Robinson et al. (San Francisco: Harper and Row, 1977), 46.

23. Quoted in Elaine Pagels, *The Gnostic Gospels* (New York: Random House, 1979), 77.

24. Compare Matt. 10:34: "Do not think that I have come to bring peace on earth; I have not come to bring peace, but a sword."

25. Garth Fowden, *Empire to Commonwealth: Consequences of Monotheism in Late Antiquity* (Princeton, NJ: Princeton University Press, 1993), 37 ff.; Jeremy M. Schott, *Christianity, Empire, and the Making of Religion in Late Antiquity* (Philadelphia: University of Pennsylvania Press, 2008), 16 ff.

26. Quoted in Erik Voegelin, *Order and History*, vol. 4, *The Ecumenic Age* (Baton Rouge: Louisiana State University Press, 1974), 155.

CHAPTER 3. THE DEBATE OVER *DHARMA*

1. My translation.

2. I discuss Constantine in the following chapter. It is worth noting that both Constantine and Ashoka held religious councils to try and eliminate doctrinal schisms in Christianity and Buddhism, respectively.

3. Romila Thapar, *A History of India*, vol. 1 (London: Penguin Books, 1990), chaps. 5 and 6.

4. Cf. Lama Anagarika Govinda, *Psycho-Cosmic Symbolism of the Buddhist Stupa* (Emeryville, CA: Dharma, 1976), 3–25.

5. Cf. Stanley Abe, "Inside the Wonder House: Buddhist Art and the West," in *Curators of the Buddha*, ed. Donald S. Lopez, Jr. (Chicago: University of Chicago Press, 1995), 63–105.

6. Alf Hiltebeitel, *Rethinking the Mahābhārata : A Reader's Guide to the Education of the Dharma King* (Chicago: University of Chicago Press, 2001), 17; Alf Hiltebeitel, *Dharma: Its Early History in Law, Religion, and Narrative* (Honolulu: University of Hawai'i Press, 2010). Patrick Olivelle has edited a book of collected essays entitled *Between the Empires: Society in India 300 B.C.E. to 400 C.E.* (New York: Oxford University Press, 2006), which has several papers on topics related to my argument here, including James L. Fitzgerald, "Negotiating the Shape of Scripture," 257–86; and, Michael Witzel, "Brahmanical Reactions to Foreign Influences and to Social and Religious Change," 457–99.

7. Following my translation; cf. James W. Laine, *Visions of God* (Vienna: Publications of the De Nobili Research Library, 1989), 177–78. Also see the *Yugapurana*, trans. John Mitchiner (Calcutta: Asiatic Society, 1986); and Sheldon Pollock, *The Language of the Gods in the World of Men* (Berkeley: University of California Press, 2006), 71. The *Yuga Purana* passage is a direct parallel, but is an explicit condemnation of the Shakas (Scythians) in the context of Satavahana rule about 50 B.C.

8. *The Questions of King Milinda*, trans. T.W. Rhys Davids (New Delhi: Motilal Banarsidass, 1965), 2: 26–28.

9. "I am" sayings equivalent to those of Jesus, for example, "I am the way, the truth and the Life" (John 14:16); or "I am the true vine . . . " (John 15:1a).

10. My translation; cf. Laine, *Visions of God*, 136–37.

11. I have followed Hendrik Kern's translation, *Saddharma Pundarika; or, The Lotus of the True Law*, Sacred Books of the East 21 (Oxford: Clarenden Press, 1884), 7–8. The original text is *Saddharmapundarika*, Bibliotheca Indica 10, ed. Hendrik Kern and Bunyiu Nanjio (St. Petersburg: Imprimerie de l'Academie des Sciences, 1912).

12. Kern and Nanjio, ed., *Saddharmapundarika*, 51.

13. Ibid., 124, 122; *Lotus Sutra* 5.19; 5.1.

14. *The Laws of Manu*, trans. Wendy Doniger with Brian K. Smith (New York: Penguin Books, 1991); *Manu's Code of Law: A Critical Edition and Translation of the Mānava-Dharmaśāstra*, trans. Patrick Olivelle (New York: Oxford University Press, 2005).

15. Olivelle, trans., *Manu's Code*, 39.

16. It is important to note here that "pagan" in the sense of "rustic" religion survived the official adoption of Christianity in the Roman world, clothing itself in the garb of local saint and Virgin Mary cults. In this regard, cf. Ramsay Macmullen, *Christianity and Paganism in the Fourth to Eighth Centuries* (New Haven, CT: Yale University Press, 1997). The differences at the level of local village religion between India and Rome in this period might be slight; but at the level of official imperial policy, kings made consequential choices.

CHAPTER 4. CONFESSIONAL RELIGION AND EMPIRE

1. Quoted in Garth Fowden, *Empire to Commonwealth: Consequences of Monotheism in Late Antiquity* (Princeton, NJ: Princeton University Press, 1993), 72.

2. Ibid., 61 and 82.

3. Cf. Paul Williams, *Mahayana Buddhism : The Doctrinal Foundations* (New York: Routledge, 1989).

4. I follow here the gist of the third chapter of the *Lotus Sutra*. Cf. Michael Pye's discussion of the story of the burning house in his *Skilful Means* (London: Duckworth, 1978), 37–40.

5. Following Hendrik Kern's translation, *Saddharma Pundarika; or, The Lotus of the True Law*, Sacred Books of the East 21 (Oxford: Clarenden Press, 1884), 413–14.

6. See Livia Kohn's discussion of millenarianism, "the belief that the world is coming to an end and a new and better one will take its place," in her *Daoism and Chinese Culture* (Cambridge: Three Pines Press, 2001). She summarizes the view that all millenarian and apocalyptic traditions from Israel to China have Persian roots, a position based on Norman Cohn's *Cosmos, Chaos, and the World to Come* (New Haven, CT: Yale University Press, 1993), but rejects that view in favor of the idea that millenarianism is produced from certain social conditions.

7. Stanley Tambiah, *World Conqueror and World Renouncer* (Cambridge: Cambridge University Press, 1976).

8. For example, Kartir was opposed to the veneration of images and popular gods, and wanted all temples to house simply a sacred fire.

9. Hormizd I, Shapur's successor, began to persecute Manichaeans under Kartir's influence. Hormizd died in the year of Constantine's birth.

10. A.K. Ramanujan, "Is There an Indian Way of Thinking?" *India through Hindu Categories*, ed. McKim Marriott (New Delhi: Sage Publications, 1990). In Ramanujan's elegant formulation, the distinctiveness of traditional Indian thought is its emphasis on context-sensitive rules rather than context-free rules. Using this grammatical model, he shows, for example, how Indian ethics tends to stress the context of the act, as opposed to the universalistic western ethic that tends to seek what is right and good in all times and circumstances. I call the Indian approach particularism, and the western style, universalism. Note that these are *tendencies*, with important exceptions on both sides.

11. For a short and clear review of Shankara's views, see Eliot Deutsch, *Advaita Vedanta: A Philosophical Reconstruction* (Honolulu: University of Hawai'i Press, 1973).

12. Daniel Overmyer, *Folk Buddhist Religion : Dissenting Sects in Late Traditional China* (Cambridge, MA: Harvard University Press, 1976). The movements that Overmyer discusses are not so much *folk* religions, the religions of the village, which the imperial state supported, but *sectarian* religions of salvation that challenged the state's claim to final authority in all things.

13. The two great Buddhas of Bamiyan in Afghanistan, standing 120 and 180 feet tall, were famously destroyed by the Taliban in 2001.

14. Cf. Kenneth Chen, *Buddhism in China* (Princeton, NJ: Princeton University Press, 1972), 220–21.

15. Kenneth Chen (ibid., 232) quotes an imperial proclamation: "More than 4,600 monasteries are being destroyed throughout the empire; more than 260,500 monks and nuns are being returned to lay life and being subjected to the double tax; more than 40,000 temples and shrines are being destroyed; several tens of millions of *ch'ing* of fertile lands and fine fields are being confiscated; 150,000 slaves are being taken over to become payers of the double tax. Monks and nuns are to be placed under the jurisdiction of the Bureau of Guests, to indicate clearly that Buddhism is a foreign religion. We are returning more than 3,000 Nestorians and Zoroastrians to lay life, so that they will not adulterate the customs of China." (A *ch'ing* is a hundred *mou;* a *mou* is about one-sixth of an acre. Thus a *ch'ing* is about sixteen acres.)

16. "So, the nations of the world were guided as though by a single pilot. They accepted the governorship of the servant of God. The Roman administration was no longer subject to disturbance. Men carried on their lives amid order and peace." Eusebius, *Life of Constantine* 4.14; cf. *The Essential Eusebius,* trans. Colm Luibhéid (New York: New American Library), 191.

17. Henry Chadwick claims: "The difference in East and West lies more in that the Byzantine world did not think of itself as two 'societies,' sacred and secular, but as a single society in harmony with the emperor as the earthly counterpart of the divine monarch." *The Early Church* (London: Pelican Books, 1967), 166.

18. Fowden, *Empire to Commonwealth,* 82–85. The monkish king (Ashoka, Constantine, St. Louis) thus poses a universalist challenge to the particularism of social roles. He represents the idea that there is one true way of life for all people, not a way of life for the religious as opposed to another way of life for the laymen of the secular world.

19. Luibhéid, trans., *Essential Eusebius,* 191, 197, translating *The Life of Constantine* 4.17, 4.29.

20. Ramsey Macmullen, *Christianity and Paganism in the Fourth to Eighth Centuries* (New Haven, CT: Yale University Press, 1997), 34.

21. Ibid., 35.

22. Ibid., 2.

23. Glen Warren Bowersock, *Julian the Apostate* (Cambridge, MA: Harvard University Press, 1978).

24. Peter Brown, *The World of Late Antiquity* (New York: W.W. Norton, 1989), 78.

25. Martin Bernal, *Black Athena* (New Brunswick, NJ: Rutgers University Press, 1987), 1: 121–22.

26. Maria Dzielska, *Hypatia of Alexandria* (Cambridge, MA: Harvard University Press, 1995), 26–65, 101–6.

27. Cf. Talal Asad, *Genealogies of Religion* (Baltimore: Johns Hopkins University Press, 1993), 35 n. Also cf. Chadwick, *Early Church,* 223.

28. "The religious policy of Constantius II showed his characteristically shrewd pursuit of a middle way. He upheld Arianism, as being the more philosophically acceptable statement of the relation between Christ and God the Father. This creed was formulated by an Alexandrian priest, Arius (c. 250–c. 336), in the face of the intransigent hostility of his ecclesiastical superior, the

authoritarian Athanasius, patriarch of Alexandria. Arius enjoyed the tacit support of cultivated bishops, such as the elder statesman, Eusebius of Caesarea. In supporting Arianism, Constantius opted for the religion of the cultivated Christian Apologists of a previous generation, against the suspect new piety of Athanasius, based on the mounting enthusiasm of the Egyptian monks. As seen by the average bishop of the age of Constantine, the victory of Christianity had been a victory of strict monotheism over polytheism. The martyrs had died for a single high God. And for the cultivated Christians of the fourth century, a high God could only manifest Himself to the physical universe through an intermediary. Christ had to be, in some way, a reflection of God; He could not possibly *be* God: for the lonely essence of the One God must stand concentrated and transcendent. The God of the Arians was the jealous God of Abraham, of Isaac, and of Jacob: but their Christ was the godlike intermediary of the Neoplatonic philosophers. Arianism also appealed to the imagination of a new court society. For Christ was thought of as 'representing' God in this world, much as a governor, sitting beneath an icon of the emperor, 'represented' Constantius II in a distant court-house." Brown, *World of Late Antiquity,* 90.

29. Marshall G. S. Hodgson, *The Venture of Islam* (Chicago: University of Chicago Press, 1974), 1: 125–45.

30. This royal name is spelled variously: Khusro, Khusrau, Chosroes.

31. It is interesting that his powerful wife Theodora continued to be sympathetic with Monophysite beliefs; and late in his career, Justinian himself supported the rather heretical position that the human body of Christ was incorruptible and only seemed to suffer (Aphthartodocetism).

32. Although Lakhmids were allied with Persia, they were (non-Chalcedonian) Christians and there is no evidence of any influence of Zoroastrianism among them.

33. Fowden, *Empire to Commonwealth,* 115–21.

34. Brown, *World of Late Antiquity,* 189.

35. Glen Warren Bowersock, *The Throne of Adulis: Red Sea Wars on the Eve of Islam* (New York: Oxford University Press, 2013), esp. chap. 6. Also cf. Fowden, *Empire to Commonwealth,* 119–20.

36. Whereas Yusuf and the Jews of his community were converts, some scholars believe the Jews of Medina fled there from Judea in the late first century when Romans destroyed the Temple.

37. On this period, cf. Fred M. Donner, *Muhammad and the Believers* (Cambridge, MA: Harvard University Press, 2010), chap. 1.

38. Fowden, *Empire to Commonwealth.*

CHAPTER 5. THE RISE OF ISLAM AND THE EARLY CALIPHATE

1. Garth Fowden, *Empire to Commonwealth* (Princeton, NJ: Princeton University Press, 1993), 106–10.

2. Marshall G. S. Hodgson, *The Venture of Islam* (Chicago: University of Chicago Press, 1974), 1: 125.

3. Some scholars would challenge this characterization of pre-Islamic Arabia. They feel that Arabia was far more influenced by Christianity and far less pagan

in the sixth century than traditional accounts allow. See Fred M. Donner, *Muhammad and the Believers* (Cambridge, MA: Harvard University Press, 2010), chap. 1.

4. Peter Brown, *The World of Late Antiquity* (New York: W.W. Norton, 1989), 189.

5. Donner, *Muhammad and the Believers*, 68 ff.

6. Cf. his discussion of the *Satanic Verses* incident in nonfictional form, in his memoir, *Joseph Anton* (New York: Random House, 2012), 41–45.

7. Ira Lapidus, *A History Of Islamic Societies* (Cambridge: Cambridge University Press, 2002), 24.

8. Ibid., 28.

PART TWO. THE ISLAMIC MILLENNIUM

1. Fernand Braudel, *La Mediterranée et le monde méditerranéen a l'epoque de Philippe II* (Paris: Armand Colin, 1966), 1: 251 (my translation). The English translation of this book is *The Mediterranean and the Mediterranean World in the Age of Philip II,* trans. Siân Reynolds (New York: Harper and Row, 1972).

CHAPTER 6. IMPERIAL ISLAM

1. Peter Brown, *The World of Late Antiquity* (New York: W.W. Norton, 1989), 201.

2. Marshall G.S. Hodgson, *The Venture of Islam* (Chicago: University of Chicago Press, 1974), 1: 223.

3. Qur'an 4.171, as quoted in Garth Fowden, *Empire to Commonwealth: Consequences of Monotheism in Late Antiquity* (Princeton, NJ: Princeton University Press, 1993), 142.

4. To paraphrase Hodgson, *Venture of Islam,* 1: 252.

5. Richard W. Bulliet, *Islam: the View from the Edge* (New York: Columbia University Press, 1994), 37–66. Bulliet notes that in the early centuries, there were no missionaries, and non-Arab subjects remained thoroughly ignorant of the Islamic religion that their masters professed.

6. "Storied," as in the stories of *The Arabian Nights,* many of which purport to tell of the caliph's adventures in Baghdad.

7. Abbasid caliphs patronized a "House of Wisdom" (*Bait al-Hikma*), an unrivaled library and center for scientific and philosophical studies, where the works of Persian, Greek, and Indian scholars were translated into Arabic. In the eighth century, Arabs learned the art of paper making from the Chinese, and were thus able to build up a massive and cataloged library. The founder of algebra, al-Khwarizmi (whose name is preserved in the word *algorithm*), worked there in the ninth century. He drew upon Persian, Babylonian, Greek and Indian traditions. In their role as patrons of learning, the caliphs followed the precedents of the Sassanid shahs, who brought scholars to Gundeshapur from India and Byzantium.

8. Ibn Battuta, a famous pilgrim of the fourteenth century from Morocco, traveled from Spain to Indonesia, and even ventured outside the Islamic world to Byzantium and China. He was respected for his learning, and often employed as a *qadi,* or judge.

9. Lord Elgin won permission from the Ottoman sultan to remove sculptures from the Parthenon in 1801. Those sculptures, now claimed by the Greeks and known as the Elgin Marbles, remain in the British Museum. In the British view, then, London, as the cosmopolitan metropolis, was the proper site of the museum of the world's heritage, not provincial Athens. Ninth-century Baghdadis would have had a similar view of their role as curators of world culture.

10. This idea is usually discussed in relation to the crowning of Charlemagne as Holy Roman Emperor on Christmas Day, 800 A.D. Alexander VI (r. 1492–1503), one of the most secular popes of the Borgia family, formed military alliances to protect Italy from French invasions. It was the age of Machiavelli, a diplomat who negotiated with the bastard son of Pope Alexander, Cesare Borgia, himself both a soldier and a cardinal.

11. Quoted in Annemarie Schimmel, *Rumi's World* (Boston: Shambala Publications, 2001), 134.

12. Annemarie Schimmel, *Mystical Dimensions of Islam* (Chapel Hill: University of North Carolina Press, 1975), 66–67.

13. In other words, essentializing Judaism as a set of beliefs rather than a complex web of cultural practices makes it more like modern Protestant Christianity. The thirteen essentials are: (1) the existence of God; (2) God's unity; (3) God's spirituality and incorporeality; (4) God's eternity (5) God alone should be the object of worship; (6) revelation through God's prophets; (7) rhe preeminence of Moses among the prophets; (8) God's law given on Mount Sinai; (9) the immutability of the Torah as God's Law; (10) God's foreknowledge of human actions; (11) reward of good and retribution of evil; (12) the coming of the Jewish Messiah; (13) the resurrection of the dead.

14. Some historians have found evidence that in the end, Maimonides felt it was best to convert to Islam, if only as a public gesture.

15. Following Carl Ernst, *The Eternal Garden* (Albany: State University of New York Press, 1992), 42. Said Amir Arjomand quotes a Sasanian tract on kingship that was translated into Arabic in the eighth century: "Know that kingship and religion are twin brothers; there is no solidity for one of them except through its companion because religion is the foundation of kingship and kingship the protector of religion. Kingship needs its foundation and religion its protector as whatever lacks a protector perishes and whatever lacks a foundation is destroyed." *The Shadow of God and the Hidden Imam: Religion, Political Order, and Societal Change in Shi'ite Iran from the Beginning to 1890* (Chicago: University of Chicago Press, 1984), 93.

16. Ernst, *Eternal Garden*, 42.

17. Ibid., 44–46.

18. *The Bijak of Kabir*, trans. Linda Hess and Shukdev Singh (New York: Oxford University Press, 2002), 42.

19. Ibid., 69–70.

20. *The Sants: Studies in a Devotional Tradition of India*, ed. Karine Schomer and W.H. McLeod (New Delhi: Motilal Banarsidass, 1987).

21. Cf. Hew McLeod, *Sikhism* (New York: Penguin Books, 1997), 33 ff., 103 ff.

22. Richard Eaton, *Essays on Islam and Indian History* (New Delhi: Oxford University Press, 2000), chaps. 9, 11.

23. Cf. Daniel Overmyer, *Folk Buddhist Religion : Dissenting Sects in Late Traditional China* (Cambridge, MA: Harvard University Press, 1976), 62 ff. Overmyer explicitly contrasts China with Japanese and European sects: "The great difference between China and both Europe and Japan is that in the Chinese situation, incipient 'denominational' or 'church' structures were never able to develop to their full potential because of official hostility" (63).

CHAPTER 7. THE GREAT ISLAMIC EMPIRES OF THE EARLY MODERN ERA

1. Salman Rushdie, *The Enchantress of Florence* (London: Jonathan Cape, 2008), 307. Also cf Abu'l-Fazl Allami, *A'in-i Akbari,* trans. Henry Blochmann (Delhi: Aadesh Book Depot, 1966). Abul Fazl presents the Mughal emperor Akbar as a rare bridge between the domains of worldly and spiritual power; he writes: "Whenever, from lucky circumstances, the time arrives that a nation learns to understand how to worship truth, the people will naturally look to their king . . . and expect him to be their spiritual leader as well; for a king possesses, independent of men, the ray of Divine wisdom, which banishes from his heart everything that is conflicting" (172).

2. Quoted by Sussan Babaie in *The Great Empires of Asia,* ed. Jim Masselos (Berkeley: University of California Press, 2010), 142. Europeans in this period, including Shakespeare, referred to the Persian emperor, here Shah Ismail I, as the Great Sophy (Sufi) because of his origins as a charismatic leader of a Sufi order, the Qizlbash.

3. Karen Barkey, *Empire of Difference: The Ottomans in Comparative Perspective* (Cambridge: Cambridge University Press, 2008), 110.

4. On the other hand, a few Europeans were beginning to take note of the Mughals. Using Mughal miniatures as his guide, Rembrandt sketched Shah Jahan, while Restoration playwright John Dryden composed an heroic tale of Aurangzeb (*Aurang-Zebe,* 1675) while the emperor was reigning.

5. *Akbar Nama* 1.65, quoted in Douglas E. Streusand, *The Formation of the Mughal Empire* (New York: Oxford University Press, 1989), 130–31.

6. *Ishraq,* the east, is the dawn, the source of light that is the first emanation of Divine Being.

7. John F. Richards, "The Formulation of Imperial Authority under Akbar and Jahangir," in *Kingship and Authority in South Asia,* ed. John F. Richards (Madison: University of Wisconsin Press, 1978), 304.

8. Annemarie Schimmel, *And Muhammad Is His Messenger: The Veneration Of the Prophet in Islamic Piety* (Chapel Hill: University of North Carolina Press, 1985), 16.

9. *Kingship and Authority in South Asia,* ed. Richards, 265.

10. See for example Leila Ahmed, *Women and Gender in Islam* (New Haven, CT: Yale University Press, 1992), 88 ff.

11. S.R. Sharma, *The Religious Policy of the Mughal Emperors* (New York: Asia Publishing House, 1972), 49.

12. Quoted in Streusand, *Formation of the Mughal Empire,* 136.

13. *Akbar and the Jesuits: An Account of the Jesuit Missions to the Court of Akbar,* ed. Pierre du Jarric (New York: Harper, 1926), 68. The word *ethnique* here seems to have baffled the English translator, but was probably a French rendering of the Greek word *ethnikos,* the New Testament word for gentile, presumably meaning a person neither Jewish nor Christian.

14. Saiyid Athar Abbas Rizvi, *Religious and Intellectual History of the Muslims in Akbar's Reign* (New Delhi: Munshiram Manoharlal, 1975), 391.

15. Harbans Mukhia, *The Mughals of India* (Oxford: Blackwell Publishers, 2004), 51.

16. Cf. Mukhia's insightful analysis of Abul Fazl's universalism: "The tracing of Akbar's descent from Adam instead of Muhammad establishes his universal, human, in lieu of Islamic, lineage. Strongly embedded in this construction was the teleological vision in which Akbar's person and reign appear as the fulfillment of human history—an inevitable divine destiny" (ibid., 42). But he further notes the complexity of these moves: "Yet, even as Abul Fazl posits a dichotomy between universalist religiosity derived from all of humanity's common God, Allah, and denominational religions—including, and above all, Islam, with its own partisan conception of God, Allah—the quiet incorporation of the suggestion of prophethood in Akbar's person and the implicit inevitability of the fulfillment of divine mission are elements pointing towards Islam as the source of this vision" (43).

17. The demotion was not to a modernist-style relativism, but to a universalism in which religions are dialects of a universal language; i.e., for Akbar and Abul Fazl the symbolism changes but the Truth behind it does not. An interesting parallel in the West, a few decades earlier, was in Renaissance Florence, where Agostino Steuco, under the Neoplatonic influence of Marsilio Ficino, coined the term *philosophia perennis,* to describe this universalism that decidedly was not "secular." Just to point this out, in case it's relevant here, since your book often makes distinctions from modernist interpretations of religion. My thanks to Andrew Frisardi for this clarification.

18. Cf. Schimmel, *And Muhammad Is His Messenger,* chap. 7. Also note Mukhia's comment: "Akbar is visualized also as 'the Perfect Man' (*Insan-I Kamil*), a complex concept primarily developed by the great mystic thinker, Ibn al-Arabi, for his millenary appearance on earth at God's command. Muhammad, for Ibn al-Arabi was the Perfect Man; Akbar was for Abul Fazl" (*Mughals of India,* 43). Note that Akbar was ruling in the millennial year of the Islamic calendar (1000 A.H. = 1592 A.D.)

19. See S.L. Goomer's statement in the introduction to the English translation of the *Ain-i Akbari,* one volume of the *Akbar Nama:* "Akbar's cult of secularism assumes a special importance and is well worth emulation in the present context of communal predilections and fissiparous tendencies [in India]" (Abu'l-Fazl 'Allami, *A'in-i Akbari,* trans. H. Blochmann [Delhi: Aadesh Book Depot, 1965], ix).

20. Quoted in Rizvi, *Religious and Intellectual History,* 409.

21. This Persian translation was the basis for the translation of the *Upanishads* into Latin not too long after this—in a version called the *Oupnek'hat.*

And this became the West's introduction to the *Upanishads,* used exhaustively by and greatly influencing, for instance, Schopenhauer. My thanks to Andrew Frisardi for this point.

22. Aurangzeb sought to assuage his conscience and gain legitimacy by becoming an ardent patron of the holy places in Mecca. Cf. John F. Richards, *The Mughal Empire,* New Cambridge History of India 1.5 (Cambridge: Cambridge University Press, 1993), 172.

23. Dara, like Akbar, had a deep interest in Hindu classical religious literature and followed an inclusivist and universalist philosophy in which Islam and Hinduism were not opposed.

24. In a previous work, *Shivaji: Hindu King in Islamic India* (New York: Oxford University Press, 2003), I have treated the history and legends of the heroic Shivaji, pointing out the ways in which he pursued both the pragmatic goals of power alongside a Hindu cultural agenda in complicated ways.

25. Cf. ibid., 41.

26. Richard M. Eaton, *Essays on Islam and Indian History* (New Delhi: Oxford University Press, 2000).

27. The *Dabistan,* a seventeenth-century text that presumes to give an encyclopedic account of many religion of the world, has an early account of the Nanak-panth (Sikhism). Consistent with Akbar's outlook, its inclusivist universalism proved still attractive two centuries later among Unitarian-influenced Bengali intellectuals.

28. Roger Savory, *Iran under the Safavids* (Cambridge: Cambridge University Press, 1980), 27.

29. Ibid., 23. It has been noted that Ismail was more of a Turkish poet than a Persian one, while his rival the Ottoman Selim composed verse in Persian. Some Turkish esoteric Sufis to this day look to Ismail as their founder.

30. Bernard Lewis, *The Emergence of Modern Turkey,* 2nd ed. (Oxford: Oxford University Press, 1966), 339.

31. With telling parochialism, the Turks reaching Austria heard spoken German and declared it a dialect of Persian.

32. Like Akbar, Suleyman married a non-Muslim. Bringing Hindu or Christian women to court no doubt influenced their cosmopolitanism.

33. Of course, even superseded identities could have their niche. William H. McNeill notes that Ottoman bureaucrats who spent their youth as Christians in Christian villages would not so totally identify with the Muslim landlord class, but would maintain a clear sympathy for their peasant Christian relatives. He even notes that one sixteenth-century grand vizier, an ethnic Serb converted to Islam, saw to it that his brother was appointed patriarch of the Serbian Orthodox Church. And when the Janissery system ended in 1638, oppression of the Christian peasants increased. Cf. William H. McNeill, *The Rise of the West* (Chicago: University of Chicago Press, 1963), 691 n.

34. Recall that when Justinian built the church in the 530s, he exclaimed, "Solomon, I have outdone thee!" It is ironic that Justinian's church would become a mosque overseen by a latter-day Solomon.

35. I have found Karen Barkey's *Empire of Difference: The Ottomans in Comparative Perspective* (Cambridge: Cambridge University Press, 2008)

especially useful for understanding Ottoman religious policy. She states: "Although Islam was understood as the religion of the state, it was subordinated to the *raison d'état*. Religion functioned as an institution of the state, and its practitioners emerged only as state officials" (106). On the Bektashis and Janissaries, Jason Goodwin writes: "The Bektashi order, to which the Janissaries were officially attached from 1543, dispensed altogether with some of Islam's striking peculiarities, like the veiling of women or the prohibition of wine. Insincere conversions didn't bother the Turks, because they supposed that a man who followed the outward forms would come to believe soon enough." See his *Lords of the Horizons: A History of the Ottoman Empire* (London: Chatto and Windus, 1998), 57.

36. "It was apparent to all that Charles VIII's France was a far more immediate threat than the Ottoman Empire to peace in Italy, and the Ottomans exploited this situation with acumen." Caroline Finkel, *Osman's Dream: The Story of the Ottoman Empire, 1300–1923* (New York: Basic Books), 90.

PART THREE. THE MODERN WORLD

1. Bruce Lincoln, "Conflict," in *Critical Terms for Religious Studies*, ed. Mark Taylor (Chicago: University of Chicago Press, 1998), 65.

2. Wendy Brown, *Regulating Aversion: Tolerance in the Age of Identity and Empire* (Princeton, NJ: Princeton University Press, 2006), 621.

CHAPTER 8. PUTTING RELIGION IN ITS PLACE

1. John Locke, "A Letter Concerning Toleration" (1689), rendered into modern English by William Popple, Constitution Society, www.constitution.org/jl/tolerati.htm (accessed June 12, 2014).

2. It is interesting that Queen Elizabeth sent a diplomatic letters to Akbar and the Ottoman sultan with adventurous merchants. The Akbar letter is quoted in J. Horton Ryley, *Ralph Fitch: England's Pioneer to India,* (London: T. Fisher Unwin, 1899), an account of sixteenth-century British adventurers. Unfortunately no reply from Akbar is extant.

3. Giovanni Boccaccio recounted a version of "The Ring Parable" in his vernacular Italian book *The Decameron*.

4. Lessing's eighteenth-century play is based on a meeting of Nathan, a wise Jew, Saladin, and a Christian knight during the Crusades. The story of the three rings is recounted to show the relativism of the three religions' claims, and the common humanity of the three men. Nathan tells a story of a father who had promised to pass a heirloom ring to his favorite son. Unable to choose a favorite among his three boys, he makes replicas, so all three receive the ring of favor.

5. Charles Taylor, in *A Secular Age* (Cambridge, MA: Harvard University Press, 2007), notes that prior to the rise of Protestantism, there were already movements to inspire lay folk to greater devotion and piety (85 ff).

6. Henry VIII's two other children had brief reigns before Elizabeth. Edward embraced a more Calvinist Protestantism, while Mary briefly returned the country to Catholicism.

7. Ronald S. Love, *Blood and Religion: The Conscience of Henri IV, 1553–1593* (Montreal: McGill-Queen's University Press, 2001).

8. Quoted in ibid., 307.

9. Quoted in ibid., 110.

10. Note that Calvin executed the humanist scientist and theologian Michael Servetus for arguing a non-Trinitarian Christology. Voltaire later condemned Calvin for that act in his "Poeme sur la loi naturelle."

11. Quoted in Love, *Blood and Religion,* 107.

12. Roland H. Bainton, *Studies on the Reformation* (Boston: Beacon Press, 1963), 224.

13. Ibid., 225. Also cf. Ivan Strenski, "The Religion in Globalization," *Journal of the American Academy of Religion* 72 (2004): 631–52.

14. Strenski, "Religion in Globalization." Carl W. Ernst also has an interesting discussion of Grotius in his book *Following Muhammad: Rethinking Islam in the Contemporary World* (Chapel Hill: University of North Carolina Press, 2003), 40–43.

15. Quoted in Strenski, "Religion in Globalization," 644.

16. Taylor, *Secular Age,* 539–93.

17. Cf. Marcel Reinhard, *La légende de Henri IV* (Saint-Brieuc: Les Presses Bretonnes, 1935).

18. Locke, *Locke, Berkeley, Hume,* ed. Robert M. Hutchins, Great Books of the Western World (Chicago: Encyclopedia Brittanica, 1952), 10.

19. John Locke, *"Epistola de Tolerentia": A Letter on Toleration,* ed. J.W. Gough and Raymond Klibansky (Oxford: Oxford University Press, 1968). The letter can also be found in online at the Online Library of Liberty, http://oll.libertyfund.org/titles/locke-a-letter-concerning-toleration-and-other-writings (accessed July 22, 2014). It is discussed in full in Perez Zagorin, *How the Idea of Religious Toleration Came to the West* (Princeton, NJ: Princeton University Press, 2003), 256–67.

20. *Locke, Berkeley, Hume,* ed. Hutchins, 3.

21. On Augustine's view of coercion in religious matters, see Zagorin, *How the Idea of Religious Toleration Came,* 24–33.

22. *Locke, Berkeley, Hume,* ed. Hutchins, 4.

23. Ibid., 3.

24. Ibid., 18.

25. Taylor, *Secular Age,* 127–28.

26. Locke's views on Muslims evolved, and later in life, he accepted that Muslims could be tolerated if not given full political rights. See Nabil Matar, "Islam in Britain, 1689–1750," *Journal of British Studies* 47 (2008): 284–300.

27. Voltaire's treatise is available in English translation online at the Washington State University website: http://public.wsu.edu/~brians/world_civ/worldcivreader/world_civ_reader_2/voltaire.html (accessed June 12, 2014).

CHAPTER 9. REVOLUTION AND RELIGIOUS FREEDOM

1. This famous statement is attributed to Diderot by Jean-Francois de la Harpe, but not found in Diderot's writings.

2. Quoted in Geoffrey Ellis, "Religion according to Napoleon," in *Religious Change in Europe, 1650–1914,* ed. Nigel Aston and John McManners (Oxford: Clarendon Press, 1997), 252–53.

3. See Steven Waldman, *Founding Faith: How Our Founding Fathers Forged a Radical New Approach to Religious Liberty* (New York: Random House, 2008), 51.

4. Noah Feldman, *Divided by God: America's Church-State Problem and What We Should Do about It* (New York: Farrar, Straus and Giroux, 2005), 51.

5. After his visit, Washington sent a letter to the synagogue expressing his views. The letter was recently exhibited in a Philadelphia museum exhibit, and discussed by CNN. See the CNN Belief Blog, http://religion.blogs.cnn.com/2012/05/23/after-decade-in-storage-washington-letter-on-religious-freedom-will-go-public (accessed July 22, 2014). One can read the entire letter on the George Washington Institute for Religious Freedom website: www.gwirf.org/index.php/the-letter-in-history/typeset-letter (accessed July 22, 2014).

6. See Robert Bellah's famous essay, "Civil Religion in America" *Daedalus* 96 (1967): 1–21, where he concentrates on the public oratory of presidents.

7. Quoted in *The Founders on God and Government,* ed. Daniel L. Dreibach, Mark D. Hall, and Jeffry H. Morrison (Lanham, MD: Rowman and Littlefield, 2004), 25. Arminians were a reformed church that opposed Calvinism in their assertion of human free will.

8. Quoted in Edwin S. Gaustad, *Faith of Our Fathers* (San Francisco: Harper, 1987), 95.

9. Feldman, *Divided by God,* 41 n.

10. Quoted in Gaustad, *Faith of Our Fathers,* 108.

11. Henry also declared: "It can not be emphasized too strongly or too often that this great nation was founded, not by religionists, but by Christians, not on religions, but on the gospel of Jesus Christ!"

12. Quoted in Frank Lambert, *The Founding Fathers and the Place of Religion in America* (Princeton, NJ: Princeton University Press, 2003), 238.

13. Quoted in Waldman, *Founding Faith,* 76.

14. "No man shall be compelled to frequent or support any religious worship, place, or ministry whatsoever, nor shall be enforced, restrained, molested, or burthened in his body or goods, nor shall otherwise suffer, on account of his religious opinions or belief; but that all men shall be free to profess, and by argument to maintain, their opinions in matters of religion, and that the same shall in no wise diminish, enlarge, or affect their civil capacities."

15. Quoted in Waldman, *Founding Faith,* 174.

16. See Waldman's discussion of the "wall of separation" language in Jefferson's letter to the Danbury Baptists; ibid., 173–77.

17. The Treaty of Tripoli (*Treaty of Peace and Friendship between the United States of America and the Bey and Subjects of Tripoli of Barbary*) was written in both Arabic and English. This portion is from the English version. It was signed in Tripoli in 1796 and ratified in 1797, during John Adams's presidency.

18. Kevin J. Hayes, "How Thomas Jefferson Read the Qur'an," *Early American Literature* 39 (2004): 247–61.

19. Jefferson Monticello website, www.monticello.org/site/research-and-collections/tunisian-envoy (accessed June 12, 2014).

20. Lambert, *Founding Fathers*, 285.

21. Ironically, in desacralizing the calendar, the revolutionaries removed names for the days of the week that were pagan (Sun, Moon, Mars, Mercury, Saturn . . .) and that predated the Christianity they were trying to disestablish.

22. Mona Ozouf, *Festivals and the French Revolution*, trans. Alan Sheridan (Cambridge, MA: Harvard University Press, 1988), xi.

23. What would most Americans make of the fact that their Statue of Liberty was a gift of the French who once attempted to replace Christianity with festivals to goddesses like her?

24. David A. Bell, *The Cult of the Nation in France: Inventing Nationalism, 1680–1800* (Cambridge, MA: Harvard University Press, 2001).

25. Ibid., 2.

26. "In 1789–90, adherents of the Revolution in the French provinces found themselves confronted with an awesome and difficult task: helping the peasant masses become good citizens of a democratic polity. The only previous enterprise that had much relevance was the Catholic Reformation's attempt to turn ancestors of those same peasants into good Catholics." Ibid., 190.

27. Ibid., chap. 6; esp. 187 ff.

28. Lynn Festa and Daniel Carey summarize this critique: "'The Enlightenment' has taken a beating in recent years at the hands of poststructuralist and postcolonial theorists. (It is hard to imagine how one might pronounce the words "Enlightenment universal subject' without a faint sneer.) The accusations leveled against Enlightenment within postcolonial theory might go something like this: irremediably Eurocentric, the ideas grouped under the rubric of Enlightenment are explicitly or implicitly bound up with imperialism. In its quest for the universal, Enlightenment occludes cultural difference and refuses moral and social relativity. Inasmuch as its values are identified as coextensive with modernity, the Enlightenment naturalizes a teleology in which all roads lead inexorably to an episteme associated with the West. *The Postcolonial Enlightenment* (New York: Oxford University Press, 2009), 8.

29. Arthur Hertzberg, *The French Enlightenment and the Jews* (New York: Columbia University Press, 1968), 266.

30. Quoted in Ziad Elmarsafy, *The Enlightenment Qur'an* (Oxford: Oneworld, 2009), 2004. Mamluks were slave soldiers who long ruled Egypt as the agents of the Ottomans, but rebelled in 1768. The "grand signior" refers to the Ottoman sultan.

31. Quoted in Ellis, "Religion according to Napoleon," 235.

32. Quoted in ibid., 252–53.

33. Bell, *Cult of the Nation*, 210–11.

CHAPTER 10. THE CONTEMPORARY ERA

1. Zastoupil devotes a whole chapter to the comparison of Jefferson and Rammohun: "Rammohun Roy, Thomas Jefferson, and the Bible," chapter 2 of his book *Rammohun Roy and the Making of Victorian Britain* (New York:

Palgrave, 2010), 23–40. Here he contests the position of R.S. Sugirtharajah, who argues in his *The Bible and Empire* (Cambridge: Cambridge University Press, 2005) that Rammohun and Jefferson reached similar conclusions in 1820 as a coincidence.

2. Letter from Thoreau to Harrison Blake Concord, November 20, 1849: "Depend upon it that, rude and careless as I am, I would fain practice the yoga faithfully. . . . To some extent, and at rare intervals, even I am a yogi." In Henry David Thoreau, *Letters to a Spiritual Seeker*, ed. Bradley P. Dean (New York: W.W. Norton, 2004), 50. Thus Indian ideas reached Thoreau in New England, while he was read by Tolstoy and Gandhi, who in turn, corresponded with each other while Gandhi was in South Africa. Gandhi influenced Martin Luther King, Jr., whose influence cycled back to South Africa in the battle to end apartheid.

3. The *Dabistan* is a survey of religions written from a universalist position in the time of Dara Shikoh and influential in the development of Sikhism.

4. A sketch of this early phase of his work and the influence of the *Dabistan* is found in Ajit Kumar Ray, *The Religious Ideas of Rammohun Roy* (New Delhi: Kanak, 1976), 20–27.

5. Zastoupil, *Rammohun Roy*, 151–62.

6. For example, Hindu converts to Christianity were still subject to the laws governing Hindus. Cf. Gauri Viswanathan, *Outside the Fold* (Princeton, NJ: Princeton University Press, 1998), 95–117.

7. Thomas Babington Macaulay, *Macaulay: Prose and Poetry*, ed. G.M. Young (Cambridge, MA: Harvard University Press, 1952), 729.

8. One can hear a recording of Vivekananda's speech at: www.youtube.com/watch?v=p4Nmvbm4WYM&noredirect=1 (accessed July 7, 2014).

9. *Sources of Indian Tradition*, ed. Stephen Hay (New York: Columbia University Press, 1988), 2:76. Note that despite the sort of bravado that Vivekananda expressed here, he also had moments when all assertiveness departed him and he fell into a spiritual state of profound passivity; cf. Sudhir Kakar, *The Inner World* (Delhi: Oxford University Press, 1988), 160–81.

10. In thinking about secularism in the South Asian context, I have learned much from two books: Gerald J. Larson, *India's Agony over Religion* (Albany: State University of New York Press, 1995); and Peter van der Veer, *Religious Nationalism: Hindus and Muslims in India* (Berkeley: University of California Press, 1994).

11. On the Shah Bano Begum case, see Larson, *India's Agony over Religion*, 256–61.

12. Cf. van der Veer, *Religious Nationalism*, 1 ff. Anand Patwardhan's documentary film *In the Name of God* also covers the Babri Masjid controversy with great sensitivity.

13. On the 2002 riots, cf. Martha C. Nussbaum, "Genocide in Gujarat," in *The Clash Within: Democracy, Religious Violence, and India's Future* (Cambridge, MA: Belknap Press, 2007), 17–51.

14. Jonathan Spence, *God's Chinese Son* (New York: W.W. Norton, 1996), 107–8.

15. For a thorough analysis of Hong and the Tai Ping Rebellion, cf. ibid.

16. *Quotations from Chairman Mao Tse-Tung* (Peking: Foreign Languages Press, 1967), 173–74.

17. For a portrayal of the Cultural Revolution in general, and the situation in hospitals in particular, see Zhang Yimou's film *To Live* (2003), based on the novel by Yu Hua.

18. Daniel Overmyer, *Folk Buddhist Religion : Dissenting Sects in Late Traditional China* (Cambridge, MA: Harvard University Press, 1976).

19. I have found David Ownby's book *Falun Gong and the Future of China* (New York: Oxford University Press, 2008) to be especially insightful in analyzing the Falun Gong movement and its relationship both to the history of sectarian religion in China, and to the current political regime.

20. In giving up Jewish practices to assimilate to French culture, how did Jews avoid simply disappearing? By becoming a *race* rather than a religious community. See Wendy Brown's argument in her *Regulating Aversion: Tolerance in the Age of Identity and Empire* (Princeton, NJ: Princeton University Press, 2005), 50–58.

21. Ibid., 6.

22. Eugen Weber, *Peasants into Frenchmen: The Modernization of Rural France, 1870–1914* (Stanford, CA: Stanford University Press, 1976).

23. John R. Bowen, *Why the French Don't Like Headscarves: Islam, the State, and Public Space* (Princeton, NJ: Princeton University Press, 2007).

24. Ibid., 11–12.

25. Bowen quotes a prominent French official as saying "there will *never* be a Sikh civil servants in France" (ibid., 14). Such a policy contrasts with British practice of accommodating Sikh dress in the military and public offices.

26. Joan Wallach Scott, *The Politics of the Veil* (Princeton, NJ: Princeton University Press, 2007), 173–74.

27. Nicolas Sarkozy, with Thibaud Collin and Philippe Verdin, *La république, les religions, l'espérance* (Paris: Cerf, 2004). It is striking that Sarkozy, like his contemporary Tony Blair, British prime minister from 1997 to 2007, became so involved with religion when they are from such secular countries. Blair converted to Catholicism after he left office and founded a major foundation on religion: see www.tonyblairfaithfoundationus.org.

28. Feversham College website, www.fevershamcollege.com (accessed June 12, 2014).

29. Since Rushdie was denounced by an illiberal Iranian cleric, British Muslims' denunciation of the author suggests that their loyalties lie not with their fellow citizens, but with their fanatical co-religionists abroad.

30. Patten authored a similar piece for *The Times* (July 5, 1989), entitled "The Muslim Community in Britain."

31. Talal Asad, "Multiculturalism and British Identity in the Wake of the Rushdie Affair," in his *Genealogies of Religion: Discipline and Reasons of Power in Christianity and Islam* (Baltimore: Johns Hopkins University Press, 1993), 239 ff.

32. Ibid., 249.

33. Cf. the record of the House of Lords ruling of 2006: www.publications.parliament.uk/pa/ld200506/ldjudgmt/jd060322/begum-1.htm (accessed June 12, 2014).

34. Merkel's remarks in a speech in 2010 were widely reported in the European press, e.g., Matthew Weaver, "Angela Merkel: German Multiculturalism Has 'Utterly Failed,'" *The Guardian*, October 17, 2010.

35. On the variety of Turkish religious associations in contemporary Germany, see Jytte Klausen, *The Islamic Challenge: Politics and Religion in Western Europe* (New York: Oxford University Press, 2005), 31 ff.

36. Quoted in Joel S. Fetzer and J. Christopher Soper, *Muslims and the State in Britain, France, and Germany* (New York: Cambridge University Press, 2005), 108. Gerhard Robbers has compiled a dense but fascinating summary of German law on religion: International Encyclopaedia of Law website, www.ielaws.com/modelreligermany.pdf (accessed June 12, 2014).

37. It is worth noting here that in France and Germany, while freedom of religion is assumed, there is a willingness to curb the activities of what are considered dangerous "cults." Scientology is banned in France and not considered a "religion" under German law. Both governments routinely investigate large numbers of "suspicious" sects.

38. According to a poll conducted by Populus, as reported in *The Guardian* ("More Young Muslims Back Sharia, Says Poll"; January 28, 2007), "Nearly a third of 16 to 24-year-olds believed that those converting to another religion should be executed, while less than a fifth of those over 55 believed the same" (www.guardian.co.uk/uk/2007/jan/29/thinktanks.religion) (accessed June 12, 2014).

39. Bruce Lincoln, *Holy Terrors: Thinking about Religion after September 11*, 2nd ed. (Chicago: University of Chicago Press, 2006), 1–61.

40. In the state of Minnesota, where I live, there are numerous examples of public schools where accommodations for Muslim students have been made. According to one informant, a teacher, bathrooms have been outfitted and marked for appropriate ablutions, and teachers given the schedule for Islamic prayer, times when students are excused for class during what is euphemistically called "culture time." It is again striking here that the word *culture* can stand in for religion as somehow more acceptably neutral.

41. Winnifred Fallers Sullivan, *The Impossibility of Religious Freedom* (Princeton, NJ: Princeton University Press, 2005).

42. President Bush, quoted in Lincoln, *Holy Terrors,* 28.

43. Ibid., 29 ff.

44. Ibid., 30–32.

45. For the transcript of the entire speech, see the Time website, www.time.com/time/politics/article/0,8599,1902738,00.html (accessed June 12, 2014).

46. Obama's speech was delivered on June 4, 2009.

CONCLUSION

1. Mahatma Gandhi, *An Autobiography: The Story of My Experiments with Truth* (Boston: Beacon Press, 1957), 504.

2. On the website of the Mind and Life Institute, one sees a description of secular ethics, beginning with a quotation of the Dalai Lama: "In today's secular world, religion alone is no longer adequate as a basis for ethics. . . . any religion-

based answer to the problem of our neglect of inner values can never be universal, and so will be inadequate. What we need today is an approach to ethics which makes no recourse to religion and can be equally acceptable to those with faith and those without: a secular ethics." See www.mindandlife.org/what-is-secular-ethics (accessed June 12, 2014).

Suggested Readings

PART ONE. RELIGION AND EMPIRE IN ANTIQUITY
Primary Sources

Analects of Confucius, trans.Burton Watson (2009).
The Bhagavad Gita. trans. Barbara Stoler Miller (1986).
The Bible.
The Edicts of Asoka, trans. Nikam A. Nikam and Richard McKeon (1959).
The Laws of Manu, trans. Wendy Doniger and Brian K. Smith (1991).
The Questions of King Milinda, trans. T.W. Rhys Davies (1965).
The *Qur'an: Approaching the Qur'an,* trans. Michael Sells (1999).
Saddharma Pundarika; or, The Lotus of the True Law, trans. Hendrik Kern (1963).
Zhuangzi: Basic Writings, trans. Burton Watson (2003).

Secondary Sources

Peter Brown, *The World of Late Antiquity* (1971).
Shaye J.D. Cohen, *From the Maccabees to the Mishnah* (2006).
Fred Denny, *Muhammad and the Believers: At the Origins of Islam* (2010).
Wendy Doniger, *The Hindus: An Alternative History* (2013).
Maria Dzielska, *Hypatia of Alexandria* (1995).
Garth Fowden, *Empire to Commonwealth: : Consequences of Monotheism in Late Antiquity* (1993).
Alf Hiltebeitel, *Dharma: Its Early History in Law, Religion, and Narrative* (2010).
Richard A. Horsley, *Jesus and Empire: The Kingdom of God and the New World Disorder* (2003).
Livia Kohn, *Daoism and Chinese Culture* (2001).

PART TWO. THE ISLAMIC MILLENNIUM
Primary Sources

Akbarnama of Abul Fazl, 3 vols., trans. Henry Beveridge (2010).
Al-Ghazali, *The Incoherence of the Philosophers,* trans. Michael Marmura (2002).
The Bijak of Kabir, trans. Linda Hess and Shukdev Singh (2002).
The Essential Rumi, trans. Coleman Barks (1996).
Maimonides, *The Guide of the Perplexed,* trans. Shlomo Pines (1974).

Secondary Sources

Said Amir Arjomand, *The Shadow of God and the Hidden Imam: Religion, Political Order, and Societal Change in Shi'ite Iran from the Beginning to 1890* (1984).
Karen Barkey, *Empire of Difference: The Ottomans in Comparative Perspective* (2008).
Richard W. Bulliet, *Islam: The View from the Edge* (1994).
Marshall G.S. Hodgson, *The Venture of Islam,* vols. 1–3 (1977).
Harbans Mukhia, *The Mughals of India* (2004).
Daniel Overmyer, *Folk Buddhist Religion* (1976).
John F. Richards, ed., *Kingship and Authority in South Asia* (1978).
Roger M. Savery, *Iran under the Safavids* (1980).
Annemarie Schimmel, *Mystical Dimensions of Islam* (1975).

PART THREE. THE MODERN WORLD
Primary Sources

Giovanni Boccaccio, *The Decameron* (fourteenth century).
Gotthold Ephraim Lessing, *Nathan the Wise* (1779).
John Locke, *A Letter concerning Toleration* (1689).
Barack Obama, "Remarks by the President at Cairo University" (2009).
Voltaire, *Treatise on Tolerance* (1763).

Secondary Sources

David A. Bell, *The Cult of the Nation in France: Inventing Nationalism, 1680–1800* (2001).
Wendy Brown, *Regulating Aversion: Tolerance in the Age of Identity and Empire* (2005).
Carl Ernst, *Following Muhammad: Rethinking Islam in the Contemporary World* (2003).
Arthur Hertzberg, *The French Enlightenment and the Jews* (1968).
Gerald Larson, *India's Agony over Religion* (1995).
Bruce Lincoln, *Holy Terrors: Thinking about Religion after September 11* (2006).
Martha Nussbaum, *The Clash Within: Democracy, Religious Violence, and India's Future* (2007).

David Ownby, *Falun Gong and the Future of China* (2008).
Ronald S. Love, *Blood and Religion: The Conscience of Henri IV* (2001).
Alyssa G. Sepinwall, *The Abbé Grégoire and the French Revolution* (2005).
Winnifred Fallers Sullivan, *The Impossibility of Religious Freedom* (2005).
Charles Taylor, *A Secular Age* (2007).
Peter van der Veer, *Religious Nationalism: Hindus and Muslims in India* (1994).
Steven Waldman, *Founding Faith: How Our Founding Fathers Forged a Radical New Approach to Religious Liberty* (2008).
Perez Zagorin, *How the Idea of Religious Toleration Came to the West* (2003).

Index

Bill of Rights, 183–84, 188, 257n14
Birbal, 149
black Africans, Enlightenment revolutions and, 195, 196, 197
Blair, Tony, 224, 225, 243n14, 260n27
blood sacrifice, 30
Boccaccio, 164, 255n3
bodhisattvas, 73–74, 83
Bonaparte, Napoleon. *See* Napoleon I (emperor of France)
Booth, Cherie, 224
Borgia, Cesare, 251n10
Bowen, John, 220, 260n25
Bowersock, Glen, 102
brahmanas and *sramanas*, 25–26, 28
brahmins, 25, 68, 94, 205, 234; Ashoka and, 20, 23, 26, 59, 236; Buddhist challenge to authority of, 77; as defenders of orthodoxy, 60; heterodox religious movements as threat to, 65–66; ideological battle over status of, 62; *Laws of Manu* as defense of, 74–75; Maitreya Buddha and, 85; Sanskrit literature of, 72
Braudel, Fernand, 119
Britain, Muslim minority in, 222–25
British Empire, 11, 22, 129, 205, 206–7; Anglo-Sikh wars, 153; "divide and rule" policy of, 209; Gandhian challenge to, 209, 233; Opium Wars against China, 213
Brown, Peter, 121
Brown, Wendy, 161, 218
Brumidi, Constantino, 185, 186
Buddhas: Amida Buddha, 138, 139; Amitabha, 91; Avalokitesvara, 83–84, 239; Maitreya (future Buddha to come), 83, 84–85; monumental statues of, 91, 247n13; pantheon of, 83. *See also* Gautama Buddha
Buddhism, ix, xii, 6, 25, 78, 180; array of doctrines and practices, 8; Ashoka's patronage of, 16, 17, 26; authorship of doctrines, x; *Bhagavadgita* as critique of, 69, 70; Buddhist visitors in Hellenistic world, 54; depoliticized, 9; European colonialism and, 203; Four Noble Truths, 6, 233; geopolitical place in ancient world, 15; imperial state patronage and, 15; Indo-Greek kingdoms and, 60; in Japan, 8, 138–39; Kanishka's patronage of, 61, 65; Mahayana, 61–62, 73, 82–83; in modern India, 212; Nichiren sect, 8,

138; as politically marginal religion, 103–4; Silk Road and, 82, 85, 91; stupas, 63, 64, 64, 72, 74; Theravada, 8; True Pure Land sect, 138; in United States, 239; universalism in, 6, 77; *upaya* ("skillful means"), 83; Zen (Chan), x, 91, 138, 139
Buddhism, in China, 34, 79, 90–92, 234, 248n15; as challenge to Confucianism, 38–39, 244n10; decline and persecution of, 78, 104, 119; Falun Gong and, 216; Mongol dynasty and, 138; Tai Ping Rebellion and, 213; Tibet under Chinese rule, 215
Bush, George W., 5, 229–30, 231
Byzantine Empire, 81, 93, 100, 107, 156, 248n17; divine kingship in, 94; One True God and, 117; Persia at war with, 102

caesaro-papism, 90
Caligula [Gaius Caesar] (Roman emperor), 45, 46–47, 48, 49
caliphs, 9, 16, 95, 178; as absolute monarchs in Persian style, 29, 121, 130, 131; global dominance of Islam and, 116; legitimacy of, 115, 126, 130–31; *shari'ah* and, 127–28; Sunni acceptance of early caliphs, 127
Calvin, John, 164, 169, 256n10
Calvinism, 165, 167, 174, 183, 186, 255n6
Carter, Jimmy, 243n14
Carter, Stephen, 7
caste, 6, 59, 76, 137, 242n4; affirmative action in modern India and, 228; *dharma* and, 69, 88; ideological battle over, 62; *sva-dharma* (caste duty), 69, 71. *See also* brahmins; *kshatriyas*; shudras
Catholicism/Catholic Church, 159, 164, 175, 222; absolutism and, 173, 176; Anglo-Catholicism, 166, 174–75; authority of nation-state above, 237; dissident views in American Catholicism, 238; Franciscan order, 139; French Revolution and, 188, 190, 191, 198; Jesuits, 147–49, 180, 194; Locke's views on tolerance and, 177–78; medieval, 3; Mexican, xi; Napoleon and, 197–99; Peace of Augsburg and, 165; Protestant challenges to, 164–69; in revolutionary America, 183, 184; rules for everyday life and, 3; secular nationalism of nineteenth century against, 199–201, 220; worldly power of popes, 130, 251n10